The economic theory of product differentiation

The economic theory of product differentiation

John Beath
University of Bristol

and

Yannis Katsoulacos
University of Liverpool

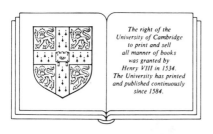

The right of the
University of Cambridge
to print and sell
all manner of books
was granted by
Henry VIII in 1534.
The University has printed
and published continuously
since 1584.

CAMBRIDGE UNIVERSITY PRESS
Cambridge
New York   Port Chester
Melbourne   Sydney

Published by the Press Syndicate of the University of Cambridge
The Pitt Building, Trumpington Street, Cambridge CB2 1RP
40 West 20th Street, New York, NY 10011-4211, USA
10 Stamford Road, Oakleigh, Melbourne 3166, Australia

First published 1991

Printed in Great Britain at the University Press, Cambridge

British Library cataloguing in publication data
The economic theory of product differentiation.
   1. Marketing. Economic aspects
   I. Beath, John II. Katsoulacos Y.S. (Yannis S.)
   380.1

Library of Congress cataloguing in publication data
Beath, John.
   The economic theory of product differentiation/John Beath,
   Yannis Katsoulacos.
      p. cm.
   Includes bibliographical references.
   ISBN 0-521-33526-4
   1. Diversification in industry.   I. Katsoulacos, Y.S., 1953– .
   II. Title.
   HD2756.B43   1991
   338.6–dc20   89-77516

ISBN 0 521 33526 4   hardback
ISBN 0 521 33552 3   paperback

IP

To Moni and Despina

Contents

Preface

While this is a book on product differentiation, it is a book about the core of economic theory that relates to this topic. The last decade has seen a rapid growth in the literature in this area. A particular problem with the literature is that it is quite widely spread across academic journals and hence someone who wanted to find out the state of the art would need to search widely and at length. What we have sought to do here is to bring this all together in a convenient form both for our fellow academics and for students at both the undergraduate and graduate levels.

In deciding what we should include in the book we have taken the view that the most significant theoretical issues in the literature have been the distinction between horizontal and vertical differentiation and the nature of their market equilibria, the advances in the analysis of locational equilibria and the limit results. We have therefore tried to provide an in-depth treatment of these topics and of some of the more fundamental applications of the theory.

In working on the manuscript we have profited from the comments of Roger Backhouse, Paul Geroski, Norman Ireland, Damien Neven, John Sutton, Jacques Thisse and David Ulph. We should also like to express our thanks to Francis Brooke and Patrick McCartan for their interest in initiating and seeing this project to fruition as well as to Anne Rix, our copy-editor.

The material in various parts of the manuscript has also been tried out on several generations of unsuspecting students at Bristol and Liverpool Universities and we have regularly been pleasantly surprised by their astute comments. We think the book has benefited from these.

Finally, and as the dedication testifies, we should particularly like to thank our wives, Moni and Despina, for their cheerful tolerance and steady encouragement.

1 Introduction

1.1 The aims of the book

We had two main aims in writing this book. The first was to explain the prevalence of differentiated goods in a modern market economy and the second was to explore the implications of this for industrial structure and market power. The literature on, and our understanding as economists of, the phenomenon of product differentiation have developed greatly in the last decade and it seemed appropriate at this point to bring this all together and see what general strands could be extracted.

A central question in the theory of imperfect competition concerns the number and kinds of differentiated goods that the market mechanism will produce. One can look at this from both a positive and normative point of view. Our objective is to provide the reader with both points of view in the course of discussing the, by now, fairly substantial literature on product differentiation. Of course, we must also recognise that product differentiation is not the only source of imperfect competition. In its absence, imperfect competition may still arise. This may be for either or both of two reasons: because firms are non-negligible in relation to the size of the market or because consumers or firms possess incomplete information. While we address both of these issues to some extent in this book, they are not the primary focus. For those who want a review of the former, we would refer them to Hart (1985c), while issues of information are dealt with by Butters (1977), Grossman and Shapiro (1984), Rothschild (1973), and Salop and Stiglitz (1977).

Our starting point is the view that what differentiates products are the characteristics that they each possess and so product differentiation involves making a particular firm's product either really or apparently different from that of its rival. However, we need to be a little more specific than this for while chalk and cheese are *different* products, Cheddar and Brie are *differentiated* ones. These examples make it clear that differentiated products are both similar *and* different.

1

We take it that these differences are grounded in the preferences of consumers. It may be that these are well-founded or they may be engineered by skilful advertising. This is not an issue in this book; we take preferences as data and do not inquire into how they may have come about. We should point out here that, because it provided a framework of reference that enables one to make precise the definition of a particular group of differentiated products, Kelvin Lancaster's (1966) paper in which he provided a framework for modelling choice over characteristics was a fundamental theoretical advance.[1]

However, although Lancaster's paper was an important and seminal one, the discussion of product differentiation did not start with it. The term as such was introduced into the literature by Edwin Chamberlin in 1933 in chapter 4 of his classic *Theory of Monopolistic Competition*. Although the idea was probably used before this, monopolistic competition provided the appropriate context. Chamberlin grappled with two particular aspects. The first was whether differentiation was 'real or fancied'. This led him to focus on things such as trademarks and branding and devote two chapters of the book to the examination of selling costs. The second was how to model these differences. Chamberlin was unhappy with the idea of treating them as 'perfect monopolies, one for each seller', but recognised that it provided a starting point. It was from this that he developed the distinction between the '*dd*' and '*DD*' demand curves that was the novel analytical feature. The former was the (downward-sloping) demand curve faced by the individual firm within a monopolistically competitive group and the latter the group demand curve. The difficulty was that these were taken as primitive ideas in his theory and it was never clear quite how the former was derived from the underlying preferences of consumers. We shall look at this in some detail in chapter 3.

A few years prior to Chamberlin, Harold Hotelling (1929) had published an analysis of competition between firms in a market in which buyers were dispersed geographically and in which firms competed by varying location as well as price. This location model is one we shall deal with in chapter 2. However, the potential application of the Hotelling location model to the analysis of product differentiation was largely ignored until Lancaster's introduction of the notion of characteristics into demand theory. It was this that allowed location and differentiation to be linked.

1.2 Methodology and overview

The approach that we shall follow in this book will be to take as given the nature of consumers' tastes, the specification of technology and a suitable notion of what would constitute an equilibrium in the particular problem under consideration. In some cases, the latter will be defined in terms of prices, sometimes in terms of characteristics and sometimes in terms of numbers of products.[2] The models that we shall be looking at try to predict the level of product differentiation that would emerge in market equilibrium. This of course is a question of *positive* economics. However, we shall also want to consider the *normative* or *welfare* economics of these market equilibria. An answer to these questions involves comparing the market equilibrium with what we would consider to be the relevant social optimum. In some instances this will be the *first-best* or optimum optimorum, but in others it may make more sense to compare the market equilibrium with a constrained optimum – the so-called *second-best*. This is very much the approach that will be followed in chapters 2 to 6.

A natural question to ask in all of this, and one that would be central in the mind of a policy-maker, is the implications of these market equilibria for industrial structure and market power. Here there are two issues: does product differentiation have an influence on the degree of concentration independent to that of technology and market size and, if the size of the maket is allowed to increase without limit, will the resulting market equilibrium correspond to perfect competition with price being driven down towards marginal cost? More precisely, is the set of limit points of imperfectly competitive market equilibria merely the set of competitive equilibria? This is the theme of chapter 7 where we show that the answer is *no*: there is something fundamental about product differentiation.

While the existence of product differentiation may imply that firms retain some market power, even in large markets with free entry, product differentiation may also impinge in a much more direct and powerful way on market power. This will be so when product differentiation can serve as an entry barrier; in particular, an incumbent monopolist threatened with entry by outsiders into the market.[3] In the product differentiation context this is the analogue of preemptive patenting in R&D. This is an issue that we look at in chapter 8 and it builds on the kind of models that are explored in chapter 2.

For the most part, the analysis we do is carried out in the context of a closed economy. This is a restriction, for competition may be at its most severe at the international level. The new and deeper understanding of product differentiation that we have as a result of recent theoretical advances has important implications for the nature of international competition and is beginning to have an impact on the theory of international trade.[4] This international dimension is an important one for, through trade relations, market size is increased. In chapter 9 we consider the implications of alternative forms of product differentiation for the theory of international trade using the ideas that we have developed in the course of chapters 3 and 6.

As should be clear from this discussion (and from the title of the book), this is a book about the *core theory* of product differentiation. This inevitably means that a number of topics, important in themselves, but side issues in terms of core theory, had to be left out. An obvious example is *advertising*. This is a topic that has been extensively and accessibly treated elsewhere (Koutsoyiannis, 1984, Schmalensee, 1972). In deciding what we should include in this book, we have taken the view that the most significant theoretical issues in the literature have been the distinction between horizontal and vertical differentiation and the nature of their market equilibria, the advances in the analysis of locational equilibrium and the limit results. We have therefore sought to provide an extensive in-depth treatment of these topics and of some of the more fundamental applications of the theory.

1.3 The formalisation of product differentiation

What differentiates products then is the characteristics that they possess. If we think of each characteristic as being represented by a dimension in some appropriate dimensional space, any product can be thought of as a point in the space spanned by the axes. The relevant set of goods is thus represented by a number of points or vectors in this space.

In explaining the widespread prevalence of differentiated goods, we focus on models in which the choice of product by the firm is endogenous. This obviously makes the question a more complicated one to consider than if we had taken brand positioning to be given, but it clearly seems to be the more relevant framework. Modern corporations take brand positioning seriously and devote considerable resources to establishing and re-establishing their different brands.

Goods can be differentiated in a number of ways. A distinction that we make considerable use of in this book is between goods that are *horizontally* differentiated and those that are *vertically* differentiated.

If all the points in the characteristics space corresponding to the set of goods on offer lie on the same ray vector through the origin, then it is natural to say that a good that is further out along this ray is better: that is to say, is of *higher quality*. If we can find a subset of goods that fits this description, then these goods can be said to be *vertically differentiated* and we could proceed to rank them in terms of some quality index. It would then follow that, if these goods were to be offered for sale at *identical prices*, every consumer would rank these goods in the same order. On the other hand, if goods cannot be ranked in terms of some quality index, then it seems natural to describe them as *horizontally differentiated*.

As our 'historical' comments above have indicated, the attempts to formalise horizontal product differentiation have followed one of two lines. The first, which has developed out of the Hotelling model, is often referred to as the *address approach*. Tastes are distributed across the characteristics space and individual consumers have their most preferred addresses or locations. In other words preferences are diverse and asymmetric. Each consumer possesses a clear ranking over all available products when they are offered at the *same* price. We can therefore refer to a consumer's 'ideal' or most preferred brand and consider brands close to it in the characteristics space as being better substitutes (and hence, better liked) than brands that are distant. The literature on location models that stemmed from Hotelling has assumed that differentiated products cannot be combined in consumption. This means that each consumer has to choose the one product that best matches his or her preferences after taking into account the costs of acquisition.

If consumers have rather varied tastes, then they will be distributed quite widely across the space whereas, if their tastes are more homogeneous, they are likely to be bunched. Consumers are taken to make rational choices and in this context that means that what they do is to balance the relative prices of goods within the competing group against the relative distances that these are from their ideal specification. Thus the demand for a particular product within the group depends on price, the distribution of consumers and the prices and locations of the rival products. In some cases, this rivalry may be between a few 'nearby' brands in which case the product will have some degree of 'local monopoly' while in other cases the immediately competitive group may be quite large. In general then, the further apart that products are in characteristics space, the less the substitutability between them and the lower the elasticity of demand for any individual product.

The alternative approach which has its roots in Chamberlin is the *non-address* approach. In this case preferences are defined over the set of all possible goods. In a sense one can say here that consumers have *a taste for variety*.[5] A central feature is preference symmetry. The implication of this assumption is that all products are in competition with all others and it means that consumer preferences cannot be used to obtain a ranking over all products when they are offered at identical prices. Thus, while each consumer can have a most preferred brand, symmetry implies an absence of 'neighbouring' brands. Hence, the fact that a consumer is observed to buy brand z provides us with no information about the nature of his preferences about some brand that is 'near' to z in characteristic space when both are identically priced.

A further subdivision within this approach is that between the case where consumers are assumed to have identical preferences and to purchase all available brands and the case where they are heterogeneous and each consumes a different subset of the available brands. The first of these two cases is the most commonly used and best-known of the models of monopolistic competition: the 'representative consumer' models. A disadvantage of such models is that they don't exactly fit in with certain of what are thought to be relevant stylised facts. Amongst these are, for example, the fact that the range of variants of a product that any consumer buys is in practice relatively limited and such goods are not often *combined* in consumption. Also, different characteristics do seem to matter in different degrees to different consumers and people can often agree on what are and are not close substitutes.

1.4 The incentive to differentiate

If firms in a particular group produce goods which are differentiated, the products of the different firms are imperfect substitutes for each other and, as we hinted earlier, this gives each firm the potential to act as a monopolist in relation to its own product. It is this potential for monopoly profits, due to the fact that it reduces the sensitivity to competitive moves, that provides firms with the basic incentive to differentiate their product. However while differentiation enables a firm to insulate its own market to some degree from the actions of its competitive rivals, the relationship is a symmetric one, and it also makes it harder for the firm to effectively compete in its rivals' own markets. Hence differentiation may well cut it off from a much larger market.

To see the argument, consider a case somewhat similar to the one that we examine in chapter 2. Suppose a situation in which two firms are initially producing the same product and are selling it at the same price. Faced with this rather limited range of products, consumers are likely to make their choice of which firm to buy from in a random manner and each firm will probably end up getting a half share of the available market. Either firm could gain the whole market, for a moment, by under-cutting on price – but it would then lose it all in the resulting price battle as its rival seeks to cut prices in retaliation. In the end price would be pushed down to the zero-profit level. However, if a firm were to vary its product, it would reduce the potential for such unstable competition, and give it some monopoly power in its own localised market. For example, think of shops located along a road. If the store we are considering were to move some distance away from its rival, this would do some but not lot of good if the vast bulk of consumers were at the original location. However, if at least half of the consumers were in the firm's new market area, the firm would find that it had just as large a market as before, but with the added bonus of a lower elasticity of demand and less competition. It will consequently be able to reap monopoly profit from the move – at least until more firms enter the market.

What this tells us is that increasing the degree of product differentiation gives a firm a far greater degree of monopoly power over an, albeit, re-stricted portion of the total market. The more varied are consumers' tastes (their own location in this example) and the more uniformly they are distributed, the greater will be the incentive to differentiate – this is, after all, the natural response to the greater taste for variety. However, if the distribution of tastes happens to be concentrated in a particular part of the characteristics space, then we are likely to find that competing firms are producing fairly similar types of good. Their products will be clustered at these high density points and they will be unlikely to differentiate into the thinner parts of the market. This is an effect which is not really taken into account in most of the locational models that we look at in chapter 2 for these assume that tastes are distributed uniformly over a large part of the characteristics space.

As we have said above, for much of this book we implicitly assume single-product firms. The reason for doing so is consistency with the existing literature which assumes single-product firms. However, it should be clear that a large firm may well differentiate its *own* product. We deal to some extent with this in chapter 8 where we explore the issue of the use of *brand proliferation* as an entry-deterring mechanism. There must hardly be a reader who is not aware of the daunting array of breakfast cereals, detergents and toiletries on the average supermarket shelf. Most of these are produced by a handful of firms: two in the case of detergents and toiletries. Indeed, firms will have an incentive to produce multiple brands even when they are monopolists. The reason is that, because consumers do in reality appear to have quite varied tastes, a single brand will appeal to only a small section of the market unless its price is reduced sufficiently to ensure it covers the market. However, the price reduction needed to do this may be one that would leave the firm with little in the way of profit. The advantage of producing more varieties is that this increases the total revenue that can be obtained from selling a given quantity because, on average, consumers find that the available products are more closely matched to what they are looking for and so they will be prepared to pay more for the privilege of having the good. However, the obverse side of the coin is that the quantity produced of any particular variety will be lower and this will reduce any benefits that are available to the firm from the presence of economies of scale. Thus the optimal differentiation strategy for a multi-product firm will involve balancing the revenue it gains from increased variety against the average cost increase that results from lowering the quantity of any single product produced. Multi-product firms are a missing element in the literature and this is clearly an area where more research is needed in order to further our knowledge about product differentiation.

1.5 Some basic propositions

Perhaps the most notable proposition in the theory of product differentiation is Hotelling's *principle of minimum differentiation*. This was his claim that two firms would locate as close to each other as possible. However, as we shall show in chapter 2, this is a very special result. In the model that Hotelling proposed, it depends on rather restrictive assumptions. We shall see that introducing other elements of imperfect competition, such as incomplete information, can restore the Hotelling result.

Chamberlin's analysis of monopolistic competition provided a theory of product variety in a market economy. He assumed that firms differentiated their products in an optimal way but provided no explicit decision structure for exactly how this happened. Given this, they then behaved like monopolists within the market for their own product equating marginal revenue to marginal cost and so pricing above marginal cost. If the number of firms were small, all would earn positive profits. However, this would attract new entry. Each new entrant would differentiate his or her product from those already available and this would cause the markets of the existing firms, and consequently their profits, to shrink. An equilibrium would be reached when profits fell to zero. The equilibrium number of firms equals the equilibrium number of products and hence measures the extent of product variety.

If profits converge to zero but price remains above marginal cost then this implies that marginal cost is less than average cost. It therefore follows that, in equilibrium, average costs must be falling. If so, we have the conclusion that a monopolistic competition equilibrium must depend on there being fixed costs or scale economies up to some point – for otherwise we could not have an equilibrium on a downward-sloping part of the average cost curve. The equilibrium degree of product variety is greater, the less the effects of scale economies and the less substitutable are group goods for one another – two basic principles in the determination of product variety that carry over to other market forms.

A zero-profit equilibrium will also emerge in the Hotelling locational model when the market is large enough. This has the advantage that location in the market, and hence variety, becomes a decision variable to be explicitly modelled. Each firm will locate far enough from others so as to have some monopoly power and will thus be able to set its price above marginal cost. Positive profits will bring additional firms into the market, reducing market size per firm and thus lowering profits until equilibrium is reached. In the equilibrium, product locations as well as the number of firms will be determind – namely the degree of differentiation as well as the extent of variety.

If the market structure is that of a single multi-product firm, the degree of variety offered will always be less than it would be under monopolistic competition. No clear results are available for an industry composed of a few multi-product firms, although this is a very important real case.

1.6 Product differentiation and welfare

Product differentiation leads to a variety of products being produced. As a result, it is possible that output levels are lower for each product than might be the case if the industry produced a single homogeneous good. If there are scale economies, the firms in the differentiated industry may not be able to take full advantage of these and so there is a potential for resource waste. In free-entry monopolistic competition, the zero-profit equilibrium in the symmetrical case (price = average cost > marginal cost) is such that all firms are producing a lower level of output than that at which costs are minimised. If the product were homogeneous, the free-entry competitive equilibrium would be one in which all firms produced at minimum average cost and so would involve a more efficient allocation of resources. It is this that gives rise to the welfare problem of product differentiation: the possible gains due to the wider range of varieties needs to be balanced against the possible losses due to the inability to take full advantage of the existence of economies of scale.

Product differentiation is also likely to have distributional consequences. If a single variety is replaced by many, there will be gains to those for whom the initial product was not their ideal – this is a gain due to the better matching of products and tastes. Of course, those who preferred the original will lose, possibly on two accounts: the original variety may no longer be available and even if it is, its price will have risen as a result of the smaller scale of its output.

Early welfare analyses of product differentiation were based on the loss that arose from the inability to fully exploit scale economies. They concluded that the monopolistically competitive market equilibrium inevitably led to a greater degree of product variety than was socially optimal. However, more recent analyses have taken fuller account of the benefits of variety and shown how the reverse relationship may sometimes be true. This is an issue that we shall continually come across in our investigation of product differentiation in the chapters to follow.

2 Spatial models of imperfect competition

2.1 Introduction

The task that we have set ourselves in this chapter is to examine the literature on product differentiation and imperfect competition that developed from Hotelling's seminal 1929 article entitled 'Stability in Competition'. The central conceptual idea is that consumers have heterogeneous tastes in the sense that each differs in what he or she considers to be the ideal brand from among the set of available products. Furthermore it is also assumed that these preferences are *asymmetric*. What this means is that if a consumer's ideal brand is i then the consumer prefers brands that are 'near' to i in terms of their specification (or combination of characteristics) more than those that are 'far' from it. This is in sharp contrast to the Chamberlinian model which we shall look at in the next chapter. In it consumers have symmetric preferences over the different brands and, in consequence, a 'representative consumer' is used to represent the whole consumer population.

In order to make the notion of asymmetric preferences clearer, it is helpful to think of brands as being represented by points in a multi-dimensional space. Asymmetry then just means that any particular consumer, identified and located by virtue of what he considers to be the ideal set of characteristics at some point in this space, will consider 'neighbouring' brands close to his 'location' to be very close substitutes. However, the further away that a brand is from this ideal point, the less close is it a substitute. Of course one must recognise that such statements are made entirely with reference to characteristics. In the market place a consumer may find that the ideal brand sells for a rather high price and some more distant brand for rather a low price and we may find that the optimal choice is the 'less-than-ideal' brand. However, this type of feature will reflect heterogeneity on the cost side, and it is not the impact of this that we want to study. The phenomenon that we want to focus on is

11

heterogeneity of preferences and its impact on the market equilibrium. Therefore for this reason we shall control for costs in our analysis by assuming from the outset that the cost function for every brand is the same.

This idea of close and distant substitutes seems like a realistic assumption when brands can be defined in terms of a *few* characteristics such as weight, size or geographical location. In such cases it is natural to assume that a consumer who values one particular brand will also put a high valuation on a brand that is its close neighbour in terms of characteristics. The conventional practice in models that use this assumption is to take the product space as a line or the circumference of a circle. In consequence, they are usually referred to as 'spatial' or 'location' models. Thus it is assumed that goods can be represented and preferences defined over a single characteristic and, if a consumer buys a brand, it will be the one that is closest to his ideal when the prices of the different brands are taken into account.

In contrast to this, in the case where each brand possesses numerous characteristics, it may be more valid to think of brands as being equally far apart as there may be no natural ordering over these characteristics. For example, Hart (1985a) comments that while chocolate bars can be described in terms of flavour, nuttiness, chewiness, etc., the overall combination of these may in some sense be unique to each bar. In a case such as this it is therefore more appropriate to use the Chamberlinian approach with the consumer maximising utility by purchasing a mix of brands on offer, the proportions of that mix varying with relative prices.

A fundamental consequence of assuming preference asymmetry is that competition between firms becomes 'localised'. Any particular firm's actions will have a powerful impact on those firms located near to it in the commodity space but will have a weak or no effect on those firms that are located very far from it.[1] Therefore, while spatial models may not be very useful in the analysis of multi-brand competition, they are ideally suited to the analysis of brand proliferation as a method of preempting entry. This is a topic that we shall return to in chapter 8.

There are three issues to be considered in the context of this model. First, given the number of products and the specification of their characteristics, firms may compete on price. We are interested then in the resulting equilibrium. While this is inevitably only a partial analysis of market equilibrium, we can usefully sort it out as a first step. However, the second step would be to allow the firms to compete in the specification of their products as well as on price. Thus in section 4 we shall allow the product to be a choice variable. The third issue that we shall want to consider is the entry of new products. The remainder of this chapter considers each of these issues in turn.

2.2 Price competition in a model of spatial duopoly

In the example that Hotelling considered, products are differentiated for
two reasons. In the first place, firms are located at different points in
geographical space. Secondly, there are positive transport costs involved
in the matching of consumers and products. In the geographical context,
as with ice-cream sellers on a beach along which potential customers are
spread out, this is fairly obvious. Where we are dealing with product
variety these transport costs can be thought of as losses of surplus to the
consumer as a result of a mismatch between the actual variety and the
consumer's ideal.

In order to fix these ideas let us assume that firms locate on a line of
length l. Suppose now that there are two sellers producing a homogeneous
commodity whose costs of production are zero and let them be located at
some points on the line. Seller 1 is assumed to be at a distance α from one
end of the line and seller 2 at a distance β from the other. Thus

$$\alpha + \beta \leqslant l; \quad \alpha, \beta \geqslant 0.$$

As we mentioned above, in this section we will treat the locations of the
products as exogenous parameters so that price becomes the only decision
variable for the two firms. Initially we shall assume that $\alpha + \beta < l$. The
market is illustrated in figure 2.1.

Consumers are taken to be uniformly distributed along the line and
each buys only *one* unit of the good. Hence demands are completely
inelastic. Since the commodity sold by the two sellers is homogeneous
a consumer will buy from the seller who quotes the lowest delivered price.
We define this to be the seller's mill price plus the cost of transporting the
good from the firm to the consumer's location.[2] For Hotelling the latter
was a constant c (>0) per unit of distance x. As we shall see, the assumptions
that the market is bounded, the goods are homogeneous, transport costs
constant per unit of distance and demands inelastic are fundamental to
Hotelling's analysis in the sense that the nature of the equilibrium in his
model may change when one or more of these assumptions are relaxed.

The first thing to note about the model is that it generates discontinuous
demand functions. In order to see this consider the case where firm 1 sets
a mill price p_1 and firm 2 p_2. At these prices there will be a consumer who

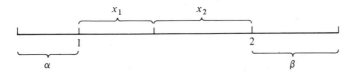

Figure 2.1

is indifferent between the two products because their delivered prices are the same. Suppose that this consumer is located at a distance of x_1 from firm 1 and x_2 from firm 2. It then follows that

$$p_1 + cx_1 = p_2 + cx_2. \tag{2.1}$$

Firm 1 will sell to all those consumers to the left of the marginal consumer and firm 2 to all those to the right. Hence we can write the sales of firm j, q_j, as

$$q_1 = \alpha + x_1, \tag{2.2}$$

$$q_2 = \beta + x_2. \tag{2.3}$$

Taking p_2 as given, firm 1 could increase its sales if it were to reduce its mill price. This would allow it to capture consumers located at a distance greater than x_1 from it. Such a policy will move the marginal consumer farther to the right and at some point this consumer will be located at the same place as firm 2. The price that achieves this, $\boldsymbol{p}_1$, is defined by the 'indifference' condition

$$\boldsymbol{p}_1 + c(x_1 + x_2) = p_2.$$

If firm 1 were now to reduce its price just fractionally below $\boldsymbol{p}_1$, it would capture all the consumers between firm 2 and the right-hand end of the market. In other words, there is a *discontinuity* at $\boldsymbol{p}_1$ in firm 1's demand curve. By a similar piece of reasoning we can find a price $\bar{p}_1$ such that the marginal consumer is at firm 1's location. This is defined by

$$\bar{p}_1 = p_2 + c(x_1 + x_2).$$

If firm 1 were to raise its price above this, it would lose all its customers to firm 2. Thus again we have a discontinuity in the demand curve. This is all shown in figure 2.2.

These discontinuities in the demand functions lead to discontinuities in the profit functions $\Pi_j = p_j q_j$ and this opens up the possibility that the reaction functions (the loci of best response) may not intersect. Thus there may well be no Nash equilibrium in prices.

Two comments are in order here. The first relates to a constraint on the set of price pairs that may constitute an equilibrium and the second relates to the size of that set. A pair of prices cannot be a Nash equilibrium pair unless they satisfy the condition that

$$|p_1 - p_2| < c(x_1 + x_2) = c[l - (\alpha + \beta)]. \tag{2.4}$$

This condition is intuitively sensible. The right-hand side of the inequality is just the cost of transporting the good between firm 1's location and firm

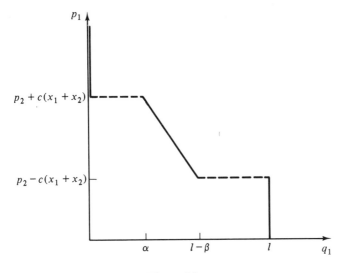

Figure 2.2

2's. The left-hand side is the difference in the mill prices. If this exceeded the cost of transporting the good there would be scope for profitable arbitrage. Thus if a price pair did not satisfy (2.4) at least one firm could increase its profits by choosing a different price.

The second point to note is that if α and β are 'large' the points α and $(l-\beta)$ will be close together. As can be seen in figure 2.2, it is only between these points that the demand function is continuous and the smaller the distance, the less, so to speak, is the extent of continuity. If we locate the firms sufficiently far apart this range of continuity can be enlarged and, other things equal,[3] we can increase the likelihood that reaction functions are continuous and that a Nash equilibrium will exist. Indeed, as d'Aspremont *et al.* (1979) have shown, a pair of prices that satisfy (2.4) and which maximise firms' profits will be the Nash equilibrium pair provided that the locations satisfy the conditions[4]

$$\left[l+\frac{\alpha-\beta}{3}\right]^2 \geqslant \left[\frac{4}{3}\right] l(\alpha+2\beta),$$

$$\left[l+\frac{\beta-\alpha}{3}\right]^2 \geqslant \left[\frac{4}{3}\right] l(\beta+2\alpha).$$

(2.5)

What condition (2.4) gives us is a necessary condition for an equilibrium. In fact, in price space it defines the set of prices within which an equilibrium must lie. However, this set of price pairs may be larger than the set of Nash equilibria. What condition (2.5) does is to provide the restriction on the size of the set defined by (2.4). Thus (2.4) and (2.5) taken together are necessary and sufficient conditions for a Nash equilibrium to exist.

For our purposes here we can suppose that condition (2.5) holds and turn now to characterising the Nash equilibrium. Using (2.1) and the fact that $l = \alpha + \beta + x_1 + x_2$ we can obtain

$$x_1 = \left[\frac{1}{2}\right]\left[l - \alpha - \beta - \frac{(p_1 - p_2)}{c}\right] \tag{2.6}$$

and

$$x_2 = \left[\frac{1}{2}\right]\left[l - \alpha - \beta - \frac{(p_2 - p_1)}{c}\right]. \tag{2.7}$$

If these are substituted into (2.2) and (2.3) and the latter into the expressions for profits, we obtain

$$\Pi_1 = \left[\frac{1}{2}\right][l + \alpha - \beta]p_1 - \frac{p_1^2}{2c} + \frac{p_1 p_2}{2c} \tag{2.8}$$

and

$$\Pi_2 = \left[\frac{1}{2}\right][l - \alpha + \beta]p_2 - \frac{p_2^2}{2c} + \frac{p_1 p_2}{2c}. \tag{2.9}$$

If we now maximise these, we can use the first-order conditions, $(\partial \Pi_i / \partial p_i) = 0$, to obtain the Nash equilibrium pair (p_1^*, p_2^*)

$$p_1^* = c\left[l + \frac{(\alpha - \beta)}{3}\right]; \quad p_2^* = c\left[l - \frac{(\alpha - \beta)}{3}\right]. \tag{2.10}$$

What we have obtained is a Nash equilibrium in which the firms are taken to be at *distinct* points. There is of course another case to consider: where the two firms are located at the same point (i.e. $\alpha + \beta = l$). Of course, if one thinks about it, this is really the case of *no* product differentiation and so it is not surprising that the Nash equilibrium in this case is simply the homogeneous duopoly Bertrand solution. In the present case in which zero marginal production costs have been assumed this just means zero prices and profits.[5]

There have been a number of approaches taken to solving the problem of existence of a Nash equilibrium. All of these involve relaxing one or other of Hotelling's original assumptions. For example, if one assumes that the firms are symmetrically located around a circle rather than along a line, then the upper discontinuity on each firm's demand curve will disappear. One can see why this should be the case. The firm faces rivals on *both* sides now and as it raises its mill price it will lose custom to both of these. When its mill price reaches the limit set by the lowest of its rivals' delivered prices at its location, then its own sales will have fallen to zero. This increases the possibility of an equilibrium as we shall see when we discuss Salop's 'circular road' model in section 5 below.[6]

The existence problem in Hotelling's model disappears when the assumption of constant marginal costs is relaxed. We shall look at this in more detail in the next section but, to get the essence of the argument, suppose that marginal transport costs increase with distance. Now consider the situation where seller 1 sets a mill price such that its delivered price just equals firm 2's mill price. Firm 2 will still be able to service *all* the consumers to its right at a delivered price that is lower than that of firm 1 by reason of the fact that its marginal cost of transport is *lower* than firm 1's. The implication then is that a small reduction in firm 1's price at this point will, given its rival's price, lead to only a small increase in sales. In other words, the discontinuities in the demand function disappear and so too will the non-existence problem. For example, d'Aspremont *et al.* (1979) consider the case where transport costs are given by cx^2 and show that there will be a unique Nash equilibrium in prices irrespective of the exogenously given locations of the two firms.[7]

In setting up this model we have given it a strictly locational interpretation by using transport costs as the differentiating factor. An alternative construction which would have made product differentiation more explicit would have been to specify a (sufficiently high, but finite) reservation price for each consumer for their ideal brand and to have appealed to the loss of utility suffered by a consumer when they purchased a 'less-than-ideal' brand. This would have had the effect of causing the reservation price to decline as the distance between a consumer's ideal brand and actual brand available increased. This device of monotonic non-linearity in the response of the reservation price has been used by a number of authors to demonstrate the existence of price equilibrium.[8]

2.3 Transportation costs and the existence problem

We shall continue to assume that there are only two firms and consider the effect of the nature of the 'transport' cost function on the profit functions facing the two firms. As we have indicated, establishing the existence of a pure strategy Nash equilibrium requires that the profit functions of each firm be continuous and quasi-concave in prices. What we shall indicate in

18   **The economic theory of product differentiation**

this section is the effect of changing the specification of the transport costs on this property of the profit function. Our discussion is based on the work of Gabszewicz and Thisse (1986).

We continue to use the same simple locational model of a linear market to examine the outcome of price and product competition under horizontal differentiation.[9] This is shown below:

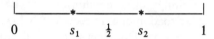

$$0 \qquad s_1 \qquad \tfrac{1}{2} \quad s_2 \qquad 1$$

The market is of unit length with consumers, who have a completely inelastic demand for one unit of the good, being uniformly distributed over that interval. It has been assumed that the two firms are symmetrically located at a distance of a from the mid-point. Thus $s_1 = \tfrac{1}{2} - a$ and $s_2 = \tfrac{1}{2} + a$.

The price that a consumer pays for any product is comprised of two parts: its mill price (p_i) and its transportation costs $t(s, s')$. The latter are given by

$$t(s, s') = c|s - s'| + d(s - s')^2, \quad c, d \geqslant 0.$$

This gives us the various cases that have been looked at in the literature. The boundary between the market areas of the two firms will be defined by

$$p_1 + t(s_1, \bar{x}) = p_2 + t(s_2, \bar{x})$$

and, as it clearly depends on just p_1 and p_2, we can denote it as $\bar{x}(p_1, p_2)$.

Taking the price of good 2 as given at $\bar{p}_2$, there are two key points in the demand schedule facing firm 1. One is where firm 1's mill price is so high that it equals firm 2's delivered price at s_1. Its only market is thus in the interval $[0, \tfrac{1}{2} - a]$. At the opposite extreme, if firm 1's mill price is so low that its delivered price equals $\bar{p}_2$ at s_2, then firm 1 will have a market of $[\tfrac{1}{2} + a]$, and firm 2 will only be able to supply one side of its potential market. The demand schedule is shown in figure 2.3.

The demand curve is comprised of three linear segments (the linearity is a consequence of the uniformity of the distribution and the assumption that each consumer only buys one unit). The prices which delimit the various segments are as follows:

$$p_1^{++} = \bar{p}_2 + 2ac + 2ad,$$
$$p_1^{+} = \bar{p}_2 + 2ac + 4a^2d,$$
$$p_1^{-} = \bar{p}_2 - 2ac - 4a^2d,$$
$$p_1^{--} = \bar{p}_2 - 2ac - 2ad.$$

Thus the slope of the two end segments is $-4ad$ and that of the middle one

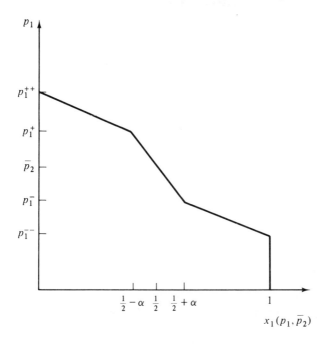

Figure 2.3

$-(4ad+2c)$. This enables us to write the demand function for 1 as

$$x_1(p_1, \bar{p}_2) = 0 \quad \text{if} \quad p_1 > p_1^{++}$$

$$= \frac{\bar{p}_2 - p_1 + 2ac + 2ad}{4ad}, \quad p_1^{++} > p_1 > p_1^{+},$$

$$= \frac{\bar{p}_2 - p_1 + c + 2ad}{4ad + 2c}, \quad p_1^{+} > p_1 > p_1^{-},$$

$$= \frac{\bar{p}_2 - p_1 + 2ad - 2ac}{4ad}, \quad p_1^{-} > p_1 > p_1^{--},$$

$$= 1 \quad \text{if} \quad p_1^{--} > p_1 \geqslant 0.$$

We may usefully note the various special cases that this gives rise to.

1 If $a=0$, then $p_1^{++} = p_1^{+} = \bar{p}_2 = p_1^{--} = p_2^{-}$. Thus if $p_1 > \bar{p}_2, x_1 = 0$ and if $p_1 < \bar{p}_2, x_1 = 1$. The demand schedule is not continuous though it is concave and is shown in figure 2.4. What we find in this case is that, when

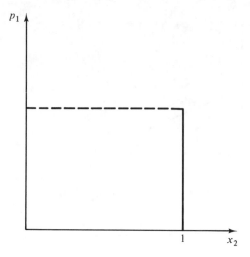

Figure 2.4

the firms are located at the centre of the market, the only equilibrium is $p_1^* = p_2^* = 0$. The market is thus shared between them.

2 If $a > 0$ and $d = 0$, we have the case of linear transport costs with $p_1^{++} = p_1^+ = \bar{p}_2 + 2ac$ and $p_1^{--} = p_1^- = \bar{p}_2 - 2ac$. The demand schedule facing firm 1 is shown in figure 2.5 (this is the case we looked at above in figure 2.2).

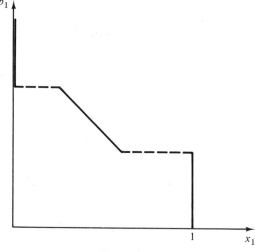

Figure 2.5

3 If $a>0$ and $c=0$ then we have a demand function (and hence profit function) that is continuous in prices and concave; as in figure 2.6.

Looking at each of these diagrams makes clear the importance of rising marginal transport costs in increasing the amount of continuity in the demand function and concavity in the demand and profit functions.

In the general case, provided that a is large enough (the firms are far enough apart), a Nash equilibrium in prices will exist and will be one in which the market boundary, $\bar{x}$, is between the two firms. In this case, the profit function for firm i is given by

$$\Pi_i(p_i, p_j) = \frac{p_i[p_j - p_i + 2ad + c]}{4ad + 2c}.$$

The graph of the reaction functions is shown in figure 2.7 and the Nash equilibrium price is $p_i^* = [2ad + c]$.

What happens as a falls is that the demand schedule changes in the manner shown in figure 2.8 and the likelihood that the best response lies on the 'interior' part of the demand schedule falls. Instead, it becomes increasingly likely that the best response will be to try to *undercut* the rival just as it was in case 1 above. In this case, an equilibrium with positive prices will fail to exist. The two firms need to be a critical distance apart to

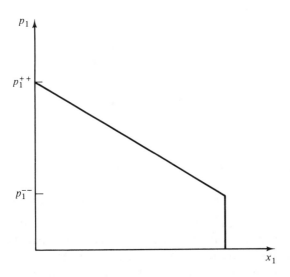

Figure 2.6

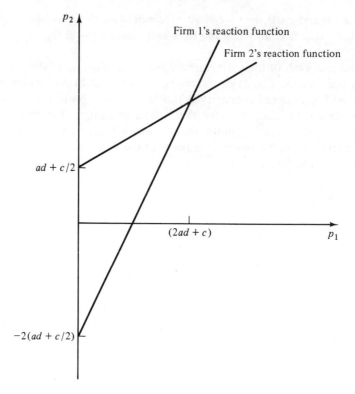

Figure 2.7

rule out this possibility. Specifically, Gabszewicz and Thisse (1986) show that the condition is that

$$2a \geqslant \min\left[\frac{1}{3}, \frac{\sqrt{c}}{2\sqrt{d}+\sqrt{c}}\right].$$

2.4 The choice of location (or product selection) in spatial models

2.4.1 Hotelling's principle of minimum product differentiation

So far we have treated a firm's location as given. It should be clear that, while this may be a reasonable assumption in a purely spatial analysis, it is less satisfactory when a more 'characteristics' interpretation is being given. For this reason we now want to see what happens when this assumption is relaxed. Thus we shall now allow firms to choose their locations optimally

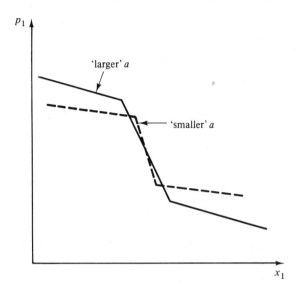

Figure 2.8

and so address in the process the issue of product selection. To start things off, and in the accepted tradition, we shall take prices as given and consider the firm's optimal locational choice.

Recalling that α and β were the distances of the two sellers from the end of the line, an inspection of (2.8) and (2.9) shows us that $\partial \Pi_1(p_1^*, p_2^*)/\partial \alpha$ and $\partial \Pi_2(p_1^*, p_2^*)/\partial \beta$ are both positive. In other words, given prices and the rival's location, each firm can increase its profits by moving away from its respective end of the market. By moving closer to its rival, each firm can encroach on its rival's market while, at the same time, losing none of the market that lies between its mill location and the end of the line. This argument therefore suggests that, in deciding on their optimal location, firms will have an incentive to *agglomerate* at the centre of the market. Hotelling thought that this type of behaviour would be widespread and termed it the 'principle of minimum product differentiation'.

It is immediately clear however, that this argument is false since we cannot, strictly speaking, use arguments that are based on the profit functions (2.8) and (2.9) because these were constructed on the assumption that an equilibrium price pair exists in the set defined by (2.4).[10] This depended on the firms being located sufficiently far apart and so the statements we made in the previous paragraph cannot be generally valid. Furthermore, suppose we consider the possibility of an equilibrium in which both firms locate at the centre of the market. The Bertrand–Nash equilibrium involves zero profits. However, the firms would be able to obtain positive profits in any other location and hence this cannot be an equilibrium where firms choose both location and price. Thus we conclude that, in its original form, the Hotelling model has no Nash equilibrium if both price and location are allowed to be choice variables.

Generally, intuition points to the existence of two forces pulling in opposite directions. Given prices, the two firms will want to increase their *market share* and this pulls them towards the centre of the market. This is the *agglomeration effect*. However, firms are aware that this essentially reduces the degree of product differentiation (the distance between them is reduced) and that this could lead to a reduction in equilibrium prices. This *strategic effect* will encourage the firms to distance themselves from one another. The question of course is which of these two countervailing effects is the dominant one. If we concentrate on symmetric locations we can see (from the equations for equilibrium prices) that in the original Hotelling model the second effect is absent. This is however due to Hotelling's special assumptions of infinitely inelastic demands and constant marginal transport costs. Thus whilst as we indicated in section 1 the conclusion that there was no Nash equilibrium in prices could easily be reversed if we were to alter some of Hotelling's assumptions, the principle of minimum differentiation will not generally survive such a change. For example, suppose that we let transport costs be given by cx^2. The firms now have continuous profit functions $[\Pi_i(p_1^*, p_2^*)]$ but these decrease with respect to distance from the *end* of the market. Firms therefore have an incentive to locate at the endpoints and the principle of minimum differentiation becomes one of maximum differentiation! In order to explore this further we will use a model, due to Neven (1985), that describes market equilibrium when firms can choose both price and location.[11]

2.4.2 A model of spatial duopoly in price and location

We assume that M consumers are uniformly distributed in terms of tastes on a product line. This is shown in figure 2.9. Consumers purchase a single unit of some variety x and spend the rest of their income on another (numeraire) commodity that represents all other goods. The utility function is additively separable in the differentiated and numeraire goods and takes the form

$$U(x^*, x) = [a - b(x - x^*)^2] + Y - p_x, \quad a, b > 0. \tag{2.11}$$

x^* is the consumer's ideal variety, Y is his income (assumed the same for all consumers') and p_x is the price of variety x. The sub-utility function $[a - b(x - x^*)^2]$ is shown in figure 2.10. The parameter a represents the

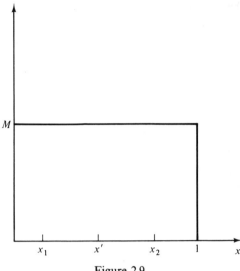

Figure 2.9

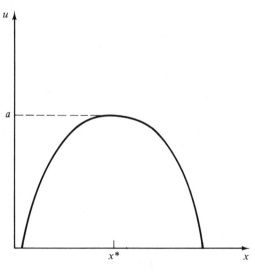

Figure 2.10

consumer's utility when he buys his ideal variety. The purchase of a less-than-ideal variety x reduces the consumer's utility by $b(x-x^*)^2$. Thus the 'utility cost' is quadratic in the distance between the actual and ideal variety, a natural assumption in non-geographic product space.[12]

Consider now the following duopoly: firm 1 is located at x_1 and firm

2 at x_2 and they are charging prices p_1 and p_2 respectively. Let the consumer whose ideal variety is x' be indifferent between x_1 and x_2 at these prices: $U(x', x_1) = U(x', x_2)$. Using (2.11) we find that

$$x' = \frac{(1/b)(p_2 - p_1) - (x_1^2 - x_2^2)}{2(x_2 - x_1)}$$

Given our assumptions, the profits of the two firms can be written as

$$\Pi_1 = p_1 x' M; \quad \Pi_2 = p_2(1 - x')M.$$

If we now use the first-order conditions for profit maximisation with respect to price, we can calculate the unique Nash equilibrium prices

$$p_1^* = (x_2 - x_1)\left[\frac{2b}{3}\right] + (x_2^2 - x_1^2)\left[\frac{b}{3}\right], \tag{2.12}$$

$$p_2^* = (x_2 - x_1)\left[\frac{4b}{3}\right] + (x_2^2 - x_1^2)\left[\frac{b}{3}\right]. \tag{2.13}$$

We now assume that firms make their location and price decisions sequentially. The duopoly game then has two stages: in stage 2 (the last stage) they choose the optimal price given their locations and in stage 1 they decide on their optimal location. Thus what we are looking for is the *perfect equilibrium* of the two-stage game.[13] In order to obtain this we simply express the profit functions in stage 1 in terms of the Nash equilibrium prices of stage 2. Since the latter are expressed as a function of *location*, we can then proceed to optimise with respect to location (x_1^*, x_2^*), and then substitute back into the price formulae so as to have everything expressed in terms of the basic parameters. The stage 1 profits are thus

$$\Pi_1 = p_1^* x'(p_1^*, x_2^*)M, \tag{2.14}$$

$$\Pi_2 = p_2^*[1 - x'(p_1^*, x_2^*)]M \tag{2.15}$$

and the optimisation yields the perfect equilibrium results

$$x_1^* = 0; \quad x_2^* = 1; \quad p_1^* = p_2^* = b.$$

In other words, the two duopolists choose the endpoints (maximum differentiation) and charge the same price.

What is important in enabling Neven to obtain this result is that, to revert to the terminology of section 3, he has assumed c to be zero and d positive. This gives him the concavity that he needs in the profit functions. In a more general analysis, it should be clear that there cannot always be a perfect equilibrium in the horizontal case. For this to be so we should need to ensure that there exists a Nash equilibrium in the second-stage price game for *any* choice of locations and we know from the work of Gabszewicz and Thisse that this is not the case.

Their analysis points in fact to a more general point. A *sufficient* condition for the quasi-concavity of profit functions is that demand functions are concave. It is clear from our analysis that the properties of the demand function hinge very much on the nature of the transport cost function. If we consider the more general (diminishing returns) function $t(s, x)$, it turns out that concavity of demand almost never holds in the horizontal case. Of course, provided that the departure is not too severe, an equilibrium may exist; but significant departures result in non-existence. Thus stability is going to be very problematic in this type of model.

A feature of the analysis that we have been doing is that it considers only *pure* strategies: strategies followed with probability one. In the light of the analysis by Dasgupta and Maskin (1986) of discontinuous games, some comments on *mixed-strategy* equilibria are called for. Dasgupta and Maskin have two results that are of direct relevance to our discussion. First, they show that the duopoly model of price competition has a mixed-strategy equilibrium for any pair of locations (theorem 3). Secondly, they show that the location choice problem when there are more than two firms – studied by Eaton and Lipsey (1975) and Shaked (1982) – possesses a symmetric mixed-strategy equilibrium (theorem 4). Osborne and Pitchik (1987) use the first of these Dasgupta-Maskin results to study the two-stage duopoly location and price game. They show that there is a unique subgame-perfect equilibrium in which the location choices of the firms are pure strategies – the firms locate at approximately the $(\frac{1}{4}, \frac{3}{4})$ points of the market. The nature of the subgame equilibrium price strategy in this case is rather interesting. It is one in which there is a 'high' price and a 'low' price. However, the probability weight attached to the latter is 'small' and they interpret this as an example of the periodic 'sales' found in high-street shops. They also find that there is a subgame-perfect equilibrium in which firms randomise over location. However, most of the probability is attached to locations that can be thought of as involving a 'moderate' amount of differentiation.

2.4.3 Equilibrium with more than two firms

Early commentators of Hotelling's analysis argued that there could be no locational equilibrium in the case of the linear bounded market when there were more than two firms. The reason is that, were a third firm to enter after the first two had located at the centre, it would choose, given the Hotelling assumption that the other firms' prices would remain constant, to locate immediately outside one of the two existing firms. Thus one firm would now find itself squeezed by the other two, have virtually no market and so would react by moving outside one of the two flanking firms. We would therefore get a pattern of locational instability.[14]

This argument ignores the problem that a Nash equilibrium in the Hotelling model may possibly not exist because it relics on Hotelling's zero conjectural variation assumption. However, even if we ensure that a Nash price equilibrium exists, there may be no Nash equilibrium in which both prices and locations are chosen. For example, Prescott and Visscher (1977) construct a model that has an equilibrium in price and location similar to that discussed in the last subsection in the case where there are two firms. However, when there are three, the model has no equilibrium.

In a model in which firms are assumed to choose price and location *simultaneously*, it is generally the case that there is no Nash equilibrium (Novshek, 1980). There can be no equilibrium in which the firms are located at different points, for then a firm could gain by locating next to one of its neighbours *and* slightly undercutting its price as long as costs were not very sharply U-shaped. Nor can there be an equilibrium in which firms are at the same location, as the only possible price equilibrium there is the Bertrand one and a firm could always gain by moving away from its rival and charging a higher price.

However, the two-stage perfect equilibrium idea that we used in the previous subsection can be applied to the case of more than two firms. Again, in the last stage, the n firms decide on their optimal Nash equilibrium prices given their locations and in the first stage they choose their optimal locations using the profit functions defined in terms of the Nash equilibrium prices of the second stage.[15] Salop's (1979) model of spatial competition could, in principle, be considered in this way – though Salop did not himself look at the issue of product choice in a sequential framework.[16] (We shall, in fact, look at his model in the next section.)

An alternative multi-stage equilibrium concept that has been suggested involves sequential foresighted entry. This has been suggested for situations in which relocation is costly. This 'foresighted sequential solution concept' has been used to prove the existence of an equilibrium in prices and product locations (or specifications) by Prescott and Visscher (1977).[17] The firms in their model locate one at a time. They argue that firms enter in a sequential fashion because some entrants become aware of a profitable market before others do. Once a firm has made its choice of location it is stuck, for it is assumed that relocating is prohibitively expensive. Thus an entering firm will observe the existing location pattern formed by its predecessors and, aware that later entrants will behave in the same rational way as itself, chooses its own profit-maximising market position. Thus the expectations that each firm holds about the response of other firms to its decision are rational in the sense that they are consistent with the predictions of the model as later entrants do indeed locate just where the firm predicted. Once each firm has made its location choice, prices are determined in a Nash equilibrium manner.

Prescott and Visscher (1977) and Lane (1980) use this approach to prove the existence of distinct equilibrium locations and equilibrium prices both in the case of an exogenous number of firms and when entry is endogenous. It should be clear that, in the case where the number of firms is given, the optimal location-price choices will be contingent on it. For instance, when $n = 3$, the locational equilibrium is one in which firms 1 and 2 locate on the unit interval at the points $(\frac{1}{4})$ and $(\frac{3}{4})$ and firm 3 at $(\frac{1}{2})$. In the case of endogenous entry, entering firms choose their optimal location taking into account the effect that this will have on potential entrants' choices. Their intention will be to deter entry because, the more firms, the nearer they are together and the more severe the resulting price competition and the lower the free-entry equilibrium profits. As a result the number of firms may well settle at a level that is lower than the maximum that the market could sustain were it impossible to deter entry.[18]

2.4.4 Agglomeration or diversity in product selection?

A central feature of the literature that we have considered in this section is its rejection of the Hotelling principle of minimum differentiation. Indeed, as we shall see in chapter 6, the same feature of firms choosing distinct qualities as an equilibrium phenomenon appears when we move from horizontal to vertical differentiation. Perhaps one should not be surprised by such a result. Commonsense arguments would probably lead one to expect that firms would use a feature like product differentiation to its full extent to enable them to lessen the adverse effects of price competition on profits. In many ways, an equilibrium with minimum differentiation as its main feature might be thought to be rather more surprising. We should therefore expect there to be a widespread tendency to use product differentiation to lessen the effects of price competition.

However we ought to ask ourselves whether or not there are counter-tendencies that just possibly might be sufficiently strong to lead firms to locate at the same point in characteristics space – if not in every dimension, at least in some. There is some suggestion that this might happen in retail trade.

De Palma et al. (1985) have looked at this and restored minimum differentiation as an equilibrium feature. They consider the case of a bounded linear market with transport costs that are linear in distance. Three assumptions are responsible for this reversal. The first is that what differentiates firms is not just location but also some other inherent characteristic. The second is that consumers are heterogeneous in the value they place on these characteristics. Finally, while firms know the distribution of these valuations across the population, they have imperfect information regarding any particular consumer's valuation. This is summed up in the following function which gives the utility that a consumer located at x will derive from buying the good at location x_i

$$u_i(x) = v_i(x) + \mu\epsilon_i, \tag{2.16}$$

where

$$v_i(x) = a - p - c|x - x_i|.$$

Each firm sells its good at a given price p (though this is endogenous and determined in the overall equilibrium). The v_i sub-utility function is essentially the one we met above. It says that a consumer's surplus is at its maximum when he or she buys a good with the ideal characteristics x and declines the further away the product is from this ideal. However, this decline is not deterministic for equation (2.16) adds a random, individual-specific element $\mu\epsilon_i$ which may be positive or negative. It is this that reflects the heterogeneity of tastes. Now the usual model would have the consumer located at x buying from firm i rather than j if

$$u_i(x) > u_j(x).$$

However, we now need to cast this in probabilistic terms: the probability that a person at x will find $u_i(x)$ greater than $u_j(x)$ and so buy from x. The surplus obtained from any commodity now has a random as well as the usual systematic element. If we denote the distance between x and x_i (i.e. $|x - x_i|$) by d_i, we can write the probability that the consumer will buy from i rather than j as

$$\Pr\left\{\epsilon_i > \epsilon_j + \frac{c(d_i - d_j)}{\mu}\right\}.$$

This probability is at a maximum if the consumer would encounter i first and at a minimum if i is encountered after j.

μ is a critical parameter here, for as it increases from 0 we move further and further away from the homogeneity in valuation of our basic model. The implications of this for the probability of purchase and for the demand schedule facing a particular firm can be seen by referring to figure 2.11.

Probability of
purchase from firm 1

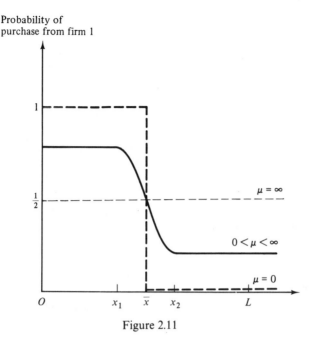

Figure 2.11

Here we consider the case of two firms located on the line OL (whose length is l): one at x_1 and the other at x_2. Consider those consumers located to the left of x_1. Firm 2 is always $\delta\,(=|x_1-x_2|)$ further away from them than firm 1 and so the probability that they will buy from 1 rather than 2 is a constant (<1). By a similar argument, this probability is also constant, but much lower, to the right of x_2. However, as we consider those consumers located between x_1 and x_2, the probability declines the closer we get to firm 2. As a result of symmetry in the distribution of the ϵ, the inflection point ($\bar{x}$) is mid way between the two. The solid line shows the probability for a positive value of μ. To see how this will vary as μ changes, suppose first that μ were zero. We are now back to the homogeneous case where the consumer buys from the nearest firm so that every consumer to the left of $\bar{x}$ buys from 1 and all to the right from 2. On the other hand, as μ goes to infinity, a consumer's location on the x-axis becomes of less and less importance in determining the valuation they place on any product so that in the limit any consumer is equally likely to buy from either firm. In other words, the probability of buying from firm 1 is $\frac{1}{2}$ over the entire interval OL. These two limiting cases are shown by the thick and thin dashed lines respectively. A further implication of the introduction of heterogeneity is that the demand function for firm 1 is a *continuous* function of x_1 over the interval.

Since we are interested in the question of the equilibrium degree of differentiation, consider now the implications of this model for the choice of location (taking price as given). The case of $\mu = 0$ is straightforward. The best-response location for 1 is to locate itself adjacent to 2. Thus firm 1's reaction function is the 45°-ray shown in figure 2.12. In other words, there are an infinity of Nash equilibria in the location game when there is homogeneity. When $\mu = \infty$, the best response for firm 1 will be to locate itself at the centre of the market as this will minimise its total 'transport' costs. The best response for firm 1 for finite μ is shown by the solid reaction function. Since the reaction function for firm 2 is the mirror image of that of 1, we see that, in the two-firm case in the presence of heterogeneity, the Nash location equilibrium will be at the centre. This is just agglomeration. Of course, the question is whether or not this tendency holds for general n. De Palma *et al.* establish that provided μ exceeds some critical value (which is increasing but asymptotically finite in n), central agglomeration is indeed a Nash equilibrium in the location game.

The next step is to take location as given and ask what will happen to prices. What is to stop Bertrand price competition from forcing profits to

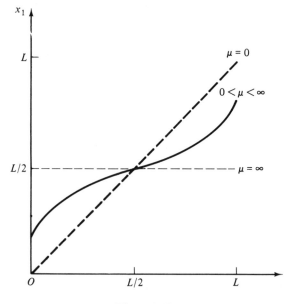

Figure 2.12

zero? This was the difficulty in the original Hotelling model. For our present purposes we can focus on the case where costs of production are zero. Then, if $\mu = 0$, we have the situation we examined earlier and we know that Bertrand competition will indeed result in the price (and profits) being driven to zero. However, the greater the degree of heterogeneity, the higher will be the equilibrium price though, given μ, this will be decreasing with the number of firms.

The final step in their analysis is to consider the nature of the overall Nash equilibrium. De Palma *et al.* show that, if μ is finite, then an agglomerated Nash equilibrium, if it exists, can do so only at the centre of the market. However, the question of existence depends on just how large μ is. If it is sufficiently great, one will exist. Essentially the reason why is that there is an interplay between the two forces we identified earlier: price competition which keeps firms distant and the desire to maximise market share which encourages firms to agglomerate in the centre of the market. Thus what the analysis shows us is that sufficient heterogeneity can indeed restore the Hotelling principle of minimum differentiation. However, what is critical is for this result is not heterogeneity *per se* but its importance in relation to the other parameters of the model. Formally, it is the ratio $[\mu/cl]$ that matters. In other words the degree of homogeneity that is needed to get agglomeration is larger the bigger the market and the more important are 'transport' costs. A final comment in this context concerns the 'folk theorem' that in large enough markets the equilibrium corresponds to the competitive outcome. Unless μ goes to zero as n goes to infinity, the equilibrium price will lie above marginal cost (here taken to be zero). We shall return to this issue again in chapter 7 where we consider limit theorems.

There is another argument that has been used in favour of agglomeration. It is based on consumers having imperfect information as to which products are on offer and where they are. Thus consumers have to *search* the product space to seek the commodity that best fits their needs. These search costs reduce the surplus that any consumer could obtain from the eventual purchase of the good and hence firms will have a profit incentive to make these as low as possible. This will maximise the pool of consumers' surplus available for them to tap and hence their expected profits. Agglomeration is the way to do this. This argument is the one that is used by Stahl (1982b). In his model consumers make, at most, one visit to a market place (a location with one or more firms). They are assumed to know the size (number of firms) and location of each market place but not its composition (the type of firms to be found there). Consumers are prepared to travel farther the larger the market place and this means that larger markets will also experience larger aggregate demand. Firms anticipate that if they join a market place rather than setting up as an isolated monopoly they can expect more visits and hence enjoy more demand. This is not due to a rise in the probability that any visit results in a sale (indeed the opposite is true), but because the search costs that consumers experience are in the nature of a fixed cost: it is the cost of getting to the market that is critical. Once there, search within that market place is costless. One can now see why the number of visits rise – consumers want to spread these fixed costs as widely as possible. A feature of Stahl's model which is unsatisfactory is that prices are exogenous so that we do not have increased price competition with agglomeration. It remains to be seen whether his conclusions would be as clear cut if prices were endogenous.[19]

2.5 Long-run equilibrium with costless relocation

Up till now we have taken the number of firms as given. We now let this number be endogenously determined by permitting free entry. We are thus going to look at long-run equilibrium. As there is, by now, quite a large literature on free-entry equilibria in imperfect markets, it may be useful at this stage to draw the reader's attention to its three main strands.

The first is the strand that is concerned with the formal description of long-run equilibrium with free entry corresponding to some particular description in terms of the parameters of technology, tastes and market size. This strand has been concerned with the questions of whether or not an equilibrium exists and, if so, what its comparative statics and welfare properties are.[20]

The second is where authors have examined the behaviour of the equilibrium of the model in 'large' economies. What they have done is to try to establish limit theorems or asymptotic results that describe the behaviour of the model as the market gets very large (of infinite size) or when fixed costs go to zero (so that tiny firms can exist). The question that they have been interested in is the truth of the 'folk theorem' that large markets approximate to perfect competition or whether such markets remain innately imperfectly competitive.[21]

The third strand in the literature is that concerned with establishing the existence of what has been termed a 'deterrence equilibrium'. Given the level of fixed costs, there is a maximum number of firms that a given size of market could profitably sustain. The question is then whether or not the actual number it *does* sustain is less than this. In a spatial context the method by which such an equilibrium might be sustained is by entry-deterring locational choices on the part of the incumbent firms.[22]

It is the first of these three strands that we are going to concentrate on in this section. The second and third strands will be considered in chapters 7 and 8 respectively. We shall consider a one-dimensional spatial market again but now represent this by the circumference of a unit circle. This has the advantage of not having to worry about endpoints. The model we use is due to Salop (1979). One reason for choosing it is because it explicitly treats the welfare issues of optimal product diversity and selection.[23] We shall concentrate on an equilibrium in which each firm earns zero profits and firms are symmetrically located around the circumference of the circle. As a result, two comments are in order. The first is that we are ignoring the 'integer problem'. This is that a free-entry zero-profit equilibrium may not be consistent with an integer number of firms. The second is that, by restricting ourselves to symmetric equilibria (so firms also produce equal output levels and charge identical mill prices), we are implicitly allowing firms to costlessly relocate as entry occurs. Potential entrants anticipate that incumbents will relocate so as to maintain symmetry.[24] Novshek (1980) notes that, while it may be legitimate to focus on the symmetric case for the purpose of showing that *an* equilibrium exists, one ought to be careful about using symmetric equilibria when one compares different markets. It is not strictly valid to do so unless one can also show that non-symmetric equilibria don't exist. Bearing this in mind let us now define a symmetric zero-profit Nash equilibrium (SZPE) as 'a price p and a number of brands n such that every equally spaced Nash price setter's maximum profit price choice earns zero profits' (Salop, 1979, p. 145).

In order to characterise an SZPE, we make the following assumptions about consumer behaviour. A consumer either purchases one unit of a differentiated commodity or else none at all. The remaining income after this choice has been made is spent on some homogeneous 'outside' commodity. We shall denote by $\bar{s}$ the surplus that the consumer would get if he were to spend all of his income on the outside good. If the consumer buys a unit of one of the differentiated goods then it must be that

$$\operatorname*{Max}_{i}[U(x_i, x^*) - p_i] \geqslant \bar{s}, \tag{2.17}$$

where x^* is the consumer's ideal brand. If there is no i that satisfies (2.17) then the consumer spends all of his income on the outside good. Salop uses a linear 'transport cost' or 'utility loss' function so that we can write $U(\cdot, \cdot)$ more explicitly as

$$U(x_i, x^*) = u - c|x_i - x^*|,$$

where u is the utility that would be obtained if he got his ideal brand x^* for free.[25] Thus (2.17) becomes

$$\operatorname*{Max}_{i}[v - c|x_i - x^*| - p_i] \geqslant 0, \tag{2.18}$$

where $v (=u-\bar{s}>0)$ is the maximum price that consumers are prepared to pay for their ideal brand.

In the n-firm symmetric equilibrium the individual firms will be $(1/n)$ apart. Consider firm i offering its brand x_i at a price p_i when its neighbours are charging $\bar{p}$. The region over which i has a local monopoly is the area x on either side of it where x satisfies

$$v-c\left[\frac{1}{n}-x\right]-\bar{p}\leqslant 0. \qquad (2.19)$$

If good x_i were not available, these people would prefer to buy the outside good in preference to the nearest available brands. The delivered price of one of these goods would exceed $[\bar{p}+c[(1/n)-x]]$, and thus the surplus they would obtain from buying it would be less than that to be obtained from buying the outside good. Of course firm i cannot charge too high a price or else they will also prefer the outside good to i. In other words we must also have

$$v-cx-p_i\geqslant 0.$$

The marginal consumer will be the one for which this last expression holds as an equality and so the boundary if i's potential local monopoly is $x=[(v-p)/c]$. If there are L consumers on the circular market of unit circumference, there will be $2Lx$ in the area of potential monopoly. Thus the monopoly demand is given by

$$q_i^m = 2Lx = 2L\left[\frac{v-p}{c}\right]. \qquad (2.20)$$

Now, when p_i is sufficiently low, i will start to attract consumers that lie beyond its monopoly area: it will start to encroach on its neighbours' market. We can refer to the consumers liable to be potentially attracted to i as its *competitive region*. The marginal consumer here is one at a distance x from i such that

$$v-cx-p_i=v-c\left[\frac{1}{n}-x\right]-\bar{p}>0. \qquad (2.21)$$

Solving this for x yields

$$x=\frac{1}{2c}\left[\bar{p}+\frac{c}{n}-p_i\right],$$

so that the firm i's demand in its competitive region is given by

$$q_i^c = \frac{L}{c}\left[\bar{p}+\frac{c}{n}-p_i\right]. \qquad (2.22)$$

Finally, note that when $p_i = \bar{p} - c/n$, the marginal consumer for i is a distance $(1/n)$ away from it: in other words, at the next neighbour's location. If the price were to fall a tiny fraction below that, firm i would capture the *entire* monopoly market of its two neighbours. In figure 2.13 we illustrate the demand curve facing i. Over the monopoly region the slope is $[-(c/2L)]$ and over the competitive region it is $[-(c/L)]$. The kink[26] reflects the fact that it is more difficult to attract consumers in the competitive region. As $\bar{p}$ and $(1/n)$ are reduced, the demand curve associated with the competitive region shifts to the left with the result that the price at which the kink occurs rises. Indeed, for sufficiently low values of these it may disappear altogether.

Now let each firm have a unit variable cost of production of m and a fixed cost of F. Three possible SZPEs are illustrated in figure 2.14 according to whether or not, in equilibrium, the declining total unit cost curve is tangent to the monopoly section, is at the kink or is tangent to the competitive section.[27] These equilibria are labelled M, K and C respectively (and the respective equilibrium prices as p^m, p^k and p^c). The kink occurs where the monopoly regions of neighbours meet. We can therefore see that at the competitive equilibrium there are no 'gaps' in the market – every consumer buys one of the differentiated brands. The same is obviously true at the 'kinked' equilibrium. However, if the equilibrium is the monopoly

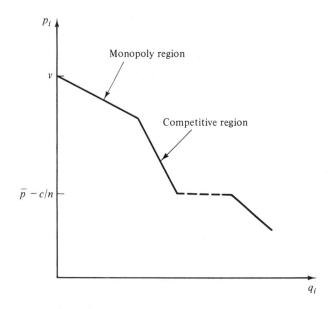

Figure 2.13

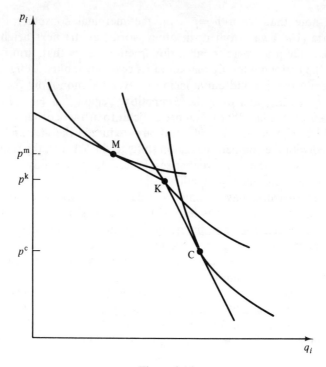

Figure 2.14

one, there are gaps as consumers sufficiently distant from the available goods prefer to spend their incomes on the outside good.

The equilibrium satisfies the profit maximisation condition that marginal revenue is less than or equal to marginal cost

$$p+q\left[\frac{dp}{dq}\right]\leqslant m, \tag{2.23}$$

the zero-profit condition

$$p=m+\frac{F}{q}, \tag{2.24}$$

and, assuming there are no gaps, the symmetry condition

$$q=\frac{L}{n}. \tag{2.25}$$

We can substitute for dp/dq from (2.20) and (2.22) and, since (2.23) holds as an equality in the monopoly and competitive regions, we obtain the following characterisation of the equilibria:

Monopoly

$$p^m = m + \left[\frac{c}{2n^m}\right]; \quad n^m = \left[\frac{\sqrt{(cL/F)}}{\sqrt{2}}\right]. \tag{2.26}$$

Competitive

$$p^c = m + \frac{c}{n^c} = m + \sqrt{(cF/L)}; \quad n^c = \sqrt{(cL/F)}. \tag{2.27}$$

Thus we can conclude that the number of firms in the monopoly equilibrium will be less than that in the competitive one.

Since, when the equilibrium is at the kink, (2.23) holds as an inequality, price will in this instance be given by the monopoly demand function. Thus using (2.20) we have

$$p^k = v - \left[\frac{c}{2n^k}\right]. \tag{2.28}$$

This, with (2.24) implies that at the equilibrium

$$\frac{F}{L}n^k + \frac{c}{2n^k} = v - m \tag{2.29}$$

and this implicitly defines the equilibrium number of firms n^k.

The natural question to ask now is what sorts of parameter configurations would be necessary for each of these types of equilibria. First note that, using (2.20) to obtain p^m, we can write monopoly profits as

$$\Pi^m = \left[v - \frac{c}{2L}q^m - m\right]q^m - F. \tag{2.30}$$

Thus (2.26), (2.30) and $q^m [= L/n^m]$ imply that if profits are to be zero in the monopoly equilibrium we must have

$$v - m = \sqrt{(2cF/L)}.$$

Since all the parameters in this expression are exogenously given, the chances of this equality holding are rather small and we can probably ignore this case. On the other hand, given that, in the monopoly region, the demand curve can (from (2.20) and (2.24)) be written as

$$p^m = v - \frac{c}{2L}\frac{L}{n^m}$$

and that, in the competitive equilibrium, p^c will be below this, we have

$$v - \frac{c}{2L}\frac{L}{n^c} \geqslant p^c.$$

Substituting for p^c and n^c from (2.27), we obtain the following condition as a characteristic of the competitive equilibrium

$$v - m \geqslant \tfrac{3}{2}\sqrt{(cF/L)}.$$

Hence we can conclude that the configuration of parameters needed to obtain the kink-point equilibrium will arise for values of $(v-m)$ in the interval $[\sqrt{(2cF/L)}, \tfrac{3}{2}\sqrt{(cF/L)}]$.

In order to compare n^k with n^m and n^c, let us denote the expression on the left-hand side of (2.29) by $f(n^k)$ and note that this is zero when $n^k = \sqrt{(cL/2F)}$ and increases in n^k for $n^k > \sqrt{(cF/L)}$. When n^k has risen to equal $\sqrt{(cL/F)}$, the value of $f(n^k)$ is $(\tfrac{3}{2})\sqrt{(cF/L)}$. Thus in the equilibrium, the number of brands must be *greater* than n^m $(=\sqrt{(cL/2F)})$, but *less* than n^c $(=\sqrt{(cL/F)})$. This is because, in the kink-point equilibrium, $(v-m) < (\tfrac{3}{2})\sqrt{(cF/L)}$ and, by definition, $f(n^k) = (v-m)$.

Among the most interesting features of Salop's model are its comparative statics properties. If one looks at equations (2.26) and (2.27), it will be seen that the comparative statics of the competitive equilibrium are straightforward and according to tradition: an increase in marginal cost (m) or fixed costs (F) raises p^c, an increase in F reduces n^c and an increase in L (the size of the market) increases n^c and reduces p^c. However, those at the kink-point equilibrium are 'perverse'. As is the case in Sweezy's analysis (the purpose of which was to explain price rigidity in oligopolistic markets), in the short run, when n is fixed, a change in either F or m has *no* effect on price (see equation (2.28)). On the other hand, in the long run, an increase in either of these two lowers the equilibrium number of brands.[28] Because this allows the now fewer brands to exploit further the available economies of scale, a lower price is the result. As we show in chapter 4, even though there is a reduction in product variety, this is not sufficient to offset the beneficial effects of the fall in price and so, as a result, consumers' welfare increases. As Salop himself notes (p. 149), this really is a rather striking result. For example, one way that costs might rise is if an excise tax were to be imposed (or raised). What this result now claims is that this tax will be welfare increasing.

By way of contrast, consider the implications of an increase in v. One interpretation that might be given to such a change might be to view it as the consequence of informative advertising. From (2.27), we can see that this will have no effect on the competitive equilibrium but that (from (2.28) and (2.29)) it increases price and product variety in the kink-point equilibrium.[29] However, this now produces a *reduction* in consumers' welfare. These are some rather awkward welfare features then and we shall devote the next but one chapter to discussing these and the other welfare issues that arise in a world of variety.

3 Symmetric preferences, the Chamberlinian paradigm

3.1 Introduction

In our analysis in chapter 2 we dealt with goods that could be defined in terms of a small number of characteristics. The implication of this was that we could easily think of goods as being close or distant neighbours to one another and hence, for some particular consumer, being good or bad substitutes. In chapter 1 we referred to this general phenomenon as preference asymmetry. It implies that any particular firm only faces localised competition from firms producing goods that are its near neighbours in the characteristics space.[1]

The aim of this chapter is to study equilibria in imperfect markets in which consumers are taken to have symmetric preferences. That is to say, any one brand is an equally good substitute for any other. There are various ways in which this can be made precise but for this chapter the way we shall do it is by assuming that there exists a 'representative consumer' with a taste for every brand on offer. The consumer's actual choice will depend on income and relative prices, but all goods are equally possible candidates *ex ante* for inclusion in the consumer's shopping basket.

Edwin Chamberlin (1933) was the first to study such markets and to refer to it as monopolistic competition. Since Chamberlin's book a substantial literature has developed in the area but not all of it is genuinely about monopolistically competitive markets nor does it all use the idea of the representative consumer. The only common feature is the assumption that consumer preferences are *symmetric*. In a number of recent models indeed the notion of the representative consumer has been dropped altogether (e.g. Hart, 1985a,b, Perloff and Salop, 1985). This is a development that we shall consider in some detail in chapter 7 but for the moment will continue to work with the representative consumer idea.

Before launching into a discussion of the Chamberlinian paradigm it probably makes sense to take a moment to set out its essential elements.

Chamberlin considered two 'group equilibria': the small group and the large group.[2] The small group was a collusive oligopoly and could be analysed by means of the standard monopoly model. The equilibrium in the large-group case however was non-cooperative but Chamberlin did not make use of oligopoly theory, instead developing his own large-group equilibrium theory – what we now refer to as *the* model of monopolistic competition.

The group as a whole faces a fixed demand curve for the differentiated product, $X(p)$. If every firm charges the same price, then we can define a *pro-rata* demand curve for any one firm as

$$x(p) = X(p)/n, \tag{3.1}$$

where n is the number of firms in the group, and $x(p)$ is what Chamberlin refers to as the '*DD* curve'. The large-group equilibrium allowing for entry is characterised by two conditions: each operating firm needs to be maximising its profits and no firm can be making positive profits. What is relevant for the first of these conditions is the '*dd* curve' for firm i

$$x_i(p_i; \boldsymbol{p}_{-i}), \tag{3.2}$$

where $\boldsymbol{p}_{-i}$ is the vector of prices excluding that of firm i. This function encapsulates firm i's twin beliefs: its belief that its actions will have no major effects on rival firms and its belief about the extent to which it will attract (or lose) customers by unilateral price variations.

By inverting (3.2) we can write p_i as a function of quantities: $p_i(x_i, \boldsymbol{x}_{-i})$. The i'th firm will seek to maximise its profits which are given by

$$p_i(x_i, \boldsymbol{x}_{-i})x_i - c(x_i). \tag{3.3}$$

Clearly firm i's price is affected by what every other firm does, but for the sake of argument here we can adopt the hypothesis that it takes others' behaviour as given in deciding on its own actions. Thus, at an optimum for firm i we have

$$p_i(x_i^*, \boldsymbol{x}_{-i}) + \frac{\partial p_i(x_i^*, \boldsymbol{x}_{-i})}{\partial x_i} x_i^* - c'(x_i^*) = 0. \tag{3.4}$$

This condition defines for each i its optimal output choice as function of the outputs of the other firms: $\zeta_i(\boldsymbol{x}_{-i})$. Therefore at a monopolistic competition equilibrium we have

$$p_i(x_i^*, \boldsymbol{x}_{-i}^*) + \frac{\partial p_i(x_i^*, \boldsymbol{x}_{-i}^*)}{\partial x_i} \cdot x_i^* - c'(x_i^*) = 0. \tag{3.5}$$

If at $\boldsymbol{x}^*$ there are positive profits being made by any firm, entry will occur and the long-run equilibrium will be characterised by the zero-profit condition

$$p_i^* = c(x_i^*)/x_i^*, \quad i = 1, \ldots, n. \tag{3.6}$$

Thus the long-run monopolistic competition equilibrium is one in which the '*dd*' curve is tangential to the average cost curve as illustrated in figure 3.1. One interesting point about this equilibrium is that, as long as the '*dd*' curve that each firm faces still has some negative slope, each firm will produce at a point above the level of minimum average cost.

The attraction of Chamberlin's model is that it offers a middle ground between monopoly and perfect competition. If there were to be only a single firm in the industry and an effective barrier to entry, there would be no difference between the monopoly and monopolistic competition equilibrium. However, if we had a number of firms, each of which was producing a very close substitute for every other good, then the '*dd*' curve would be very flat and the monopolistic competition equilibrium would closely approximate the competitive equilibrium. Indeed were the goods to be exact substitutes, so that there was no longer any differentiation, the two would coincide.

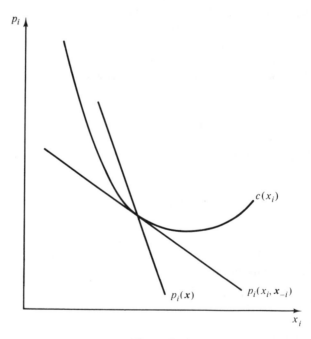

Figure 3.1

Recently Hart (1985a,b) has sought to formulate Chamberlin's ideas in a rigorous and careful way. He takes the view that a model of monopolistic competition in the spirit of Chamberlin needs to have the following four ingredients:

1 it should have many firms each producing a differentiated commodity;
2 each firm should be negligible in the sense that it can ignore its impact on, and so the reaction of, other firms;
3 free entry should lead to a situation in which each firm that is operating earns zero profits; and,
4 each firm should face a downward-sloping demand curve for its product with the result that, in equilibrium, price will exceed marginal cost.

As Hart notes, both (2) and (3) will be violated by any model in which markets are taken to be of a fixed, finite size and in which the entry process is limited by the existence of set-up costs. Only a finite number of firms can enter and operate in the market so that one cannot then claim that firms are negligible in the sense of (2). There is also the 'integer problem' that we referred to in chapter 2: the marginal operating firm will generally be making strictly positive profits so that condition (3) will be violated. For these reasons models in which we assume such markets are actually oligopolistic rather than monopolistically competitive in nature.

It follows from this that models that assume a finite market size and fixed costs are essentially oligopolistic rather than monopolistically competitive.[3] The study of monopolistic competition therefore properly involves the study of very large markets and their limiting market equilibria as either size goes to infinity or fixed costs go to zero.[4] Such equilibria have been studied by Hart in the papers we have already mentioned, by Perloff and Salop (1985) whose analysis we consider in chapter 7, and, subject to the qualification below, by Dixit and Stiglitz (1977). All of these take preferences to be symmetric. In this chapter we are going to consider a model that is close to that of Dixit and Stiglitz. This is a model in which it is assumed that the firm's behaviour is conditioned by the preferences of a representative consumer. Although the Dixit and Stiglitz paper does not concern itself with infinitely large markets, it does allow us to capture the essence of monopolistic competition in the sense that conditions (2) and (3) will be approximately true when the market has attained a sufficiently large size.

Some might argue that the twin assumptions of symmetric preferences and the absence of neighbouring effects which characterise monopolistic competition restrict the applicability of this model. However it is still likely to be the case that some markets are more closely approximated by monopolistic than by oligopolistic competition and this seems a reasonable argument for studying them. In this study there are two issues of interest. The first of these is the question of whether the market will produce too many or too few brands as compared with the social optimum. This is a question that is relevant whether or not we are dealing with symmetric preferences and one would be interested in the answer to it both in the case of oligopoly and monopolistic competition. The model that we shall develop in the next section is needed to allow us to study this issue in chapter 4.

A second, and perhaps more fundamental, issue is that of trying to discover if there are (reasonable) conditions under which even very large markets remain imperfectly competitive in the sense that the equilibrium price exceeds marginal cost. This is important because 'large markets' is often given as a justification for analysing some problem or other using perfect competition. An obvious example is in open-economy macro-economics and the theory of international trade where it has been quite standard to assume a country is a price-taker in world markets.[5] We discuss the conditions that are needed in chapter 7 but the discussion in the present chapter is a valuable preliminary to that.

There are, finally, a couple of technical reasons for developing a model of monopolistic competition. The first is that, since we assume that no firm has a significant impact on any other, we can sidestep the rather complex issues of conjectures and reactions. The second is that, in contrast to the analysis of entry and equilibrium in oligopoly, we don't have to worry about the 'integer problem'. That is, that firms can only enter in discrete lumps and that while an industry with n oligopolists might all earn positive profits, with $(n+1)$ they may all make losses because, in a sense, the market could only sustain a fraction of an entrant.

Thus we shall devote the remainder of this chapter to developing a model of imperfect competition based on the two key assumptions of symmetric preferences and that the market can be represented by a typical consumer. In the next section we look at the oligopoly equilibrium (ignoring the integer problem) and then in the final section we establish what the monopolistically competitive equilibrium looks like and compare the two of them. We make no claims to provide a formally rigorous analysis of monopolistic competition. It seemed to us that to do so would take the discussion beyond the scope we intended for this book. Those who do want to find such an analysis are referred to Oliver Hart's original papers. Despite this we do think our rather less formal approach gives a valuable insight into the workings of imperfect competition in the absence of neighbouring effects and provides just enough of a basis to analyse the welfare issues that we deal with in chapters 4 and 8.[6]

3.2 The oligopoly equilibrium

3.2.1 The specification of commodity demands

We consider an industry that is composed of n firms, each producing one distinct brand whose output is denoted by x_i, $i = 1, \ldots, n$. It is assumed that consumers like all brands and that there is a representative consumer whose tastes over the various brands are symmetric. Thus there are no neighbouring goods.[7] Symmetric demands for the brands, and the assumption that fixed and marginal costs are identical for each brand imply that it really doesn't matter how we label them. It is only the total number of brands that matters and it is this that acts as the measure of product diversity in the industry.

The representative consumer's utility function is assumed to be

$$V = \left(\sum_{i=1}^{n} x_i^{\alpha} \right)^{1/\alpha}, \quad 0 < \alpha \leqslant 1 \tag{3.7}$$

or

$$V = \left[\sum_{i=1}^{n} x_i^{(\sigma-1)/\sigma} \right]^{\sigma/(\sigma-1)}, \tag{3.8}$$

where $\sigma = 1/(1 - \alpha)$ is the elasticity of substitution between any two brands.

The marginal rate of substitution between any two brands is given by

$$\mathrm{MRS}_{ji} = \left. \frac{dx_j}{dx_i} \right|_{V = \text{const.}} = - \left[\frac{x_j}{x_i} \right]^{(1-\alpha)}. \tag{3.9}$$

Thus the indifference curves in any two dimensions are symmetric about the 45-degree line along which $x_i = x_j$. This they cross with a slope of -1. Their degree of curvature as one moves away from that line depends on the (constant) elasticity of substitution.

We do not explicitly introduce a numeraire commodity but, instead, assume that a fixed amount Y is spent by the consumer population on the industry's products. This is equivalent to assuming a unit elasticity of substitution between the numeraire commodity and the weighted sum of the industry's outputs as given by the bracketed term in (3.8). This assumption implies that the representative consumer allocates a constant share of his budget to buying the products of the imperfectly competitive sector.

In order to see this consider the following two-stage budgeting procedure. In the first stage consumers allocate income between the products of the differentiated industry and the numeraire good (which may be thought of as a Hicksian composite commodity) by maximising a Cobb–Douglas utility function

$$U = x_0^{1-s} V^s. \qquad (3.10)$$

V is a quantity index representing the differentiated brands and s is a constant $(0 < s < 1)$. This maximisation is subject to

$$x_0 + qV = I, \qquad (3.11)$$

where I is the economy's endowment of the numeraire and x_0 is the amount of the numeraire consumed. q, the price index that corresponds to V, is given by

$$q = \left[\sum_{i=1}^{n} p_i^{(1-\sigma)} \right]^{1/(1-\sigma)}. \qquad (3.12)$$

The solution to this problem yields the 'demands'

$$V = \frac{sI}{q} \quad \text{and} \quad x_0 = I(1-s). \qquad (3.13)$$

Note that this last equation implies that the budget shares are constant: $qV/I = s$, and that the marginal rate of substitution between the numeraire and the differentiated commodity in equilibrium is

$$\frac{\partial U/\partial x_0}{\partial U/\partial V} = \frac{1}{q}. \qquad (3.14)$$

Thus we can set Y equal to sI and drop the numeraire from the analysis until chapter 4 when we shall have to deal explicitly with it again. We can now turn to the second stage of the budgeting procedure where the representative consumer allocates Y between the differentiated brands.

However, before we do this we should stress a crucial feature that arises because we have used a utility function like (3.7). As noted by Koenker and Perry (1981) this is that all products are in direct competition with each other. Every time a new product appears the dimensionality of the product space expands and this product is an equally good substitute for those already in existence. This fact is in stark contrast to spatial models where the number of (single-product) firms typically exceeds the dimensionality of the product space. As a result products compete directly only with those that are adjacent to them.[8]

A consumer optimally allocating her income between brands i and j will choose that consumption pair for which the marginal rate of substitution equals the relative price of goods i and j – at least in an interior solution.

Referring back to (3.9) we see that this implies that

$$\frac{x_i}{x_j} = \left[\frac{p_j}{p_i}\right]^{\sigma}, \quad i \neq j; \quad i, j = 1, \ldots, n. \tag{3.15}$$

In the case, where $\sigma = \infty (\alpha = 1)$, the products are perfect substitutes and so can be considered as a homogeneous good. At the lower limit $\sigma = 1(\alpha = 0)$ they are quite distinct goods and are consumed in fixed proportions. Thus as σ falls the goods become increasingly imperfect substitutes for one another.

The marginal utility of brand i is, in equilibrium, proportional to its price. Thus, from (3.7), we have

$$\left[\frac{V}{x_i}\right]^{1/\sigma} = \lambda p_i. \tag{3.16}$$

Substituting this into the budget constraint, $Y = \Sigma^n p_i x_i$, yields

$$Y = \left[\frac{V}{\lambda^{\sigma}}\right] \sum [p_i]^{(1-\sigma)} = V\lambda^{-\sigma} q^{(1-\sigma)}, \tag{3.17}$$

where λ is the shadow price of consumption of the differentiated good: the implicit value attached by the representative consumer to the consumption of the differentiated commodities. Equation (3.17) can be solved for λ which, if substituted for in (3.16), yields the demand function for x_i:

$$x_i = \frac{Y}{p_i^{\sigma} q^{(1-\sigma)}}. \tag{3.18}$$

If we transform (3.18) into logarithms we have

$$\ln x_i = \ln Y - \sigma \ln p_i - (1-\sigma)\ln q \tag{3.19}$$

and we can now use this to straightforwardly derive expressions for the own- and cross-price elasticities of demand. However, recalling that we have assumed that firms hold Bertrand–Nash conjectures[9] about their rivals' pricing decisions, note, using (3.12), that

$$\frac{\partial \ln q}{\partial \ln p_k} = [p_k/q]^{(1-\sigma)}. \tag{3.20}$$

Hence we have the following expressions for the elasticities

$$\eta_{ii} \equiv \frac{\partial \ln x_i}{\partial \ln p_i} = -\sigma - (1-\sigma)[p_i/q]^{(1-\sigma)}, \tag{3.21}$$

$$\eta_{ij} \equiv \frac{\partial \ln x_i}{\partial \ln p_j} = -(1-\sigma)[p_j/q]^{(1-\sigma)}. \tag{3.22}$$

Given our assumption that firms have identical costs, the natural case to consider is the symmetric one in which $p_i = p$ and $x_i = x$. In this case $[p/q]^{(1-\sigma)}$ equals $(1/n)$ and (3.18), (3.21) and (3.22) become

$$x = \frac{Y}{np}, \tag{3.23}$$

$$\eta_{ii} = -\sigma - \left[\frac{1-\sigma}{n}\right], \tag{3.24}$$

$$\eta_{ij} = -\left[\frac{1-\sigma}{n}\right]. \tag{3.25}$$

While (3.18) can be thought of as Chamberlin's '*dd*' curve, (3.23) is the '*DD*' curve: the demand curve facing the firm when all firms change their prices simultaneously. Its price elasticity is unity, a consequence of the assumption that we made above that the elasticity of substitution between the differentiated good and the numeraire was unity.

We can also see in (3.23)–(3.25) several limiting features of a symmetric equilibrium as n tends to infinity

$$x \to 0,$$
$$\eta_{ii} \to -\sigma,$$
$$\eta_{ij} \to 0.$$

Furthermore, the usual condition that the '*dd*' curve be more elastic than the '*DD*' curve is just the condition that

$$(\sigma - 1) - \left[\frac{\sigma-1}{n}\right] > 0.$$

Having established the various features of our model on the demand side we need to specify costs before we can proceed to analyse the n-firm symmetric Nash equilibrium. We assume that each firm has a fixed cost of F and a constant marginal cost of c. Hence the firm's total costs are given by

$$C = cx + F. \tag{3.26}$$

3.2.2 The free-entry equilibrium

In a free-entry Nash equilibrium, each firm must be maximising profits but no operating firm making positive profits. From the profit-maximising condition that marginal revenue equals marginal cost, and using (3.24), we have the following expression for p

$$p = \frac{c[\sigma(n-1)+1]}{(\sigma-1)(n-1)}. \tag{3.27}$$

If we now substitute out p in (3.23) we find the equilibrium output to be

$$x = \frac{Y(\sigma-1)(n-1)}{nc[\sigma(n-1)+1]}. \tag{3.28}$$

From the zero-profit condition we have

$$(p-c)x = F. \tag{3.29}$$

These last three equations can be used to solve for the number of firms in the free-entry equilibrium. This is

$$n^e = \left[1 + \frac{1-\gamma}{\gamma\sigma}\right], \tag{3.30}$$

γ denoting the ratio (F/Y). For economic feasibility γ must be less than unity. If per firm fixed costs exceeded the maximum amount that consumers were prepared to spend on the good the industry could not exist at all and any attempt at analysis would be futile.

In order to obtain the expressions for equilibrium price and output we can substitute back into (3.27) and (3.28) to get

$$p^e = \frac{\sigma c}{(\sigma-1)(1-\gamma)} \tag{3.31}$$

and

$$x^e = \frac{(\sigma-1)F(1-\gamma)}{c[1+\gamma(\sigma-1)]}. \tag{3.32}$$

Recall that the higher is σ, the better are the brands substitutes for one another. What these last three equations show is that the effect of an increase in σ is to lower the equilibrium price and increase the equilibrium output per brand. As a consequence the number of brands in the free-entry equilibrium falls. This is as one might have intuitively expected. The more readily available a suitable substitute, the more intense is likely to be the competitive pressure on price. Any particular firm's market power is consequently reduced and price-cost margins are lower. This fact reduces the incentive to enter so that in the eventual equilibrium there are fewer firms.

In the limit as σ goes to infinity the brands of the differentiated good cease to be distinct in consumers' eyes and become perfect substitutes in that case. It follows from equations (3.30)–(3.32) that

$$n^e \to 1,$$

$$p^e \to \frac{c}{1-\gamma},$$

$$x^e \to \frac{(1-\gamma)F}{c\gamma}.$$

Unit cost in this limiting scenario is

$$c + \frac{F}{x^e} = \frac{c}{1-\gamma}, \tag{3.33}$$

so that we have in the case of the free-entry, homogeneous product, Bertrand–Nash equilibrium, price equal to unit cost. This is of course just the outcome that one would obtain under the assumption of *contestable markets*.

By restricting ourselves to a significant value for fixed costs we have, in this section, really been considering an oligopolistic equilibrium. In section 3 we consider what happens as these fixed costs become very small. Here we now move on to the analysis of monopolistic competition.

3.3 Monopolistic competition

As we have already noted in the introduction to this chapter, for monopolistic competition we need to have a sufficiently large number of firms in operation. This is necessary to be able to reasonably assume that each firm is of negligible size and can ignore the effect of its actions on other firms. Furthermore, the fact that each firm is of negligible size allows us to sidestep the integer problem and assume that each firm will earn approximately zero profits in the free-entry equilibrium. In this section we shall use the results of section 2 to help us characterise the monopolistically competitive equilibrium.

First, note that, from (3.30), the Nash equilibrium number of firms increases as γ decreases; that is, as aggregate expenditure on the industry's products relative to cost increases. In the limit as γ tends to zero, the number of firms goes off to infinity. Now, the notion that each firm is negligible may be translated into the condition (sometimes referred to as the 'large numbers' assumption) that each firm neglects its influence on (or takes as given) the weighted average industry price q. This is given in equation (3.12). (3.20) and (3.21) then show that in this case

$$\eta_{ii} = -\sigma. \tag{3.34}$$

Equation (3.24) confirms that this is indeed a reasonable assumption when n is sufficiently large. Indeed, $\partial q/\partial p_i$ goes to zero as the number of firms goes off to infinity, irrespective of the value of conjectures.[10] This explains our earlier remark that one of the virtues of the analysis of monopolistic competition is that the issue of reactions can be sidestepped. Note also, from (3.25), that η_{ij} equals zero when $(\partial q/\partial p_i) = 0$. This indicates that in a monopolistically competitive equilibrium any one firm's actions have (approximately speaking) no effect on any of its rivals. Hence the Bertrand–Nash conjecture is approximately correct.

Now with elasticity given by (3.34), the profit maximisation condition implies that the equilibrium price in a symmetric, monopolistically competitive equilibrium is given by

$$p^* = \left[\frac{\sigma}{\sigma - 1}\right] c. \tag{3.35}$$

With this we can solve for the other two conditions that characterise the symmetric equilibrium

$$x^* = \frac{(\sigma - 1)F}{c} \tag{3.36}$$

and

$$n^* = \frac{1}{\gamma\sigma}. \tag{3.37}$$

These are the output per firm and the equilibrium number of brands. A comparison between (3.35) and (3.31) and (3.36) and (3.32) reveals that

$$p^* < p^c \text{ and } x^* > x^c.$$

In other words, under monopolistic competition, given the degree of product substitutability, market price will be lower and output per firm greater than under oligopoly. On the other hand, since it may be reasonable to think that the value of γ in (3.37) is smaller than the corresponding value of γ in (3.30), we cannot say which market structure will generate the greater number of products. However, we can predict that industry output, for given Y, will be larger under monopolistic competition since

$$n^* x^* = \left[\frac{\sigma - 1}{\sigma} \right] \frac{Y}{c} > n^e x^e = \left[\frac{\sigma - 1}{\sigma} \right] \frac{Y}{c} (1 - \gamma). \tag{3.38}$$

Notice that even though we are considering a 'very large' market we can see from (3.35) that price exceeds marginal cost so that property (4) in our initial list of ingredients of a monopolistically competitive equilibrium is also satisfied. On the other hand, as substitutability between the brands (the value of σ) increases, price falls towards marginal cost.

The number of firms defined by (3.37) may not be an integer number and so, we should draw a distinction between n^*, the number corresponding to the zero-profit equilibrium, and $\tilde{n}$, the (integer) number of firms in the free-entry equilibrium.[11] This is just the largest integer that is less than or equal to $[1/\gamma\sigma]$. In other words, $\tilde{n} = 1/\gamma\sigma - \epsilon$ where $0 < \epsilon < 1$. To this value of n will correspond a level of per-firm output

$$\tilde{x} = \frac{Y(\sigma - 1)}{\sigma c \left[\dfrac{1}{\gamma\sigma} - \epsilon \right]}.$$

It therefore follows that $\tilde{n}/n^*$ and $\tilde{x}/x^*$ tend to 1 as $1/\gamma\sigma$ tends to infinity. But this is just equivalent to γ going to zero. As γ will be very small in monopolistic competition, we can therefore claim that the value of n obtained from the zero-profit condition will be a good approximation to the free-entry equilibrium value in this instance.

In conclusion we should emphasise again that in the model that we have used in this chapter we have restricted our attention to the special case where consumers spend a fixed share of their budgets on the differentiated products. In a more general model, such as that examined by Dixit and Stiglitz, where full account is taken of the numeraire commodity, the analysis of monopolistic competition is not quite so straightforward. As Hart has pointed out, that analysis itself suffers from two shortcomings. The first is the question of the uniqueness of the equilibrium. It is not clear that one can rule out the presence of additional non-monopolistically competitive equilibria. The second is that the Dixit and Stiglitz analysis relies on there being a discontinuity in the marginal rate of substitution between a typical brand and the numeraire at the equilibrium per capita consumption bundle in the limiting economy (i.e. as the number of products goes off to infinity). As Hart notes 'if this marginal rate of substitution is a continuous function, perfect rather than monopolistic, competition will result' (Hart, 1985b, p. 890).

However, despite the simplifying assumptions we have used in building up the model in this chapter, it has the important advantage that it provides an easily understood basis for the comparison between the oligopoly and monopolistically competitive equilibria that we have just looked at. It also allows us to compare these with the social optimum. This comparison is the task to which we now turn in chapter 4.

4 Product diversity and product selection: market equilibria and social optima

4.1 Introduction and some preliminary results

It is well-known that, in the presence of scale economies, one cannot rely on the market mechanism to produce the socially optimal quantities of goods. Optimality requires that the demand price is equal to marginal cost. Such an optimum cannot be sustained as the equilibrium of a perfectly competitive market as each firm would have negative profits. An imperfectly competitive market equilibrium, on the other hand, while it would allow firms to make positive profits, would violate the condition.

What is less well-known, but at least as important a market failure in terms of its welfare implications, is that the market equilibrium may not sustain the optimal number of commodities. In other words, the amount of product diversity is not ideal. Thus Spence, writing in 1976, noted:

In the past, some of the costs of imperfect competition have been measured by the cost of the nonmarginal cost pricing of the existing set of products. Using some numerical examples, I have tried to show that a significant fraction of the cost of imperfect competition may be due to the currently unmeasured cost of having too many, too few, or the wrong products. This analysis is far from decisive empirically, since it is based on numerical examples. It is however suggestive, that over a range of assumptions about the structures of demand and costs, product selection failures may be significant components of welfare costs.[1]

To see intuitively why the market may fail to provide the optimal degree of product diversity note that, on social welfare grounds, a commodity should be produced if the change in gross surplus (the sum of revenues and consumer surplus) minus the total cost of production, generated by its introduction, is positive. On the other hand, the criterion for production used by the market is profitability and there is no reason why the maximisation of net social surplus will occur at the same point (i.e. at the same number of commodities introduced) at which the anticipated profit from the introduction of an additional commodity becomes zero.[2]

56

To clarify this point it may be useful to think of the following two forces that affect the decision to introduce a new product. The first is a direct effect that will be familiar from the classic problem of when to build a bridge. It may be that, in the absence of some form of price discrimination, sales revenues fail to cover costs even though the product has positive social value. This is a force tending to eliminate products and is illustrated in figure 4.1.

The second effect is that, when a product is introduced, in addition to increasing consumers' surplus, it affects the profits being earned by existing firms. To the extent that the product is being introduced by a new firm (recall that we assume single-product firms), this effect will not be taken into account. If the products are substitutes this effect will be adverse – it is often referred to as 'cannibalisation'. This feature is shown in figure 4.2, and is just the location model again although for illustrative purposes we have assumed that firms can behave as perfect price discriminators. Consumers value their ideal good at a and the price obtained is shown by the lines that decline from A′, B′ and C′. Here it is assumed that firm C enters between firms A and B. Its decision to enter is based on comparing its fixed costs with the profits to be earned. The latter comprise the two shaded areas. However, it is only the stippled area that represents a contribution to net

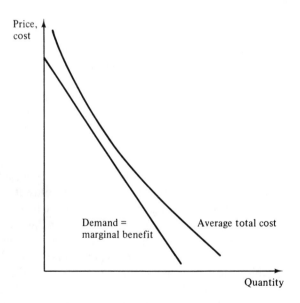

Figure 4.1

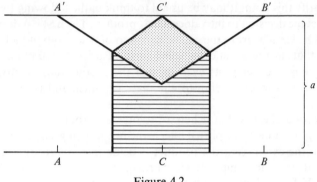

Figure 4.2

surplus; the horizontally shaded area is 'cannibalised' profits. Because the entering firm doesn't take this effect into account in reaching its decision, it may enter when it is not generating a social benefit. This is a force tending to generate too many products in the case of substitutes. However, if the products are complements both forces tend towards the introduction of too few products.[3]

A little reflection on the above arguments makes clear that they point to the fundamental conflict that lies at the root of the problem. This is the conflict between the desire for greater *efficiency*, on the one hand, and greater *variety* (product diversity) on the other. The former requires that each commodity is produced at as low a unit cost as possible. Hence, if scale economies are present, output should be as great as possible. The desire for variety is of course an untested assumption in all of this analysis though most people would probably consider it a basic fact of economic life. Consider the utility function we assumed in chapter 3 for the representative consumer (equation (3.8)) and suppose that we are in a symmetric equilibrium: $x_i = x, \forall i$. In this case, the utility function can be written as

$$V = (nx) \, n^{1/\sigma - 1}. \tag{4.1}$$

This makes clear that an increase in n holding industry output (nx) constant – spreading a given amount of industry output over more brands – increases utility. This suggests that n should be increased without bound. However, this benefit from diversity has to be balanced against the fact that each product must be produced more and more inefficiently as more products enter the market; it is because the market doesn't fully take into account this trade-off that we may get 'too many' or 'too few' products.[4]

Chamberlin (1933, 1953) claimed that, as compared with the competitive standard, his free-entry long-run monopolistically competitive equilibrium would involve (i) excess capacity – i.e., production to the left of the minimum unit cost output by each firm, (ii) a higher price and (iii) more firms. However, he also suggested that this equilibrium might be some 'sort of ideal' when account was taken of consumers' desire for more variety.[5] There are two things to note about this. The first is that Chamberlin's assertion concerning the number of products in monopolistic competition as compared with the social optimum was based on informal and imprecise theorising and, as we shall see below, may not always be valid. The second is that despite his remarks about equilibrium under monopolistic competition constituting a 'sort of ideal' when the desirability of variety is taken into account, the traditional view among economists since the publication of his work has been that monopolistic or, more generally, imperfect competition would result in too many firms each producing at less than optimal scale.

One of our main objectives in this chapter is to examine the validity of this view using the models of imperfect competition developed in the last two chapters. We shall show that the traditional view seems to be pointing in the right direction when one considers oligopoly – that is, in circumstances where market size is not very large relative to fixed set-up costs. However, the case is much more difficult to establish for monopolistic competition proper.[6] The latter may indeed constitute a 'sort of ideal'. As we shall see, it is a second-best optimum and, even though generally the direction in which the first-best optimum lies is unclear (i.e. monopolistic competition could involve too many or too few products), the welfare costs of having the wrong number of products is likely to be small.[7]

To conclude this section, we should finally note that above (as in much of the chapter) we have been thinking of product diversity under the assumption of symmetric market equilibria. In such cases, it is only the total number of products, n, that is relevant. That is, there is nothing unique about such an equilibrium, for, as Dixit and Stiglitz put it, 'any group of n [is] just as good as any other group of n'.[8] In the final section of this chapter we take a look at what we may call the issue of product selection: will the market produce biases against particular *types* of products? The answer, we shall see, is unambiguously 'yes'; the market equilibrium will show a bias against products whose demand elasticity is low and whose fixed costs are high.

4.2 A digression into the case of homogeneous products[9]

The discussion above has implicitly assumed that the market under consideration is one of differentiated commodities. This is certainly the most interesting case in the present context and the one most extensively analysed in the literature. However it is worthwhile digressing at this point to examine the question of whether there will be excessive or insufficient entry in homogeneous but imperfect markets. The advantage of doing this is that it throws additional light on some of the forces mentioned above that tend to make for excessive entry. In addition, it clarifies the reason why the market for a differentiated product is more likely to be characterised by insufficient entry than is the case for a homogeneous one.

To be more specific, consider again the second effect mentioned above: the cannibalisation effect. This effect leads to excessive entry. To see this, consider the social welfare function in the homogeneous product case. We can write this as

$$W(n) = \int_0^{nq_n} p(z)\,\mathrm{d}z - n[c(q_n) + f\,],$$

where $p(z)$ is the inverse demand function, n the number of firms, q_n the output per firm and $c(\cdot)$ and f are, respectively, variable and fixed cost per firm. The cannibalisation or, as Mankiw and Whinston (1986) term it, the 'business stealing effect' means that, as the number of firms increases, output per firm falls: $\partial q_n/\partial n$ is negative. Differentiating $W(n)$ and using the definition of profit per firm, we can write

$$\frac{\mathrm{d}W}{\mathrm{d}n} = \pi(n) + n\left[p - \frac{\partial c}{\partial q_n}\right]\frac{\partial q_n}{\partial n} \qquad (4.2)$$

However, in the free-entry equilibrium, profit per firm, $\pi(n)$ is zero and so we can claim that at that equilibrium, $\mathrm{d}W/\mathrm{d}n < 0$. In other words, the free-entry equilibrium number of firms exceeds the socially optimal number: there is excessive entry.

On the other hand, when product differentiation is present, there is the desire for variety. This now biases entry in a direction opposite to that of the business-stealing effect: 'the marginal entrant creates surplus by increasing product variety that he does not capture as profits'.[10] In many cases the latter will dominate the former effect with the result that there will be insufficient entry in the market equilibrium.

4.3 Product diversity: first- and second-best optima and the market equilibrium

In this section we characterise the social optimum for two of the models that we have looked at in previous chapters. These are Salop's spatial model (chapter 2) and the Chamberlin-type model of chapter 3. We shall compare these optima with the corresponding market equilibria. In the case of the latter, we shall look at both the first- and second-best optimum. Our examination of the second-best may be justified on the grounds that, with scale economies, the first-best (or unconstrained) optimum would require lump-sum transfers to firms to cover losses. There are clearly formidable conceptual and practical difficulties to doing this. This is why a more appropriate notion of optimality is probably the constrained one: where each firm must have non-negative profits. This may be achieved by regulation, or by excise or franchise taxes or subsidies. The important restriction is that lump-sum subsidies are not available.

4.3.1 The social optimum in Chamberlinian models

We start by comparing the constrained (second-best) optimum with the market equilibrium under monopolistic competition. The social planner's objective here is to obtain the values of n and x that maximise social welfare (the representative consumer's utility function (3.10) of chapter 3) subject to the constraint that each firm is making zero profits. This utility function $[U = x_0^{1-s} V^s]$ can be expressed in terms of q (using equations (3.11)–(3.13). In addition, note that in a symmetric equilibrium, $q = n^{[-1/\sigma-1]}p$. Thus the problem of maximising U becomes one of

$$\operatorname*{Min}_{p,n} [n^{-1/\sigma-1}p] \quad \text{subject to} \quad (p-c)\frac{Y}{np}=F,$$

where we have used $x = Y/np$ in the zero-profit constraint. From the first-order conditions for the solution to this we obtain

$$\tilde{p} = \left(\frac{\sigma}{\sigma-1}\right)c \tag{4.3}$$

and

$$\tilde{n} = \frac{1}{\gamma\sigma}, \tag{4.4}$$

where $\gamma = F/Y$ (as in chapter 3). Thus, from $x = Y/np$,

$$\tilde{x} = \left(\frac{\sigma-1}{c}\right)F. \tag{4.5}$$

If we now compare equations (4.3)–(4.5) with their counterparts, (3.35)–(3.37), in chapter 3, we see that the monopolistically competitive market equilibrium is identical to the constrained (second-best) optimum. Thus Chamberlin's observation that such an equilibrium is a 'sort of ideal' is indeed vindicated.

Let us now compare the market equilibrium with the first-best optimum. To achieve the first-best optimum, a social planner will maximise $U(x_0^{1-s}V^s)$ taking into account the fact that $x_0 = I - n(cx + F)$. Thus the objective is to

$$\underset{n,x}{\text{Max}} \left[I - n(cx + F) \right]^{1-s} \left[n^{\sigma/\sigma-1} x \right]^s.$$

The first-order conditions with respect to x and n, respectively are

$$\frac{\partial U}{\partial x_0}(-nc) + \frac{\partial U}{\partial V} n^{\sigma/\sigma-1} = 0 \qquad (4.6)$$

and

$$\frac{\partial U}{\partial x_0}(-cx - F) + \frac{\partial U}{\partial V} x \left(\frac{\sigma}{\sigma-1} \right) n^{1/\sigma-1} = 0. \qquad (4.7)$$

From (4.6), using equation (3.14) we obtain the result that the price, p_u, at the unconstrained optimum will be

$$p_u = c. \qquad (4.8)$$

In addition, from (4.7) and (4.8), again using (3.14), we find that

$$x_u = \left(\frac{\sigma-1}{c} \right) F. \qquad (4.9)$$

Finally, with $p = c$, lump-sum transfers to firms of nF are required. Hence, now expenditure on the differentiated industry is $s(I - nF)$, so that

$$n = \frac{s(I - nF)}{px} = \frac{Y - snF}{(\sigma-1)F}.$$

Thus

$$n_u = \frac{1}{\gamma[\sigma - (1-s)]}. \qquad (4.10)$$

We can now compare (4.8)–(4.10) with the corresponding equations for the constrained optimum and the monopolistically competitive equilibrium. As Dixit and Stiglitz (1977) have pointed out, the most striking fact is that the output of each active firm is the same in all three situations. As a result of the fact that in a Chamberlinian equilibrium each firm operates to the left of the point at which average costs are minimised, it has been common to say that there is excess capacity. However, when variety is desirable, i.e. when the different products are not perfect substitutes, it is not in general optimal to push the output of each firm to the point where all economies of scale are exhausted. These results therefore undermine the validity of the 'folklore' about excess capacity from both a first- and second-best viewpoint.

While the output per firm is socially optimal (compare (4.9) and (3.36)), the number of firms in the monopolistically competitive market equilibrium is smaller than is called for in the first-best optimum (contradicting yet another piece of economic folklore). On the other hand, if we compare (4.4) with (3.30), we can see that, in the case of the model we are using here, the market will generate the second-best optimal degree of product diversity.

These results are illustrated in figure 4.3, where D indicates the firm's demand curve and AC, MC its unit and marginal cost curves respectively. Unfortunately, however, these results are not general. We can say this because Dixit and Stiglitz (1977) have also considered the case where the utility function for the imperfect industry's products is not of the constant elasticity of substitution form. Their analysis shows that in fact the bias could go either way.[11] In other words, the market equilibrium could involve fewer and bigger firms than the constrained optimum, and fewer but smaller firms than the unconstrained one. This ambiguity in the results has

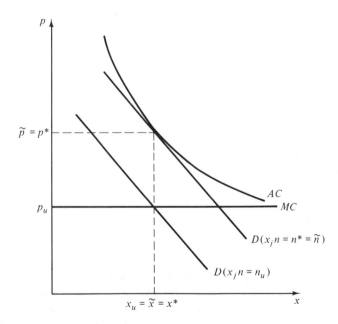

Figure 4.3

been confirmed more recently by Hart (1985b) using a model of monopolistic competition which did not use the device of a representative
consumer. In his conclusion, he notes that 'the laissez-faire number of
brands may either exceed or fall short of the optimal number depending on
the parameters of the model. Moreover, this is true both for the first-best
optimum and the second-best optimum.' These results are very much in
accordance with our earlier intuitive arguments where we drew attention to
the conflicting forces that would influence the characteristics of the market
equilibrium and socially optimal solutions.

Given this, the question arises as to just how big, relative to the first-best
optimum, is the welfare loss that arises because monopolistic competition
results in the wrong number of products being produced. Using a partial
equilibrium framework with a utility function similar to (3.7), Yarrow
(1985) employs the following device to enable him to provide an answer to
this question.[12] He notes that if

$$z_i = x_i^\alpha \quad \text{and} \quad z = \sum_i z_i$$

are used in (3.17) – z_i being labelled 'the utility-output of firm i' – these
transformed output variables of the firms are perfect substitutes for one
another so that one can obtain for any firm a demand function that depends
only on total utility-output z. With the cost conditions expressed in terms of
utility-output too, a comparison between the market and the first-best
optimum can then be made in price/utility-output space. This is shown in
figure 4.4. Utility-output per firm and the 'price' of this output is the same in
the two situations but $z(=z_u)$ is greater in the first-best optimum than in the
market solution (z^*). As figure 4.4 shows, the welfare loss is then seen to be
equal to the shaded area. Yarrow does some illustrative calculations of
a Harberger type to show these to be of very small order. Thus, at least for
the type of model we developed above, it seems that the welfare cost of
monopolistic competition from non-optimal product diversity may well be
very small.

4.3.2 Oligopoly and the social optimum

There is a good intuitive reason why the monopolistically competitive
equilibrium does not involve too large a welfare loss in the case of the model
that we have been using in this chapter. The reason is that, while there are
losses due to sub-optimal product diversity, there are none due to
sub-optimal scale (each firm producing the socially optimal amount)
because we are dealing with a situation where market size is large relative to
fixed set-up costs. The opposite is true under oligopoly. We looked at its

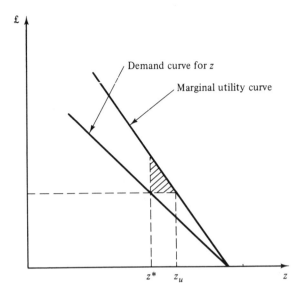

Figure 4.4

equilibrium in chapter 3 and equilibrium (3.30)–(3.32) gave the equilibrium values of n^e, p^e and x^e, respectively. If, first of all, we compare these with the constrained equilibrium values, $\tilde{p}$, $\tilde{n}$ and $\tilde{x}$, we see that

$$p^e > \tilde{p}, n^e > \tilde{n} \quad \text{and} \quad x^e < \tilde{x}. \tag{4.11}$$

Thus the equilibrium in our model is characterised by too many firms, each producing too little output (at too high a price) relative to the second-best welfare optimum. (Remember that, whilst $n^e > \tilde{n}$, we cannot compare n^e with n^*, the number of firms in monopolistically competitive equilibrium, since the value of γ will be different under monopolistic competition and under oligopoly.) Thus a two-way comparison is needed: given a 'large' market relative to fixed cost (γ 'small'), we can prove that $n^* = \tilde{n}$, while for a 'large' γ, we can prove that $n^e > \tilde{n}$.

Secondly, comparing the market equilibrium with the unconstrained optimum values p_u, n_u and x_u we see that

$$p^e > p_u, \quad x^e < x_u \tag{4.12}$$

and

$$n^e \gtreqless n_u \text{ as } \frac{\gamma\sigma(\sigma-1)}{1+\gamma(\sigma-1)} \gtreqless (1-s). \tag{4.13}$$

These conditions tell us that, relative to the first-best optimum, firms in equilibrium will also be characterised by sub-optimal scale and, in addition, there may be too many firms in the market.

These results are based on the assumption that the firms hold Cournot-Nash conjectures. However, if firms' behaviour is less competitive than implied by this, the possibility that the free-entry oligopoly equilibrium will be characterised by too many firms relative to the first-best optimum increases. The intuition here is that, as the market becomes less competitive, more firms are attracted into the market.[13] Thus we have the result that welfare losses may be large under oligopoly both because firms operate at a sub-optimal scale *and* because an excessive number of products is produced – the latter being more likely the 'less competitive' is the behaviour of firms. Yarrow's (1985) calculations show a loss 'considerably in excess' of the level calculated for monopolistic competition.

4.3.3 The social optimum and market equilibrium in spatial models

In this section we complete our comparison of the market-generated and socially optimal amount of product diversity. To do so we use the Salop spatial model of imperfect competition of chapter 2. This gives us an insight into the nature of these two equilibria in the case of those industries for which the spatial approach is appropriate.

Using the notation we employed in chapter 2 (section 5), we first note that if n firms operate in the circular market (of unit-circumference) at a distance $1/n$ apart, the marginal consumer travels a distance $\frac{1}{2}n$ to the nearest firm. Thus, a consumer located at distance $x \leqslant \frac{1}{2}n$ obtains a surplus in excess of marginal cost (m) of $[v - m - cx]$ where c is the unit transportation cost and v the consumers' reservation price.[14] Hence, with L consumers around the market, the total net surplus when brands are offered at marginal cost is

$$W = 2n \int_0^{(1/2)n} (v - m - cx) \, L \, dx - nF, \qquad (4.14)$$

which on integration yields

$$W = \left(v - m - \frac{c}{4n} \right) L - nF. \qquad (4.15)$$

Since $\frac{1}{2}n$ is the distance travelled by the marginal consumer and zero that travelled by the consumer located next to his ideal brand, the average distance travelled (at a cost of c per unit distance) is $\frac{1}{4}n$. Thus the term in brackets in (4.15) is the average net surplus per consumer, and hence W, as given by (4.15), *is* total net social surplus. Maximising (4.15) with respect to n we obtain

$$n^* = 1/2 \sqrt{\frac{2L}{F}}. \qquad (4.16)$$

If we compare this with the values for the various market equilibria (see chapter 2), we can see that

$$n^* < n^m < n^k < n^c, \qquad (4.17)$$

where the superscripts 'm', 'k' and 'c' refer to 'monopoly', 'kinked' and 'competitive' equilibria respectively. There is, however, a caveat. According to this result, a circular market will have an excessive number of product varieties. Unfortunately, as Salop has noted, it is not robust, but depends rather crucially on the distribution of consumers and preferences around the circle.

We can obtain a helpful diagrammatic illustration of this model and of the result given in (4.17) by using an equivalent way of solving the social planner's problem. This is to maximise average consumer welfare less the price paid subject to the breakeven constraint that the mill price covers average total costs. Formally we

$$\text{Max } \bar{W}(n, p) = v - p - \frac{c}{4n} \qquad (4.15')$$

$$\text{subject to } p = m + \frac{F}{L} n.$$

Figure 4.5 indicates the solution to this problem in $(p, L/n)$–space. This is at the point E_o, where the constraint (of slope $-F/(L/n)^2$) is tangent to a linear indifference curve generated by (4.15') – of slope $- c/4L$.[15] The (zero-profit) competitive and monopoly equilibria are indicated by points E_c and E_m, respectively. They represent the points of tangency between the unit cost curve and the relevant demand curves (of slope $-c/L$ and $-c/2L$ respectively) in the competitive and monopoly regions.

As a final point, consider figure 4.6 and note that an increase in unit cost leads to an increase in welfare in the long-run if equilibria are kinked. This was something that we had asserted in chapter 2. It arises because of the fact that the slope of the monopoly region of the demand curve $(-c/2L)$ is greater (in absolute value) than the slope of the indifference curves $(-c/4L)$, so that moving down the curve to a new kinked equilibrium (from E to E') when unit costs increase from AC to AC' must increase welfare.

4.4 Biases in product selection

Throughout the present chapter we have concentrated on the issue of product diversity under the assumption of symmetry. This meant that in

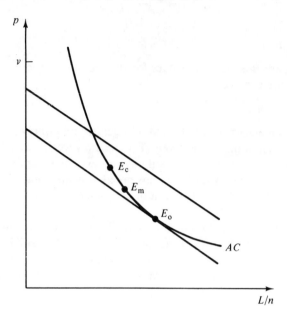

Figure 4.5

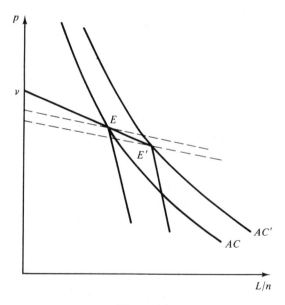

Figure 4.6

our comparison of the market equilibrium and social optimum only the total number of products n was relevant. In this section we shall briefly turn our attention to the issue of whether the market will be biased against the introduction of certain types of products.

That such biases may exist is suggested by what we have already said concerning the market's ability to generate the right number of products. As we had occasion to note more than once, its ability to do so is hampered by the fact that firms entering the market cannot capture all the consumer surplus that their entry will generate (but which is taken into account by the social planner in deciding on optimal variety). Now it seems intuitively plausible that firms' ability to capture surplus will depend on the type of product introduced and thus that the market will tend to discriminate against the introduction of certain products.

Spence (1976a, b) was one of the first economists to deal rigorously with this issue. He noted that not all products are equally subject to the same degree of imperfect appropriability that tends to eliminate products that should be produced. As he himself said, 'although revenues, in the absence of price discrimination, do not capture all of the gross surplus generated by a product, the fraction of the gross surplus that is or can be captured varies from product to product. The ratio of revenues to gross surplus depends upon the properties of the demand functions' (Spence, 1976a, p. 409).

In order to simplify the analysis of this question, consider the case of a constant elasticity (η) demand function. It is easily shown[16] that in this case

$$\text{Total Revenue } (TR) = \left(1 - \frac{1}{\eta}\right)(\text{Gross Surplus } (GS)) \qquad (4.18)$$

or

$$\pi = \left(1 - \frac{1}{\eta}\right)GS - [c(Q) + F], \qquad (4.19)$$

where Q is output and $c(.)$ the variable cost function. From (4.18), the fraction of gross surplus that appears as revenues to the selling firm is larger, the higher the price elasticity of demand. And, since

$$\text{Net Surplus } (NS) = GS - [c(Q) + F] \qquad (4.20)$$

we see by comparing (4.19) and (4.20) that, when products vary in terms of their elasticity, it is quite plausible for a product with a lower price elasticity to have a higher net surplus and lower π than a product with a high price elasticity. In such a case, the market will choose the high elasticity one when the low elasticity one should have been chosen on social welfare grounds. This point is illustrated in figures 4.7 and 4.8.[17]

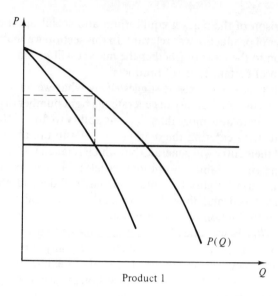

Product 1

Figure 4.7

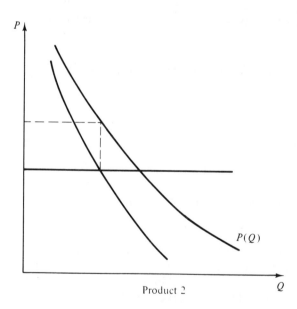

Product 2

Figure 4.8

In these diagrams, it is assumed that products 1 and 2 have the same marginal and fixed costs. The first product has a lower surplus and higher profits than the second, though gross profits (i.e. profits before fixed costs are deducted) are positive for both products. However, at some fixed cost the first product could be profitable and survive while the second would not, even though the latter contributes more to the surplus. If the two products are substitutes and if the market mechanism selects the more profitable, then again the first product will be taken.[18] A demand curve such as that for product 2 is likely to be generated

if the potential consumers of a product have a highly variegated set of willingness to pay for it, so that there is a small group with a high willingness to pay, and then rapidly declining reservation prices after it; then the selling firm will have difficulty capturing the surplus... With some caution, one might refer to such products as special-interest ones. They tend to be supplied by clubs or other institutional devices that do not use the pure price system.[19]

An analysis similar to the above can be applied to commodities with the same demand curves but different cost structures. In figure 4.9, commodity 1 is assumed to have the lower fixed cost and the higher marginal cost (MC). Thus the average cost (AC) curves cross once as shown. We might also note

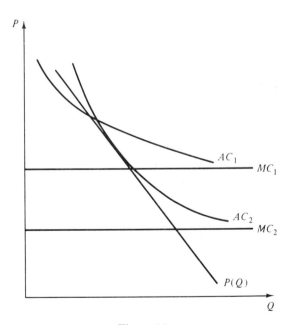

Figure 4.9

that it is profitable to produce commodity 1 but not commodity 2 (though it is just at the margin of being produced). On the other hand, were we to choose on the basis of social optimality, we would have gone for commodity 2 (which would be produced at a much higher output level than commodity 1 and so would generate a much larger consumer surplus). Thus, as with commodities with inelastic demands, the market will discriminate against high-fixed-cost/low-marginal-cost commodities.

5   Product quality and market structure

5.1 Introduction

The feature of product differentiation on which we have focused up till now has been variety. In some cases (as with Hotelling), we have had in mind a taste parameter which we have thought of as being distributed across consumers. In others, such as our discussion of Chamberlin, we assumed a primitive desire for variety. In each case we have looked at the optimal variety to service the needs of consumers and what it is that limits the market's ability to achieve this. In this chapter we start our examination of another dimension of product differentiation that matters for people's utility: the question of product quality and the relationship between quality choice and market structure. In this chapter we shall restrict the discussion to the choice of a single quality level or, to be more precise, when we consider market structures other than monopoly, we shall only consider symmetric equilibria in which firms choose the same quality level. The discussion of product differentiation by quality is the theme of the next chapter on vertical differentiation. In that, the market equilibrium may be characterised by the co-existence of several levels of quality.

In the current discussion we follow the approach originally taken by Dorfman and Steiner (1954) in supposing that it can be represented by some scalar measure, z, such that the higher is z the higher are unit costs and the more highly do consumers value any particular quantity of the good. We also assume that consumers know the quality of the goods that they purchase. In section 6 we shall relax this to some degree when we discuss the idea of quality as reliability.

It may be argued that there is a wide range of products for which a scalar representation of quality is unsuitable. More precisely, that products are differentiated by a multiplicity of characteristics and that any good can only be represented by a vector w of these. Let us suppose this to be true and that all logically feasible brands lie in some compact, convex set. Now, endow consumers with preferences given by a utility function defined over both some undifferentiated numeraire good y and the set of feasible characteristics. If we now assume that these preferences are separable between the numeraire and characteristics so that we can write any individual's utility function as

$$u(y, w) = v(y, z(w)) \qquad (5.1)$$

and, if we also assume that the $z(\cdot)$ functions are identical across individuals, then we can talk about quality as if it were a scalar. Of course, as equation (5.1) makes clear, 'quality' is not a physical characteristic but rather a subjective sub-utility index. Though it may not be absolutely compelling, this justification may be plausible as a first approximation and it has an obvious convenience value in doing analysis. Since we have only imposed identity at the sub-utility level, the preferences of equation (5.1) still allow individuals to differ in their marginal rates of substitution between the numeraire and the quality good.

There are three different ways in which one can think about quality improvement. In drawing this distinction we are following Levhari and Peles (1973). The first type of quality improvement is that which increases the demand for a good. What we have in mind here could include the whole range of non-price competitive factors like advertising, promotional offers, such as those glasses and games offered by the oil industry, and, in the professions, minimum qualifications for entry. A thorough discussion of this in fact involves considering the quality of a set of differentiated goods rather than just a single good. However, since the analysis of this is a little more complex we shall not worry about this problem until later on in this chapter. For the bulk of our time we shall restrict ourselves to the single-good case. In the second place, quality may be a perfect substitute for quantity. This we refer to as the 'shaves' model since the obvious example is that of the life of a razor blade. What the consumer cares about is *total service*, the number of shaves, but this can equally be provided by buying a large number of not very durable blades or a small number of highly durable blades. Another example is of course the electric light bulb of a given wattage. The final type of quality improvement is that which increases the durability of a good. This gets us into a discussion of dynamic issues for changes in durability have implications for the stock of the good on the market. Although there is quite a long literature on this we shall concentrate on the important papers by Swan (1970, 1971) and the survey by Schmalensee (1979).

Sections 2–4 of this chapter concentrate on the case of monopoly. In section 5 we analyse oligopoly using the ideas of Spence (1977) and Dixit (1979). A particular feature of all of this discussion is the assumption that consumers know the true quality of the good they buy. However, imperfect information is an issue that seems to us to be very closely associated with quality goods and we conclude this chapter with a discussion of a particular aspect of this: consumers' uncertainty about the *reliability* of products.

5.2 Quality choice: welfare optimum and market equilibria

In the analysis of quality choice it is customary to start from the inverse demand function. This shows, for a given quality, how price varies with quantity

$$p = p(x, q), \tag{5.2}$$

where x is quantity, q is quality, $p_x < 0$ and $p_q > 0$. The reason for this last condition is that in what follows we shall want to consider various cases. For example, when we consider the 'shaves' model to which we have already referred, what matters will be the product xq. To start the formal analysis in this chapter we shall look at the polar cases of monopoly and competition and compare these market equilibria with the social optimum. This analysis can be carried out quite satisfactorily using the inverse demand function. However, this type of single-good framework doesn't allow us to consider the intermediate oligopoly market forms which lie between monopoly and competition in a very satisfactory way. An interesting dimension of the quality/quantity problem is where one variable is set in a collusive fashion while the other is set competitively. In monopoly of course, both variables are set collusively (see Spence, 1975), while under monopolistic competition both are competitively set (see Spence, 1977). However, it is quite likely that some variables in the choice problem are easier to set collusively than others and hence a framework that allows this richness is desirable. For this reason we shall approach the issues in the spirit of Dixit's 1979 paper when we extend the analysis to the case of oligopoly. In (5.2) we have already specified the inverse demand curve for the case of the single quality good. One interpretation which can be given to this curve, and one that is useful in discussing welfare issues, is to treat it as indicating the gross surplus (S) obtained by consumers from their consumption of some given quantity x of a good of quality q

$$S(x, q) = \int_0^x xp(s, q) \, ds, \tag{5.3}$$

so that consumers' surplus is given by

$$[S(x, q) - xp(x, q)].\tag{5.4}$$

This is illustrated in figure 5.1 where S is the hatched area under the inverse demand curve.

We now need to introduce production costs. Total production costs will be given by the cost function

$$C = c(x, q), \quad c_x > 0, \quad c_q > 0.\tag{5.5}$$

With this and the inverse demand function we may write the profits to be obtained from the production of this good as

$$\Pi(x, q) = xp(x, q) - c(x, q).\tag{5.6}$$

Since a distribution-neutral measure of welfare is the sum of consumers' surplus and profits, we can see that, since sales revenue $[xp(x, q)]$ cancels out as a mere transfer between producers and consumers, welfare can be written as

$$W(x, q) = S(x, q) - c(x, q).\tag{5.7}$$

Let us first of all establish the conditions necessary to achieve optimum welfare. If we consider first the choice of output, we can see immediately by superimposing the marginal cost curve on figure 5.1 that welfare is an

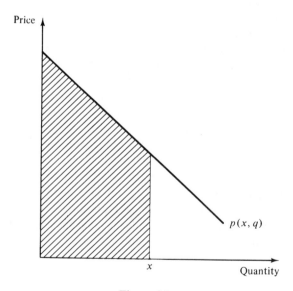

Figure 5.1

increasing function of x, given q, for as long as $p(x, q)$ exceeds $c_x(x, q)$. Hence the optimal choice, given q, is defined by

$$p(x, q) = c_x. \tag{5.8}$$

This is illustrated in figure 5.2.

In order to determine the optimal level of quality we must maximise $S + \Pi$ with respect to q. Doing so yields the necessary condition

$$S_q(x, q) = c_q(x, q),$$

i.e.

$$\int_0^x x p_q(s, q) \, ds = c_q(x, q). \tag{5.9}$$

In words, what this condition says is that the aggregate benefits accruing from a marginal change in quality should, at the optimum, equal the additional costs that have been incurred. An alternative way of expressing this involves dividing both sides of the expression by the level of output. Then, the right-hand side is simply the marginal cost of quality per unit of output (a sort of 'average' marginal cost), while the left-hand side is just the average valuation of the marginal change in quality.

Consider now the two market equilibria. The monopolist will seek to

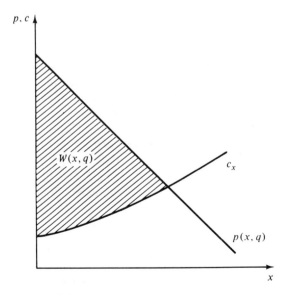

Figure 5.2

maximise profits and the relevant first-order conditions for this are

$$\Pi_x = 0 = p(x, q) + xp_x(x, q) - c_x(x, q), \tag{5.10a}$$

$$\Pi_q = 0 = xp_q(x, q) - c_q(x, q). \tag{5.10b}$$

Without being explicit about the relationship between costs under monopoly and competition, we can characterise the competitive market equilibrium as involving marginal cost pricing, with each firm choosing quality so as to maximise profits at this price. That is

$$p(x, q) - c_x(x, q) = 0, \tag{5.11a}$$

$$xp_q(x, q) - c_q(x, q) = 0. \tag{5.11b}$$

At this stage we may as well assume that there are constant returns to scale in production. This is because we are not concerned with the relationship between scale and quality choice, but instead with that between market structure and quality choice. To avoid any complications that might arise due to scale/structure interactions, it seems sensible and natural to assume that[1]

$$c(x, q) = xc(1, q), \quad \text{for all } q.$$

With this equation, (5.11a) is now consistent with zero profits in equilibrium.

There are several points to note now about these various equilibria. The first of these is that, in comparing monopoly and competition, the output that satisfies (5.10a) is smaller than that which satisfies (5.11a). This is a quite standard result reflecting the fact that average revenue is always at least as large as marginal revenue. However, the conditions that characterise the profit-maximising level of quality are identical. Of course, this does not mean the quality level so defined will be the same. The reason why this will generally not be true can be readily seen if the first-order conditions are graphed in quality/output space. This is done in figure 5.3.

The contours are iso-profit contours and $\Pi_x = 0$ and $\Pi_q = 0$ are the loci of the respective first-order conditions. Though both have been drawn with a positive slope in figure 5.3, there is no reason in general why this need be so. Implicit differentiation of these conditions yields equations that define their slopes. These are

$$dq/dx|_{\Pi_q=0} = -[\Pi_{xx}/(p_z + p_{xq} - c_{xq})], \tag{5.12a}$$

$$dq/dx|_{\Pi_q=0} = -[(p_q + xp_{qx} - c_{qx})/\Pi_{qq}], \tag{5.12b}$$

where $\Pi_{xx} = 2p_x + p_{xx} - c_x$ and $\Pi_{qq} = p_{qq} - c_{qq}$ are the second-order conditions. At a maximum, each of these will be negative. Thus the slopes of

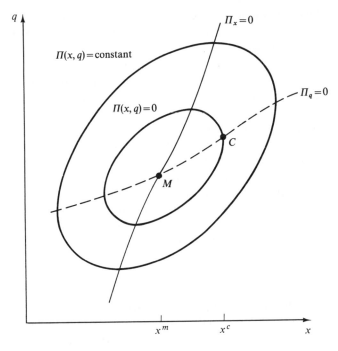

Figure 5.3

these loci depend critically upon the sign of the terms $(p_q + p_{qx} - c_{qx})$ and $(p_q + xp_{qx} - c_{qx})$ respectively. Note here that we have used the assumption that $p(x, q)$ and $c(x, q)$ are continuous functions to let $p_{xq} = p_{qx}$ and $c_{xq} = c_{qx}$.

Under both monopoly and competition the market equilibrium lies on the locus $\Pi_q = 0$. Since the monopoly equilibrium must also satisfy $\Pi_x = 0$, this equilibrium will be at the point M in figure 5.3. We have, however, already established that monopoly output x^m is less than the competitive output, so that the competitive equilibrium must lie on $\Pi_q = 0$ to the right of M. Since we have assumed constant returns to scale in production this point would be that where the zero-profit contour intersected the $\Pi_q = 0$ locus. This we may take to be the point C.

A second point to note is that a sufficient condition for quality to be invariant to market structure is that $\Pi_q = 0$ is horizontal. In fact, one of the vexed issues in the literature is this very point – the relationship between market structure and quality. The 'old orthodoxy' (see, for example, Kleiman and Ophir, 1966, Levhari and Srinivasan, 1969 and Schmalensee,

1970) had been that monopoly would produce goods of lower quality than a competitive industry. In other words it took the view that both the loci in figure 5.3 sloped upwards. However, this view, at least as it related to the important quality dimension of durability, was questioned in a series of papers by Swan (1970, 1971). In these he showed that as far as durability was concerned the 'quality' locus was horizontal and that it was invariant to market structure. Swan's result was a consequence of his imposing conditions that ensured that the locus was horizontal, but the papers had the effect of stimulating work in which these assumptions were relaxed. We shall explore the durability issue in section 5.3.

The third point is the issue of how these market equilibria relate to the social welfare optimum defined by conditions (5.8) and (5.9). Now, as we have defined it, welfare is the sum of consumers' surplus and profits. Therefore to see what impact a change in quality would have on this we need to consider the following condition

$$\frac{\partial W}{\partial q} = \int_0^x p_q(s, q) \, ds - x p_q(x, q) + \Pi_q(x, q). \tag{5.13}$$

However we already know that in the market equilibrium $\Pi_q = 0$. What this means then is that the quality level chosen in the market equilibrium will be too high or too low as compared with the social optimum depending on whether the first two terms are negative or positive. In other words it will depend upon whether

$$(1/x) \int_0^x p_q(s, q) \, ds \gtrless p_q(x, q). \tag{5.14}$$

The left-hand side of (5.14) is a term we have already met in equation (5.9). It is the average benefit from a marginal change in quality. The term on the right-hand side of (5.14) has a very obvious welfare interpretation: it is the benefit to the marginal consumer from a marginal change in quality. Hence the issue of optimality hangs on the sign of the basically ambiguous cross-derivative p_{qx}. It is probably easiest to see this point by referring to figure 5.4. This shows two demand schedules: one for quality q_0 and the other for quality $q^0 + \epsilon$. In the case that is illustrated, intra-marginal consumers place a higher value on the increase in quality than the marginal consumer – at x^0. This is a case where p_{qx} is negative and the left-hand side of (5.14) will exceed the right-hand side and quality will be too low in both the market equilibria. Conversely, if it is positive, the market choices of quality will be too high.

The conclusion to be drawn from our discussion so far would seem to be that the quality problem is as much a problem due to the inappropriateness of market price signals as it is to do with structure. This is an

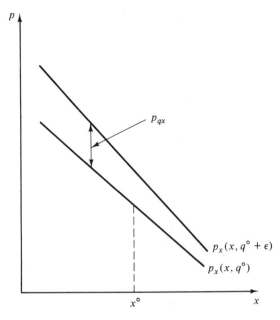

Figure 5.4

important point and it may be useful to make it in a slightly different way. Imagine that we had decided to regulate the behaviour of our monopolist in the following way: that he should set his price equal to marginal production cost. First note that the variations in x and q that would be consistent with marginal cost pricing are given by totally differentiating the price equals marginal cost equation. This yields

$$p_x dx + p_q dq = c_{xx} dx + c_{xq} dq,$$

i.e.

$$dx/dq = -[(p_q - c_{xq})/(p_x - c_{xx})]. \tag{5.15}$$

Since the denominator is unambiguously negative as long as we have non-increasing returns to scale, the sign of dx/dq depends on the sign of $(p_q - c_{xq})$. This is a result which we shall use in a moment. The second point to note is that the impact of the constraint is to determine output as a function of the, as yet, unspecified quality: $x(q)$. Given this, we can now seek to choose the socially optimal quality level. This would maximise

$$W(x(q), q) = \int_0^{x(q)} p(s, q)\, ds - c(x(q), q). \tag{5.16}$$

This, $\hat{q}$, is defined by the appropriate first-order condition

$$\int_0^{x(q)} p_q(s, q) \, ds = c_q(x(q), q). \tag{5.17}$$

We might now ask the following question. If, for some reason, the constrained firm were to find itself at this level of quality, would it indeed wish to stay there? In other words, what is the sign of $d\Pi/dq$ at $q = \hat{q}$? Well, since

$$\Pi(x(q), q) = p(x(q), q)x(q) - c(x(q), q), \tag{5.18}$$

we have

$$d\Pi/dq = [(p - c_x) + x p_x](dx/dq) + x p_q - c_q. \tag{5.19}$$

However, since the constraint holds, $(p - c_x) = 0$, so that this condition, which we have to evaluate at $\hat{q}$ is

$$(1/x)(d\Pi/dq) = p_x(dx/dq) + (p_q - (c_q/x)). \tag{5.20}$$

A necessary condition for this to be an equilibrium for the firm is that $p_x = c_{xq}$ (and hence, from (5.15), $dx/dq = 0$) and $p_q = c_q/x$. In other words, that

$$c_{xq} = c_q/x. \tag{5.21}$$

This equality would hold in the specific case of constant returns to scale that we have argued we may fairly focus on. This is because

$$c(x, q) = xc(1, q) = xc^*(q)$$

and hence

$$c_q/x = c_q^* = c_{xq}. \tag{5.22}$$

However we know that at the welfare optimum

$$\bar{p}_q \equiv (1/x)\int_0^{x(\hat{q})} p_q(s, q) \, ds = c_q/x, \tag{see (5.9)}$$

and that whether $\bar{p}_q \gtrless p_q$ depends on p_{qx}. If $\bar{p}_q > p_q$ then both terms in equation (5.20) will be negative at the social optimum and a profit-oriented firm would increase its profits were it to reduce quality. This is, our marginal cost-price constrained firm would set its quality level too low, while, if $\bar{p}_q < p_q$, it will set it too high.

The relationship between the social optimum and the two market equilibria that we have been considering can be illustrated by reference to figure 5.5. This is constructed for the case where $\bar{p}_q < p_q$, that is the

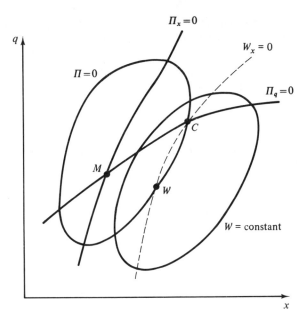

Figure 5.5

competitive and marginal cost constrained firms would choose to operate at point C with a level of quality that lies above the optimum. However note that in this case it is conceivable that the monopolist (located at M) might choose the same quality of good as the social optimum (W) would require. However, even if this were so, output would be too low. In other words, too few goods of the right quality would be produced for sale at too high a price.

5.3 Durability: quality and quantity as pure substitutes

The analysis which we have conducted so far has been concerned with a completely general specification of the inverse demand curve. We shall now consider a more specific form for this and at the same time move to the second of the distinctions to which we referred earlier. That is, we shall now consider the case where quality and quantity are pure substitutes. What this means is that there is no demand for quality as such. The example we can usefully think of is razor blades. What matters to consumers is the number of shaves s. Thus, x blades of life q will yield xq shaves. However clearly the demand for blades will now be a derived demand because it arises from the basic demand for shaves. Hence we should start the analysis from this, more fundamental, inverse demand curve $\xi(s)$. Since the number of blades of quality q that has to be purchased to deliver a service level of s shaves is $x=(s/q)$, it must be a feature of equilibrium that the quality-adjusted price of blades of different qualities is equal. In other words the inverse demand function for blades must have the form

$$p(x, q)=q\xi(xq)=q\xi(s), \quad \xi_s<0. \tag{5.23}$$

The monopolist will seek to choose that combination of x and q that maximises

$$\Pi(x, q)=\xi(s)s-c(x, q) \tag{5.24}$$

and this yields the first-order conditions

$$\Pi_x=0=s\xi_s z+\xi q-c_x$$
$$=q(\xi+s\xi_s)-c_x, \tag{5.25}$$

and

$$\Pi_q=0=x(\xi+s\xi_s)-c_q. \tag{5.26}$$

Taking these together gives us the condition

$$(c_x/c_q)=q/x. \tag{5.27}$$

What would the competitive industry do in this example? Suppose that we treat q as given for the moment. Then an extra unit of output (x) is valued at $q\xi$ by the marginal consumer. Its marginal production cost is s_x. Hence the competitive market equilibrium and the social optimum will be characterised by the condition that

$$q\xi=c_x. \tag{5.28}$$

Turning now to the incentives that the competitive firm has to increase its quality, given the level of output, we can see that this will have an immediate impact on the level of service equal to ds/dq. Consumers value this marginal change in s at $\xi(s)$. Hence the marginal revenue is $\xi(ds/dq)=\xi x$. Since the marginal cost of quality is c_q we have the following optimum condition for quality choice

$$x\xi=c_q. \tag{5.29}$$

The obvious feature to note about (5.28) and (5.29) is their similarity to (5.27). However, although the conditions look identical they do not mean that the actual levels of x and q chosen will be the same in the competitive and monopoly equilibria. What these conditions are, in fact, are conditions that tell firms to produce *efficient* combinations of x and q and *not the same* levels. In other words, every firm should choose its (x, q) combination so as to minimise the cost of delivering the relevant service level s. Now we know that it is not true that monopolists and competitors will deliver the same overall level of service. By restricting the quantity of this the monopolist will be able to earn profits in excess of normal.

We can illustrate all this in the following way. Consider some iso-cost curve $c(x, q) =$ constant. Along this curve we have $dq/dx = -(c_x/c_q)$. Suppose that the firm wishes to produce some level of service s then it can do this with any combination of x and q that satisfies $xq = s$; that is, any combination that lies on the relevant rectangular hyperbola. But the slope of this is $dq/dx = q/x$. Hence the first-order conditions merely tell us to choose the (x, q) pair where these are tangential. This is the efficient point E which is illustrated in figure 5.6.

Although we know that the monopoly level of service will be less than the competitive level, there is nothing in general that one can say concerning the respective output and quality levels. The actual result will depend crucially on the nature of the cost function. For example the case we have chosen to illustrate in figure 5.7 has $x^m < x^c$ but $q^c < q^m$.

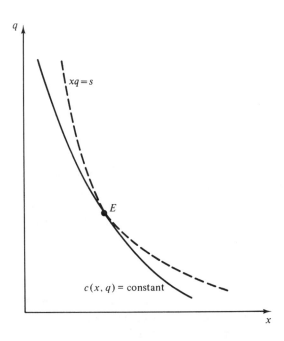

Figure 5.6

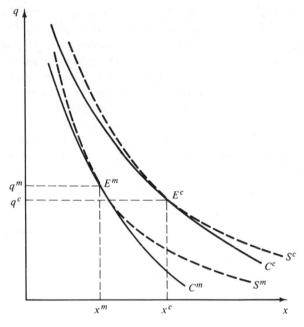

Figure 5.7

Nevertheless we may perhaps want to concentrate on the constant returns to scale case where $c(x, q) = xc^*(q)$. If so, we have in equilibrium

$$c_x/c_q = c^*/(xc_q^*) = q/x,$$

i.e.

$$(qc_q^*)/c^* = 1. \tag{5.30}$$

This condition, which now defines q, is completely independent of x which appears nowhere in (5.30). In other words it is only in the constant returns to scale case that the competitive industry and the monopoly firm will produce goods of the same quality and, furthermore, that this will be the socially optimal level as well. Figure 5.8 illustrates this.

5.4 Durability: stock and flow equilibrium

The way in which we have introduced durability in the 'shaves' model is really not very satisfactory. This is because we have not paid attention to the fact that what firms are producing is a *stock* of blades while consumers are concerned with the consumption of a *flow* of shaves. Hence our next

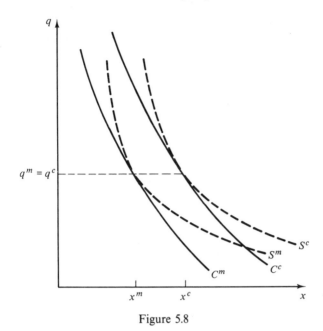

Figure 5.8

task is to specify how in a more general framework s is related to the firm's choice variables x and q.

The simplest way to model this is to let s be proportional to the stock that is held. If we do this we may also make the further simplifying assumption that they are equal for this is merely a matter of how we choose our units. How then is this stock itself related to x and q? The standard way that the literature has tackled this is to suppose that the good is an example of the 'one-hoss shay': that the units held by consumers yield a constant flow of services throughout their lives, q years, and then collapse. Note that the important thing about this is that we are treating depreciation as exogenous. It is this that is a crucial assumption and not the particular pattern of depreciation that we have chosen. Sieper and Swan (1973) have shown that the choice of this pattern has no important implications. The way in which we shall analyse the choice of durability is to suppose that we are in the following kind of stationary equilibrium. At some particular date, call it zero, let the firm produce x units of a good of durability q. These units yield a constant flow of services over their service life of q periods. After these q periods, the good collapses and the stock has to be replaced by producing another x units. Thus in planning terms the firm sees itself as producing x units every q'th period ad infinitum. The decision problem for the firm is the choice of x and q. The relevant demand side information is contained in what we might refer to as the 'average revenue' function $p(x, q)$. The exact meaning of this will become clear in a moment but it is intended to reflect the potential profitability of the following strategy which the firm may feasibly pursue: produce x units of a good of durability q every q'th period.

If we now turn to the consumers, we know that what they value is the flow of services that are yielded by this stock of x units. The durability of the good has no relevance in this valuation. A useful way to think about how to reflect these preferences is to suppose that they can be encapsulated in a rental function. This will indicate the maximum rental charge per period that they would be prepared, at the margin, to pay for x units of stock. Let this be $\xi(x)$. Given that the good lasts q periods, the present value of these rentals per unit is

$$v(x, q) = \int_0^q \xi(x) e^{-rt} \, dt = [\xi(x)/r][1 - e^{-rq}]. \tag{5.31}$$

Thus the strategy choice for the firm can be thought of as getting v at date 0, v at date q, v at date $2q$, and so on ad infinitum.

We can now forge the link with $p(x, q)$ in the following way: it is simply the present value of the set of returns from following this strategy per unit of production of the stock. In other words

$$p(x, q) = v + v e^{-rq} + v e^{-2rq} + \cdots$$
$$= [v/(1 - e^{-rq})] = [\xi(x)/r]. \tag{5.32}$$

Thus we now have a formal relationship between the unit price relevant to planning as far as the firm is concerned and the underlying valuation of this plan by consumers as summarised in their rental function. What equation (5.32) indicates is the following: if the producing firm were to increase x by one unit, this will have the effect of raising the service flow by one unit at every point in time, regardless of the actual durability q. However, as in the simple 'shaves' story, consumers only care about the service flow and so the net amount they will pay for one more unit of the good will simply be the capitalised rental charge or service price. Thus, in the case where what we mean by quality is durability, we have the result that p_q and $p_{xq} = p_{qx}$ are identically zero. If we were now to let the cost function, corresponding to the average revenue function, be $c(x, q)$, we would have the following conditions to characterise the optimum choices of x and q for the monopolist

$$\Pi_x = 0 = [(\xi + x\xi_x)/r] - c_x(x, q), \tag{5.33a}$$

$$\Pi_q = 0 = -c_q(x, q). \tag{5.33b}$$

In other words, given x, the monopolist would seek to find that durability that minimised costs per unit of output. However, a welfare-maximising social planner would also want to choose the durability level defined by this condition.

Recall now equations (5.12a,b). These told us the slopes of the loci $\Pi_x = 0$ and $\Pi_q = 0$. In the durability case these become

$$dq/dx|_{\Pi_x = 0} = \Pi_{xx}/c_{xq}, \tag{5.34a}$$

$$dq/dx|_{\Pi_q = 0} = c_{xq}/\Pi_{qq} = -c_{xq}/c_{qq}. \tag{5.34b}$$

We may reasonably suppose that $c_{qq} > 0$, so that the exact nature of the market and welfare equilibria will depend very much on what we choose to assume about $c(x, q)$.

Let us assume that the cost function $c(x, q)$ is separable. In this case we may write it as

$$c(x, q) = a(x)b(q), \tag{5.35}$$

with

$$c_q(x, q) = a(x)b_q. \tag{5.36}$$

If we now compare (5.33b) and (5.35), we can see that the level of q that satisfies equation (5.33b) is independent of x. Another way of stating this is that the locus of points that satisfies both $\Pi_q = 0$ and $W_q = 0$ is horizontal and hence durability is independent of market structure. Thus along these two loci we have

$$dq/dx = -[a_x b_z/a(x)b_{qq}] = 0. \tag{5.37}$$

This result is quite independent of the nature of scale economies in production, it is purely a matter of separability of the cost function into an output component and a durability component.

In his seminal paper, Swan (1970) supposed constant returns to scale in production and hence imposed separability since this is equivalent to the specification $c(x, q) = xc(1, q)$. As we argued earlier, this is perhaps a sensible assumption to make when what one wants to do is to compare how optimal choices depend upon market structure. If we do make this assumption then $c_q = c_{xq} = 0$ and taking (5.33b) and (5.34b) together yields the result that Π_q is horizontal and that durability is independent of market structure. A further implication of constant returns to scale is that the zero-profit competitive equilibrium corresponds to the social optimum. Hence we may illustrate Swan's result on optimal durability as in figure 5.9. The loci of the first-order conditions that solve the profit- and welfare-maximising conditions are indicated by Π_x, Π_q, W_x and W_q. Therefore, we once again have the result that the monopoly offers the same

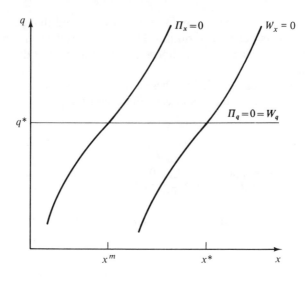

Figure 5.9

product as the competitive industry, but that it charges a higher price for it. In other words, we have derived in a more careful way the result which was illustrated in figure 5.8.

There are two points to note with regard to this result. The first is the result that the optimum is characterised by $c_q = 0$. It is possible that some may find this result a little unusual when they first come across it. However, it should be borne in mind that $c(x, q)$ is actually a function in present value terms in the same way that $p(x, q)$ was. Hence, were we to write the instantaneous cost function, call it $d(x, q)$, we would define $c(x, q)$ as follows

$$c(x, q) = d(x, q) + d(x, q)e^{-rq} + \cdots$$
$$= [d(x, q)/(1 - e^{-rq})]. \tag{5.38}$$

If we now substitute for c_q in equation (5.33b) using (5.38) we get the condition defining the optimal q as

$$d = r/(e^{rq} - 1). \tag{5.39}$$

However, this is simply a condition defining the durability or lifetime that minimises $c(x, q)$.

We commented earlier that work done subsequently to Swan's original paper has suggested that his independence result does not depend on the assumption of exogenous depreciation (e.g. Auernheimer and Saving,

1977, Swan, 1977). However, with non-separability and non-constant returns to scale, c_{xq} is non-zero. This means that the loci Π_q and W_q are no longer horizontal. However, they are equivalent in that the same conditions characterise them. That is to say, they will coincide but may slope either upwards or downwards so that both market output and durability levels will diverge from their social optimum levels.

We have been slightly cavalier in the way we have treated returns to scale in production. In the quasi-dynamic way that the durability model in the last section was set up we had supposed that production was periodic inasmuch as there was an initial and immediate building up of stock to its steady-state level and that, after that, the only production needed was that needed to meet replacement demand. If there are constant returns to scale in production then this would be an appropriate adjustment path for our economy in which there is perfect knowledge. However, if there are increasing marginal costs, say, then the natural tendency would be to try and spread the adjustment to the equilibrium stock over a period of time.

Auernheimer and Saving (1977) have attempted to explore this issue by analysing a model in which marginal costs are constant in the long run once the stock has adjusted to its steady-state level but where they are increasing in the short run. The way that they do this is to consider the following cost function

$$c(x, q) = xb(q, \dot{x}, \dot{q}),$$

where $b_q > 0$ and $\dot{x}$ and $\dot{q}$ are derivatives with respect to time. If the rate of output or durability is increasing then so are b_x or b_q. Their analysis shows that in the limit, as the steady-state is reached, the durability chosen is indeed independent of market structure. However, they do not provide any results on how durability might vary before this point. Nevertheless they do extend their analysis to show that this result also holds in the case where the inelastic supply of inputs means that, even in the long run, marginal production costs are increasing. The general conclusion then seems to be that Swan's independence result is pretty robust with respect to cost assumptions.

An attempt to look at the adjustment path prior to the steady-state has been made in a recent paper by Muller and Peles (1986). They assume that one is dealing with the decreasing returns (increasing marginal cost) case. Given this, they show that if the marginal cost of quality per unit of output is non-increasing, as might be the case where the major cost of quality improvement was in the form of fixed-product development costs

$$(1/x)cq < 0,$$

then in the trajectory to the steady-state both the competitive firm and the monopoly will choose a path of decreasing durability. Along these paths the monopoly level will always be less than the competitive level. This latter fact merely reflects the lower output trajectory chosen by the monopolist. Along any path, as the actual stock builds up to its steady-state level, the rental price will be above that which would hold in the eventual equilibrium and it is this that makes it profitable in the short run to produce a durability level in excess of the steady-state level. Of course this does seem to depend a lot on our assumption of perfect knowledge. If consumers were initially unaware of the exact nature of the product, it might pay firms not to produce too durable a good to start with so as to be able to offer it at a relatively low introductory price and create consumer awareness.

Our analysis of durability assumed that there was no demand for durability as such. However, in practice this may well not be so. For example if there are non-trivial transactions costs in renewing one's stock of the durable good every q'th period, then this will create a demand for durability itself. Thus, if it cost something significant to fit a new razor blade or to change a light bulb, $p(x, q)$ would no longer be independent of q. In a way this is the issue that Schmalensee (1974) and Su (1975) consider when they look at the sensitivity of Swan's result to the assumption that maintenance cannot be performed on durables. If it were possible to prolong the life of a durable by performing maintenance then the independence result may well not go through. If the impact of maintenance spending is on the service flow of the durable then the commodity that interests consumers, service, has effectively two characteristics: maintenance and built-in durability. If the good is one that is rented then both competition and monopoly will lead to production of the good at minimum cost. If the good is sold by the competitive industry then the same choice will be made. However, what about a monopoly seller? Suppose that in an attempt to increase his profits he raises the price. Those who buy the good will now value it more highly and will consequently find it worthwhile to undertake a little more maintenance in order to prolong its life. Thus the monopolist who sells faces a constraint in that customers have control over maintenance and this will make selling less profitable than renting. However it is not clear just what that sales equilibrium will look like, it might involve a higher or lower durability than in the rent equilibrium.

An element of costs associated with owning a durable good that we have so far neglected is operating costs. This has been studied by Parks (1974). Suppose that owning a unit of a good with lifetime q involves the flow outlay operating costs $d(q)$. Assuming stationarity and perfect markets, the purchase and rental prices are related as follows

$$v = \int_0^q [\xi(x) - d(q)]e^{-rt} \, dt. \tag{5.40}$$

If we now integrate this and substitute into equation (5.32) we obtain

$$p(x, q) = [\xi(x) - d(q)]/r. \tag{5.41}$$

It is clear that p_q is not generally zero so that we shall no longer have the first-order condition in the form of equation (5.33b). Thus separability will no longer be sufficient for independence. However, p_{qx} does equal zero with the result that, under constant returns to scale, the $\Pi_q = 0$ locus is horizontal and we once again have the Swan independence result. A final corollary on this is to note that the way we have modelled operating costs is to assume they are constant. If we had made them depend on both x and q the result would no longer hold.

What about transactions costs? Let us suppose that every time that a good wears out the consumer incurs a transaction cost of T. This must now be added to the replacement price v which is now defined by

$$v = [\xi(x)/r][1 - e^{-rq}] - T. \tag{5.42}$$

Using equation (5.32) we get

$$p(x, q) = [\xi(x)/r] - [T/(1 - e^{-rq})]. \tag{5.43}$$

Again we find that $p_{qx} = 0$ with the consequence that durability is again invariant to market structure. If we have constant returns to scale, the first-order condition characterising the monopolist's choice of q can be written as

$$bq/[b(q) + T] = r/[e^{rq} - 1], \tag{5.44}$$

so that durability is increasing in T. That is to say, though the actual choice is independent of market structure, it is not independent of the transaction costs themselves.

There is one final assumption which we have yet to consider. This is that both consumers and producers face the same rate of time discount: that capital markets are perfect. What if this were not so? If the durable good is rented nothing is affected since both the competitive firm and the monopoly will want to produce that service level which minimises their production costs. However, when the good is sold to consumers it is a different story. Let us take the consumer's discount rate to be the common one of ρ. Then the relationship between the service price, which determines demand, and the sale price, which determines producer revenue, is given by

$$v = [\xi(x)/\rho][1 - e^{-\rho q}].\tag{5.45}$$

From equation (5.32) the resulting sale price is

$$p(x, q) = [\xi(x)/\rho]\left[\frac{(1 - e^{-\rho q})}{(1 - e^{-r q})}\right].\tag{5.46}$$

If r and ρ differ then there is a demand for durability as such.

5.5 Quality choice under oligopoly: symmetric equilibrium

The way in which we shall analyse oligopoly follows that suggested in the papers by Spence (1977) and Dixit (1979). We consider a number, n, of differentiated goods. The output of the i'th good will be denoted by x_i and its quality level by q_i. We have already introduced the numeraire good which we take to be produced at constant unit cost. To each of the n differentiated goods there corresponds a gross surplus[2] given by the function $\phi(x_i, q_i)$. It seems reasonable to suppose that ϕ is increasing in q and concave in x. Given that n products are on sale, the total gross surplus from these is

$$s = \sum_{i=1}^{n} \phi(x_i, q_i).\tag{5.47}$$

We assume that the analysis can be carried out using a representative consumer and so can write the gross benefit function as

$$B(x, q, y) = G(\Sigma_i \phi(x_i, q_i)) + y.\tag{5.48}$$

The demand for any particular differentiated product can be derived from the solution to the problem of maximising benefits over costs. That is, quantities, x_i, are chosen so as to

$$\text{maximise } [B(x, q, y) - \Sigma_i p_i x_i - y].\tag{5.49}$$

This gives us the inverse demand functions

$$p_i = G'(s)\phi_x(x_i, q_i), \forall i.\tag{5.50}$$

Notice that oligopolistic interactions, the effects of the actions of producers other than i ($\partial p_i/\partial x_j$ and $\partial p_i/\partial q_j$), appear in the value of s and so get channelled through the function G. Obviously these are going to depend on the sign of the second derivative, G''. For this reason we would not want to restrict G too much at the outset. Thus although G will be increasing in q there is no *a priori* reason to impose, say, concavity. Whether or not this is appropriate would depend on the character of the industry. It may perhaps be plausible to suppose the following. When the number of firms is rather low, and so s is small, goods are more likely to be complementary, so that G would be convex. However, as the number of products gets larger, goods are less clearly differentiated and are more likely to be substitutes. If so, then we would have G concave. Hence we assume that there is some critical s^* such that for $s < s^*$, $G'' > 0$ and $s > s^*$, $G'' < 0$. This is illustrated in figure 5.10.

There are now three dimensions of choice: the number of products and the quantity and quality of each. It is useful to have the additional richness produced by the first of these since one may wish to consider cases where this number is limited. For example, the differentiated good that we are considering might be some professional service. Professions may engage in practices to restrict entry as well as engaging in others whose effect is to determine the standard of service provided. Alternatively, such professional bodies might simply limit entry and allow their members to compete over quality. However, were there no barriers to entry, collusion over quantity and quality would serve no purpose since profits would be driven to zero by entry.

Whatever it is that is collusively set, we shall assume that the other variables are set in a profit-maximising non-cooperative way. This seems a fairly natural way to look at matters. Thus, the nature of the non-

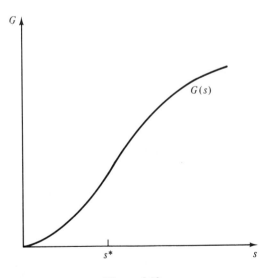

Figure 5.10

cooperative equilibria in the analysis is Nash and to simplify the presentation we shall assume at the outset that they are symmetric. That is to say, $x_i = x$ and $q_i = q$. Thus we can now write the expression for total gross surplus as

$$s = n.\phi(x, q). \tag{5.51}$$

Each firm is assumed to face the same cost conditions and these we write as the cost function $c(x, q)$. A property that we shall assume at the outset is that this function exhibits economies of scale. The reason for this is that we need something to place a limit on the number of firms so that we may talk of oligopoly. To illustrate some results, a more specific form will be put on this function at a later point. Since we are restricting our discussion to the case of identical, symmetric firms, we know that, if each were to choose the pair (x, q), then aggregate welfare could be written as

$$W(x, q, n) = G(s) - nc(x, q) = G(s) - s[c(x, q)/\phi(x, q)] \tag{5.52}$$

by appropriately choosing the origin to eliminate y, the numeraire commodity. While this function depends on n, x and q, we could for the moment take n to be given. If we do so then we immediately see that the optimum choice of x and q will involve minimising

$$c(x, q)/\phi(x, q). \tag{5.53}$$

The two conditions that characterise this are

$$\phi_x/\phi = c_x/c \tag{5.54}$$

$$\phi_q/\phi = c_q/c. \tag{5.55}$$

Consider (5.54). For any particular q this equation will define some $x(q)$. If we now substitute that into (5.53) we have a 'minimised' value of c/ϕ, conditional on q. Denote this $m(q)$. To solve for the welfare optimum we now need to choose the relevant values of q and s. The choice of the latter implicitly defines n by way of $s = n\phi$. Thus we want to solve the 'concentrated' problem of maximising

$$W(s, q) = G(s) - sm(q). \tag{5.56}$$

The conditions that characterise the solution to this are

$$G'(s) = m(q), \tag{5.57}$$

$$m'(q) = 0. \tag{5.58}$$

These equations can be solved recursively since (5.58) defines q^*, and we can then look for the s^* that solves $G'(s^*) = m(q^*)$.

Consider for a moment equation (5.57). If we take its total differential we see that

$$\mathrm{d}s/\mathrm{d}q = m'/G''.$$

Recall that for $s < s^*$, $G'' > 0$, and for $s > s^*$, $G'' < 0$. The implication of this is that the locus of equation (5.57) is an ellipse about the axes $s = s^*$, $q = q^*$. This is illustrated in figure 5.11. Since, for a given q, we should want s to be as large as possible, we can restrict our attention to the upper part of the ellipse. The welfare optimum is thus the point W which satisfies the conditions (5.57) and (5.58).

Now that we have established the characterisation of the social optimum, let us now turn our attention to the market equilibria. Recall that, in introducing oligopoly, we referred to the example of a professional body. Such an organisation, whose actions are such as to force a collusive outcome, can be treated as another market participant. Although it may be permissible in some instances to treat the resulting equilibria as Nash equilibria, there must also be cases where the organisation has superior powers. In such cases we should think of it as a leader in the choice of some decision variable and the individual firms as Stackelberg followers. Thus the organisation itself behaves as a Stackelberg leader and so takes account of individual firms' reaction functions when it takes its own decision.

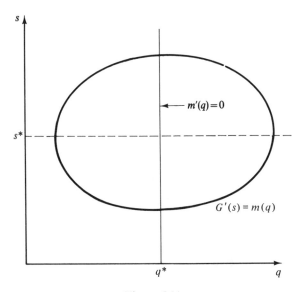

Figure 5.11

What then can we say about the objectives of the firms? Individual firms will have single objectives: to maximise their own profits

$$\pi = G'x\phi_x - c, \qquad (5.59)$$

with s being treated as a constant (this is the 'large numbers' assumption in this context). If we allow free entry to take place then profits will be pushed to zero for the marginal firm. However, the organisation's objective could be one of two. It may either wish to see profit per firm (π) maximised or it may wish to maximise group profits, $n\pi = \Pi$.

Let us first consider the case where the organisation and its members both wish to see profit per member maximised. The extreme case would be the cartel form in which n, x and q were all collusively chosen. In this case the maximisation of (5.59) yields the following three conditions

$$G''(s) = 0, \qquad (5.60)$$

$$G'(s)\partial(x\phi_x)/\partial x = c_x, \qquad (5.61)$$

$$G'(s)\partial(x\phi_x)/\partial q = c_q. \qquad (5.62)$$

The first of these tells us that s should equal s^*. This makes sense since this is the point at which the products switch from being complements to being substitutes. The organisation would not wish to see the unnecessary competition which would be created by goods being substitutes. While we know that this value of s is less than is socially optimal, we are unable to go further and compare the values of x and q with their optimal levels.

An alternative way in which the organisation might be run is that its function is merely to control entry. In such a case each firm would treat n as fixed and then set x and q according to equations (5.61) and (5.62). These two conditions implicitly define reaction functions for the firms, $x(n)$ and $q(n)$. The organisation will then choose n so as to maximise $\pi[s(n), x(n), q(n)]$. However, since firms have chosen their x and q optimally for any given n, the condition that characterises the optimal choice of n is just

$$(\partial\pi/\partial s)\cdot(ds/dn) = G''(s)\phi = 0.$$

Notice, however, that this is effectively the same as equation (5.60). We can therefore conclude that an organisation that fixes its membership results in an outcome that is the same as if there were full collusion.

Let us turn now to the question of group profits. If membership is chosen to maximise this then the first-order condition is

$$\partial\Pi/\partial n = G'(s)x\phi_x + nx\phi_x G''(s)\phi = 0,$$

i.e.

$$G'(s)/G''(s) = -n\phi < 0. \qquad (5.63)$$

Since $G' > 0$, this implies that $G''(s)$ is negative at the optimum. In other words, the optimum will be where $G(s)$ is concave. In the light of this condition, and to facilitate analysis, we can assume specific functional forms for G and ϕ. These, iso-elastic, functions are respectively

$$G(s) = (1/\beta)s^\beta, \quad 0 < \beta < 1$$

and

$$\phi(x, q) = Ax^{\alpha(q)}, \quad 0 < \alpha < 1.$$

From these it follows that

$$sG'(s) = \beta G(s)$$

and

$$x\phi_x = \alpha(q)\phi.$$

Hence, total group profits are

$$\Pi = n[G'(s)\alpha(q)\phi(x, q) - c(x, q)]$$
$$= sG'(s)\alpha(q) - nc(x, q)$$
$$= \beta\alpha G(s) - nc(x, q). \tag{5.64}$$

For any given n, and hence s, each firm will choose x and q to maximise its own profits and the two conditions that reflect these choices are

$$G'\alpha\phi_x = c_x, \tag{5.65}$$

$$G'(\alpha\phi_q + \phi\alpha') = c_q. \tag{5.66}$$

If there is no control over entry, then entry will occur until profits are zero. That is, until

$$G'\alpha\phi = c. \tag{5.67}$$

Taking this condition along with equation (5.65) tells us that in the zero-profit equilibrium we will have

$$\phi_x/\phi = c_x/c.$$

However this condition also implies that, given q, we minimise c/ϕ with respect to x. We have already met with this above where we called the minimised value $m(q)$. Hence we can substitute for c/ϕ in the zero-profit condition to get

$$G'(s) = m(q)/\alpha(q). \tag{5.68}$$

If we now take the ratio of equations (5.66) and (5.67) we obtain

$$\alpha'/\alpha = c_q/c - \phi_q/\phi.$$

Since $m = c/\phi$, we also have

$$m'/m \equiv \partial \log m/\partial q = c_q/c - \phi_q/\phi,$$

so that a second condition which characterises the zero-profit equilibrium is

$$m'(q) = [m(q)/\alpha(q)]\alpha'(q). \tag{5.69}$$

There are two things to note about conditions (5.68) and (5.69). The first is that the locus defined by (5.68) lies inside that on which the social optimum is. Furthermore, its slope is given by

$$ds/dq = [m' - (m\alpha')/\alpha]/\alpha G''. \tag{5.70}$$

This will be zero at the point where equation (5.69) is satisfied. The second point is that the location of the locus described by (5.69) in relation to the optimum depends critically on the sign of $\alpha'(q)$. If it is negative, it lies to the left, and, if it is positive, it lies to the right of the socially optimal quality level.

Let us now consider the 'cartel' solution in which n, x and q are collusively chosen. The necessary first-order conditions are

$$\beta\alpha G'\phi = c, \tag{5.71}$$

$$\beta\alpha G'n\phi_x = c_x, \tag{5.72}$$

$$\beta(G\alpha' + \alpha G'n\phi_q) = nc_q. \tag{5.73}$$

The first two of these once again give us the condition for minimising c/ϕ with respect to x, so that (5.71) can be written as

$$G' = (1/\beta\alpha)m. \tag{5.74}$$

Taking the ratio of (5.73) and (5.71) yields

$$\left[\frac{1}{n\phi}\right]\left[\frac{G}{G'}\right]\left[\frac{\alpha'}{\alpha}\right] = \left[\frac{G}{sG'}\right]\left[\frac{\alpha'}{\alpha}\right] = \left[\frac{\alpha}{\beta\alpha}\right]$$

$$= \left[\frac{c_q}{c} + \frac{\phi_q}{\phi}\right] = \left[\frac{m'}{m}\right],$$

so that we have a second condition

$$m' = (m/\beta\alpha)\alpha'. \tag{5.75}$$

A final solution that we shall look at is where membership and output is fixed so as to maximise group profits but the choice of quality level is left up to the individual firms. Looking at the group decisions first we see that these are characterised by

$$\beta G' \phi = c, \tag{5.76}$$

$$\beta \alpha G' n \phi_x = c_x. \tag{5.77}$$

Thus one condition that will hold true in this equilibrium is (5.74). Each firm, independently choosing its q, sets

$$G'(\alpha \phi_q + \phi \alpha') = c_q. \tag{5.78}$$

If we take the ratio of (5.78) and (5.76) we get

$$m'(q) = [(1/\beta \alpha)\alpha' + (1 - \beta/\beta)(\phi_q/\phi)]m. \tag{5.79}$$

This last condition is a new one. To work out where this locus lies in relation to the others that we have derived we need to compare (5.79) and (5.69). Subtracting the latter from the former yields

$$(1 - \beta/\beta)[(\alpha'/\alpha) + (\phi_q/\phi)]m. \tag{5.80}$$

However before we can put a sign to this we need to consider the impact of an increase in quality on the maximum price obtainable for any particular unit. It would seem quite reasonable to suppose that this, p_q, is positive. Since

$$p = G'(s)\phi_x = (G'(s)/x)\alpha\phi,$$

we have

$$p_q = (G'\alpha\phi/x)[(\alpha'/\alpha) + (\phi_q/\phi)] > 0,$$

and this can only be true if the term in square brackets is positive, irrespective of the sign of α'. However this is just what we need to interpret (5.80). We can therefore conclude that the locus defined by (5.79) lies to the right of that which corresponds to the monopolistic competition equilibrium.

The equilibria that we have examined in equations (5.62) to (5.80) are illustrated in figure 5.12a (for $\alpha' < 0$) and figure 5.12b (for $\alpha' > 0$).

In both of these diagrams W is the welfare optimum, MC the zero-profit equilibrium with free entry, FC the fully collusive equilibrium and C that which corresponds to collusion over membership and quantity. The first thing to note is that, in all three of the market equilibria, quantity is chosen so as to minimise c/ϕ. This at least is one point of efficiency. However, as is clear from the diagrams, the choice of quality is unlikely to be optimal. To say something about welfare we need to consider the iso-welfare contours. Totally differentiating equation (5.56) gives us an expression for the slope

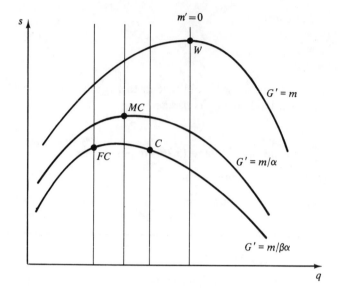

Figure 5.12a

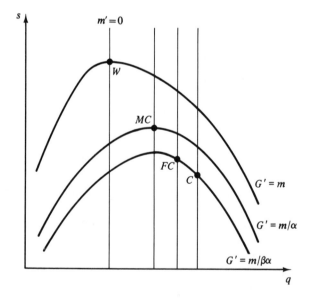

Figure 5.12b

of these

$$ds/dq = -[sm'/(G'-m)].$$

From this it should be clear that these are concentric about W. Given this we can see that, in the case of $\alpha' > 0$, the market equilibria are clearly ranked

$$MC > FC > C.$$

However, matters are not so simple when we come to look at $\alpha' < 0$. The zero-profit equilibrium MC is better than full collusion FC, but there is no way that we can rank FC and MC with respect to C and so there remains some ambiguity.

What about market equilibrium output levels? For a start we know that x is chosen to minimise c/ϕ. However to get specific results we shall need to assume that $c(x, q)$ is separable and linear in its arguments, so that $c_{xx} = c_{xq} = 0$. If we do so we may use the first-order condition (5.5) to claim

$$x(q) = \alpha c/c_q.$$

From this it follows that

$$(1-\alpha)x'(q) = (\alpha'c + \alpha c_q)/c_x,$$

so that

$$x'(q)/x(q) = [(\alpha'/\alpha) + (c_q/c)][1/(1-\alpha)]. \tag{5.81}$$

In evaluating equation (5.80) we established that $(\alpha'/\alpha) > -(\phi_q/\phi)$. This then enables us to claim, using (5.81), that

$$x'/x > [(c_q/c) - (\phi_q/\phi)][1/(1-\alpha)]$$
$$= -(m'/m)[1/(1-\alpha)]. \tag{5.82}$$

if $\alpha' > 0$, then by (5.81) (x'/x) is also positive. If $\alpha' < 0$, we can see from figure 5.12a that, in the region of interest, $m' < 0$, so that again (x'/x) is positive. It therefore follows that $x(q)$ is increasing in q. In the case where $\alpha' > 0$ the output and quality levels clearly move in the same direction. Since as we move through the various market equilibria s is decreasing while x and q (and so ϕ) are increasing, it follows that the number of firms in the industry must be declining. Unfortunately no such clear picture emerges for the case where $\alpha' < 0$.

If the group that we are modelling can only choose to limit membership then, in order to maximise group profit $n\pi$, it will set n to satisfy

$$\pi + n\pi' = 0.$$

This implies that in the group equilibrium π' is negative so that this is not consistent with maximising profit per product. Given n, the individual members are then free to choose output and quality so as to maximise their individual profits π. The x and q that achieve this are defined by

$$G'\alpha\phi_x = c_x, \tag{5.83}$$

$$G'(\alpha'\phi + \alpha\phi_q) = c_q. \tag{5.84}$$

From the definition of Π, $\partial\Pi/\partial n = 0$ yields

$$\beta\alpha G'\phi = c. \tag{5.85}$$

Taking the ratio of (5.83) to (5.85) gives the condition

$$(\phi_x/\phi) = \beta(c_x/c). \tag{5.86}$$

If we compare this with (5.54), we can see that it is no longer the case that c/ϕ is minimised. Just as we used (5.54) to define $x(q)$, we can use (5.86) to define $\chi(q)$. The upper part of figure 5.13 shows (5.54) and (5.86) as functions of x along with $x(q)$ and $\chi(q)$. In the lower part we graph c/ϕ indicating that the 'minimised' value when (5.86) is satisfied $\mu(q)$ exceeds $m(q)$.

Having now defined $\mu(q)$, we can substitute this in (5.85) which can be usefully rewritten now as

$$G'(s) = \beta[\mu(q)/\zeta(q)]. \tag{5.87}$$

If we now look back to figure 5.12 we can see that this defines a locus which lies below those for G' that we have previously established. That is to say, for every q, s is smaller in this case. The point that this indicates is that when a group has no control over quality, it will seek to compensate for this by restricting entry. The equilibrium level of q is defined by considering the ratio of (5.84) to (5.85). This yields

$$(\alpha'/\alpha) = (1/\beta)c_q/c - \phi_q/\phi, \tag{5.88}$$

which has to be evaluated at $\chi(q)$. There is no general answer we can give but, in the case of the linear cost function we considered earlier, it defines a vertical curve which lies to the right of the previous ones. So the equilibria in this case involve a lower s and a higher x and q and hence a smaller n.

There is one final permutation which we have as yet not considered. A feature of certain professions might for example be that they collusively set membership and standards but allow the individual firms to choose output levels. In this case (5.87) still holds, but (5.88) is replaced by a slight variant

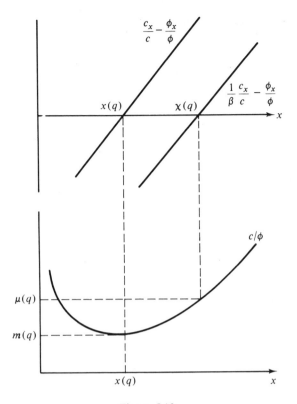

Figure 5.13

$$(\alpha'/\alpha) = (1/\beta)[c_q/c - \phi_q/\phi]. \tag{5.89}$$

This equation is like a condition which characterised the fully collusive decision which we discussed above. However, what distinguishes the two is that this is evaluated at $\chi(q)$ rather than $x(q)$. In the case of $\alpha' > 0$ this involves choosing a quality level that lies above that for full collusion. Looking back to figure 5.12b one can see then that if a regulator were to enforce quantity competition from a position of full collusion then society would find itself on a lower welfare curve in this instance.

5.6 Product reliability

In all of the discussion so far in this chapter, we have assumed that consumers were certain about the quality of any particular good. This is quite a strong assumption and it would be wrong to finish this chapter without some discussion of the effect of uncertain information on the quality of goods. The way we shall do this is by taking a look at the question of product reliability. This is an important aspect of product quality, and one which touches on the issue of how well consumers are informed (a similar aspect is product safety). We shall therefore round off this chapter on single-dimensional quality with a brief discussion of the relevant issues.

We can think of the consumer as buying x units of a good, only q of which are functional. Thus the fraction of non-defective units (q/x) is the natural measure of quality in this case. Let the probability that, in a purchase of x units, q are 'good' be $f(q, x)$ with mean value $\omega(x)$. The expected fraction of satisfactory goods is then $\omega/x \equiv \gamma$. The utility that consumers get depends on the number of satisfactory units, defective units will have a cost that is the sum of the price paid (p) plus a sum to compensate for defectiveness (w). The effect of uncertain reliability then is to make the budget constraint stochastic

$$px + w(x - q) + y = m, \tag{5.90}$$

where m is income and y the numeraire good whose price we can take to be unity (normalisation). Letting $v\,(=p+w)$ be the cost of a defective unit, we can write the constraint as

$$pz + (p + w)(x - q) + y = pq + v(x - q) + y = m. \tag{5.91}$$

Where w is non-zero, the amount of income that is available for expenditure on the numeraire good is $(m - vx - wq)$. We may suppose that consumers will choose x so as to maximise expected utility

$$\int_0^x u(q, y) f(x, q)\, \mathrm{d}z = \int_0^x u(q, m - vx + wq) f(q, x)\, \mathrm{d}z. \tag{5.92}$$

With experience, consumers will learn that when they buy x units they will on average only get ω good units. This means that to them the expected cost of buying these x units is

$$c = px + w(x - \omega), \tag{5.93}$$

and the effective per unit price

$$p^* = c/q = (p/\gamma) + (1 - \gamma/\gamma)w = \sigma + \tau w, \tag{5.94}$$

Oi (1973) refers to this as the 'full-price'. A natural interpretation to place on σ is to think of it as a warranty price, and to treat τ as the actuarially fair premium per unit of insurance cover. The reason for the latter is that given the risks $(\gamma, 1 - \gamma)$ of making the payouts 0 and 1 respectively, a company that charged a premium of τ would just break even on average. That is its 'premium income' would be $\tau\gamma$ and its 'expected claims' $(1)(1-\gamma)$ and since these have to come to zero if the premium is actuarially fair we have

$$\tau = [(1-\gamma)/\gamma].$$

Suppose that there were a competitive market for such 'defective-claims' insurance, then the consumer could behave as if q could be acquired for the price p^* and this would make the budget constraint non-stochastic

$$p^*q + y = m. \tag{5.95}$$

If we now maximise $u(q, y)$ subject to this we get

$$u_q/u_y = p^*, \tag{5.96}$$

which with the budget constraint yields the demand function for q, $D(p^*)$ say. Using the fact that $q = \gamma x$ we have then the demand function for x

$$x = q/\gamma = D(p^*)/\gamma. \tag{5.97}$$

We can now see that an improvement in product quality will increase γ. This will reduce p^*, given p, and so increase the demand for q. However, there remains another one of these ambiguities that has dogged us in our discussion of quality for, as both q and γ have risen, we cannot say what will have happened to the overall quantity bought, x.

Let us close the chapter by considering an issue in regulating such markets and which conveniently leads in to the discussion of vertical differentiation in the next chapter. A legislator might wish to consider two possible liability assignment rules. One of these, referred to by lawyers as 'caveat emptor', assigns the liability to the buyer. The other extreme would be if the seller were to be fully liable – 'caveat vendor'.

We shall suppose two goods: x_1 with defective probability γ_1 and x_2 with defective probability γ_2. If we assume that $\gamma_2 < \gamma_1$, we can refer to good 2 as the high quality one.

The first point to note is that we must have $\sigma_1 > \sigma_2$ for otherwise no one would demand the low quality good. Good 1 will be preferred to good 2 if and only if

$$p_1^* < p_2^*,$$

i.e. $\sigma_1 + \tau_1 w < \sigma_2 + \tau_2 w,$

i.e. $w > (\sigma_1 - \sigma_2)/(\tau_2 - \tau_1). \tag{5.98}$

The numerator in (5.98) is the warranty price differential and the denominator the insurance differential. There will be some value of

w ($=w^*$) at which (5.98) is satisfied as an equality. Thus consumers are segmented into two sorts depending on their w relative to w^*. Those whose w is less than this critical value will buy the high quality good (2), those whose w is greater will buy the low quality good (1). Denote, now, the total quantity bought by those consumers who have a compensation value w by $g(w)$. With consumers segregated into these two markets, we can work out the aggregate compensation charge. This is

$$\lambda = \int_0^{w^*} (1-\gamma_2)wg(w)\,dw + \int_{w^*}^{\infty} (1-\gamma_1)wg(w)\,dw. \tag{5.99}$$

If legislation were now to be passed to ban the sale of good 1, consumers of this product would now have to switch to the high quality good but will buy less of it. Let this be $h(w)$. The new aggregate compensation charge is

$$\lambda' = \int_0^{w} (1-\gamma_1)wh(w)\,dw + \int_{w^*}^{\infty} (1-\gamma_1)wg(w)\,dw. \tag{5.100}$$

Since $(1-\gamma_1)<(1-\gamma_2)$ and $h<g$, it follows that $\lambda'<\lambda$. However, consumers are worse off for they would freely have traded the higher risk of defective units for the lower price p_2.

If we now consider the case of producer liability, then they will have to take out an insurance policy to cover this risk. If they are liable they will have to pay out both the purchase price and damages. The fair premium is τ. Thus the total supply price for good j will now be

$$z_j = p_j + \tau_j(p_j + w).$$

w is distributed across the population and, if producers cannot discriminate, then they have to take account of the mean w, $\bar{w}$. Therefore

$$z_j = p_j + \tau_j(p_j + w) = (1+\tau_j)p_j + \tau_j\bar{w}$$
$$= (p_j/\gamma_j) + \tau_j\bar{w}$$
$$= \sigma_j + \tau_j\bar{w}. \tag{5.101}$$

Since the consumers now bear no costs they will simply buy that good with the lowest supply price. In an equilibrium in which all goods are on sale then q_j has to be the same for all j. What we have then is a problem that involves questions of adverse selection and it is not clear whether we shall see high drive out low or vice versa. It is on this rather open question that we shall end the chapter.

6   Vertical product differentiation

6.1 Introduction

In chapters 2 to 4 we were concerned with the type of product differentiation that Lancaster (1979) has termed 'horizontal'. Its distinguishing property is that, if such products are offered at the same price, consumers, if asked to do so, would *rank them differently*. Thus, if a number of firms were offering distinct 'horizontally' differentiated products at the same price, each would obtain a strictly positive market share. It is in this sense that the equilibrium might be one of product *variety*.

However, an equally important aspect of product differentiation is *quality*, the idea that some goods are just of a higher specification than others and that it is this that is the source of their higher valuation. We started the analysis of this in chapter 5 but there, by assumption, a feature of the equilibria was that there was only a single quality on sale. What we want to do in this chapter is to remedy this 'single-quality' feature by turning to the analysis of what is termed 'vertical' product differentiation.

Products are said to be 'vertically' differentiated if, when offered at the same price, *all consumers choose to purchase the same one*: that of highest quality. Of course, in equilibrium, assuming that consumers differ in their willingness to pay for quality improvement, products will sell at different prices with the higher quality products being sold at a premium over the price of rival lower quality products.

The original contributions to the analysis of 'vertical' product differentiation proceeded by considering the 'pure' case where products are assumed to be differentiated solely in terms of a vertical attribute (e.g. miles per gallon) referred to as the 'level of quality'. This case was contrasted to the 'pure' horizontal differentiation case where products are assumed to be differentiated solely in terms of a horizontal attribute in the tradition of the Hotelling spatial competition paradigm. In practice products are differentiated with respect to both kinds of attributes and recently an attempt has been made to provide an analysis of the general case where products are assumed to be differentiated both horizontally and vertically. We. will return to this in section 5 of this chapter and, until then, we will deal with the pure vertical case. However, in order to help readers relate the discussion in this chapter with that contained in chapters 2 to 4, we shall start by reconsidering the simplified location model that we introduced in section 2 of chapter 2. This model involved a simple linear market and to assist in recall we have reproduced the basic diagram below.

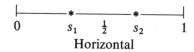

Horizontal

This model can be easily adapted to produce a 'prototype' model of vertical differentiation if, instead of placing the two firms at locations s_1 and s_2 inside the market, we locate them outside the market. This is what we show in the next diagram below.

Vertical

Recall that the market is of unit length and consumers, who have a completely inelastic demand for one unit of the good, are uniformly distributed over the interval. In the horizontal case, consumers will rank the two firms differently depending on where they are located, whereas in the vertical case they will agree that firm 1 is 'better' than firm 2.

In this prototype model of vertical differentiation, rising marginal costs of transport are essential if it is to be possible for both firms to co-exist in the market. If this were not so, the 'higher quality' firm, located at s_1, could always undercut its rival's delivered price and still earn positive profits. Given the mill prices, the market boundary is defined by the intersection of the two delivered-price schedules as shown in figure 6.1. It is clear from this that, in equilibrium, the price of the 'lower quality' good must be less than that of the 'higher quality' good, for otherwise it could not gain any sales. Consider now firm 1. For it there are two critical prices (given p_2). The first, $p_1^+ (=p_2 + c(s_2 - s_1) + d(s_2{}^2 - s_1{}^2))$, is that at which firm 1 loses all of the market to firm 2. The other, $p_1^- (=p_1^+ - 2d(s_2 - s_1))$, is that at which it holds the entire market. The profit function for firm 1 is shown in Figure 6.2. If $p_1^- > 0$, this is quasi-concave and, given p_2, firm 1's best response is $p_1^* = p_1^+/2$. A similar graph exists for firm 2. If we make the assumption that an internal equilibrium exists (i.e. both firms are present in the market), the

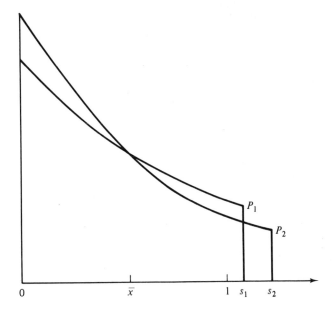

Figure 6.1

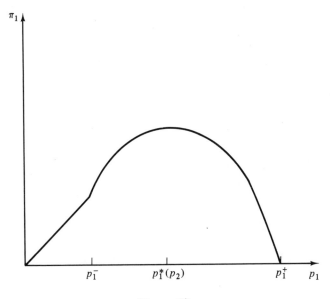

Figure 6.2

Bertrand reaction functions are given by

Firm 1: $p_2 = 2p_1 - c(s_2 - s_1) - d(s_2^2 - s_1^2)$,
Firm 2: $p_2 = (1/2)p_1 + (d - c/2)(s_2 - s_1) - (d/2)(s_2^2 - s_1^2)$,

and the equilibrium prices are

$$p_1^* = (s_2 - s_1)\left[\frac{d(s_1 + s_2 + 2) + c}{3}\right],$$

$$p_2^* = (s_2 - s_1)\left[\frac{d(4 - s_1 - s_2) - c}{3}\right].$$

Notice that $p_2^* = 0$ if $(c/d) \geqslant (4 - s_1 - s_2)$. This is the condition that the intersection of the two reaction functions shown in the figure 6.3 lies in the

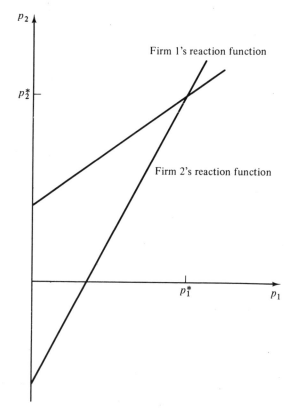

Figure 6.3

south-east quadrant. If one recalls the discussion of Nash price equilibria in chapter 2, one can see that there is much greater price stability in the vertical case.

This analysis has, of course, taken location (product attributes) to be fixed. A more general analysis of the differentiation model would ask us to consider varying location. The natural way to consider this is to treat the choice of price as the second stage in a two-stage process in which firms make their product choices knowing what the resulting price equilibrium will be. In other words, we look for a perfect equilibrium.

We saw that perfect equilibrium was problematic in the case of horizontal differentiation. This was because we needed to ensure that there existed a Nash equilibrium in the second-stage price game for any choice of locations. We discovered that this was not the case. On the other hand, a perfect equilibrium exists in the vertical case.[1]

The analysis above is, of course, special since it uses a specific model. However, even with a more general (diminishing returns) specification of the transport cost function, a price equilibrium will be supported. While this doesn't necessarily guarantee the existence of a perfect equilibrium, it gives much more hope for stability in this type of model.

The analysis of markets in which firms sell products that differ in terms of some vertical attribute has thrown light on important differences that may exist between the equilibrium characteristics of these as opposed to horizontally differentiated markets. What gives rise to these differences is not the mere presence of a vertical attribute. There is an important additional condition. This is that the unit variable costs associated with increased quality rise more slowly than consumers' willingness to pay for this. We shall make this statement a little more precise shortly. However, this sort of interrelationship between technology and tastes means that the main burden of quality improvement falls on fixed rather than variable costs. In other words what we are talking about is a class of goods where quality improvement comes about as a result of research and development or design rather than as a result of the use of higher cost materials or more expensive methods of quality assurance. Perhaps as an example we might think of computers where enhanced performance may well depend on a computer's architecture (a design feature) rather than on higher specification and hence more costly circuitry materials.

When this sort of interplay between technology and tastes happens the most fundamental difference is that the market cannot sustain more than some maximum number of products in equilibrium. In other words there is a limit to the number of products for which price can exceed unit variable cost and which have a positive share of the market. Furthermore, this maximum will be independent of the set of products on offer, of the size of fixed costs and of the number of potential buyers in the market. What determines it is in fact the range of the distribution of consumers' incomes.[2] This property of a limit to the equilibrium number of products has been labelled the *finiteness property* by Shaked and Sutton and those markets in which this is a feature of equilibrium are referred to as *natural oligopolies*.

In section 2 we shall look at why it is that finiteness may arise when goods are vertically differentiated but will not arise when the differentiation is horizontal. To help in this we make use of a stylised model that enables us to highlight the main assumptions that have been used in the analysis of vertical differentiation and we use it to look at the case of *natural monopoly* as an example. In section 3 we look more closely at the critical assumption one needs for finiteness. In section 4 we consider the important issue of quality selection and its relation to market size. Section 5 summarises the discussion and considers the implications of vertical differentiation for the theory of industrial structure. In this we draw a comparison with the recent literature on contestable markets.

6.2 The finiteness property and natural oligopolies

Perhaps the sensible place to start is by explaining why the finiteness property is not a characteristic of horizontally differentiated markets. Consider the type of Hotelling or 'circular' models that we dealt with in chapter 2. Additional products can be introduced into the market in these models in the following way. Suppose that all products have the same unit cost. If the new product sells at unit variable cost it will obtain a positive share of the market. This is because it will attract those consumers that are located nearest to it in terms of their ideal choice. Given fixed costs of entry and a finite market size, a point will be reached where additional products will not get sufficient sales to cover *total* costs. Hence, in a market economy, they will not in fact be introduced. But, and this is the important point, as the fixed cost of entry falls or the market gets larger, more and more products can be introduced. As a result the distance between any two products will be reduced. Thus for small enough entry costs or a large enough market size one can guarantee that an arbitrarily large number of products will be present even though each of them will have an arbitrarily small market share.[3]

We can now turn to the finiteness property in vertically differentiated markets and will start by discussing the set of assumptions that we shall be using in the rest of this chapter. We assume that n distinct products are available for sale by n single-product firms and we label these in increasing order of quality which we denote by q, i.e. $q_1 < q_2 < ... < q_n$. For the moment we take these as exogenously specified. Let the unit variable cost of quality k be denoted by $c(q_k)$. Since the quality levels available are given, the natural type of competition to consider is competition between the firms on price. Hence we will be looking for a Nash equilibrium in prices. Finiteness is in fact a property of a price equilibrium. Of course the analysis needs to be extended to deal with quality choice and entry and this is a step that we take in section 4. However, for the moment, we take these qualities as fixed.[4]

Consumers are assumed to buy either a single unit of one of the qualities on offer or else no quality good at all. They also differ in their willingness to pay for quality improvement. This could be the result of differences in tastes (i.e. sensitivity to quality) or in income (or both). To keep our discussion consistent with Shaked and Sutton we assume it is due to differences in their incomes and we shall specifically assume that these are different and can be described by the following uniform distribution

$$f(y) = \begin{bmatrix} s & \text{for } 0 < a \leqslant y \leqslant b, \\ 0 & \text{otherwise.} \end{bmatrix}$$

This is shown in figure 6.4. The lowest and highest incomes are a and b respectively. We can treat s as a measure of the size of the economy and think of $s(b-a)$ as total spending power.

Every consumer has identical preferences and these are given by the utility function

$$U(y, k) = q_k(y - p_k), \quad k = 1, \ldots, n \tag{6.1}$$

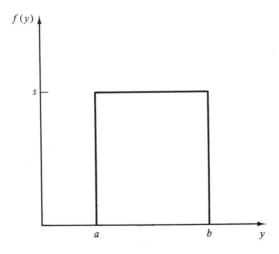

Figure 6.4

and

$$U(y, 0) = q_0 y. \tag{6.2}$$

Having decided to buy one of the quality goods on offer, $(y - p_k)$ is the income left over to spend on other goods. Indeed, one can think of (6.1) as saying that the 'effectiveness' or satisfaction attached to any given sum spent on other goods is the higher, the higher the quality of the vertically differentiated good one has purchased. Of course, we need to allow for the fact that someone may not buy the good at all. In that case the entire income y is available for spending on other goods and q_0 is the relevant 'satisfaction multiplier', so to speak. (6.2) gives the utility level in that event. It is assumed that $0 < q_0 < q_1$ and that $U(0, k) = 0$.[5]

If two products k and $k - 1$ sell for prices p_k and p_{k-1} respectively, then a consumer will be indifferent between them who has the income y_k, where this is given by the condition

$$U(y_k, k) = U(y_k, k - 1), \tag{6.3}$$

i.e. $\quad q_k(y_k - p_k) = q_{k-1}(y_k - p_{k-1}).$

Notice that the marginal utility of income at y_k is equal to q_k if good k is bought and q_{k-1} if good $k - 1$ is bought. In other words to the right of y_k the left-hand side of (6.3) exceeds the right-hand side and vice versa to the left of y_k. The upshot is that, given prices, y_k is the critical income level that defines the lower limit of the market that firm k enjoys.

A second point to notice is that we can re-arrange the last expression as

$$p_k = \frac{1}{r_k} y + \left[1 - \frac{1}{r_k}\right] p_{k-1}, \tag{6.4}$$

where $r_k = q_k / q_k - q_{k-1} > 1$. In other words, given p_{k-1}, p_k is the maximum price that firm k can charge and just attract the customer whose income is y. It also shows that in response to a unit cut in the price of its nearest lower quality rival, firm k needs to cut its price by less than a unit in order to retain its marginal customer. This is of course just a reflection of the fact that consumers place some value on quality itself.

This stylised model is illustrated in figure 6.5. Suppose for the moment that good k was available at a zero price. Then $U(k, y)$ is given by $q_k y$. This is just a straight line from the origin with slope q_k and is shown by the dashed line labelled $q_k y$. Of course, the good is actually available at a price p_k and the utility cost of giving up p_k to get the good is $q_k p_k$. Thus the utility schedule for good k is just the straight line with slope q_k and a vertical intercept of $-q_k p_k$. The two solid lines in the diagram show this and the utility schedule for good $k - 1$.

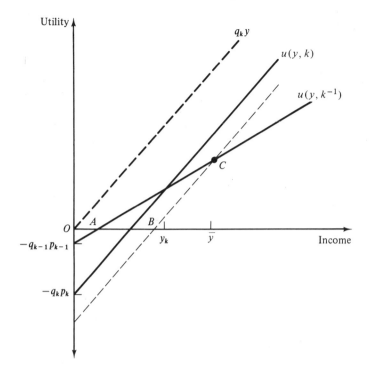

Figure 6.5

y_k is the income of the consumer who is indifferent between goods k and $k-1$. Given the prices, consumers with incomes less than y_k will be better off buying good $k-1$ and those with incomes above y_k will strictly prefer good k. It is also clear from elementary geometry that the points where the utility schedules cut the horizontal axis measure the prices of the two goods.

Although we have only illustrated this for two goods, it is clear that adding goods would add more lines and we should get a whole series of points like y_k: one for every pair of adjacent qualities. Thus, given prices, we can partition the distribution of consumers by income into a set of markets, in each of which a single quality is chosen. For example, product n will sell to all those whose incomes lie between b and y_n and hence the quantity sold will be $s(b-y_n)$. In a similar fashion, since good $n-1$ sells to all those whose incomes lie between y_n and y_{n-1}, the quantity sold will be $s(y_n-y_{n-1})$, and so on until we reach the lower income bound of a.

Consider the consumer whose income is $\bar{y}$. Given that good $k-1$ sells at p_{k-1}, we can find the maximum price that the consumer would pay for quality k by drawing a line with slope q_k that passes through the point C. It is clear that this consumer would not be indifferent between goods k and $k-1$. This maximum price can be read off from the horizontal axis and it is given by the distance OB. Since $k-1$ is selling at a price equal to OA, the maximum premium for quality that can be charged by the producer of good k to this consumer is AB. It is obvious that this is *increasing* in income.

We want to examine critical income levels like y_k but, before we do so, we shall make one more, important, assumption. This is that we shall assume that, if each of the n products were to be offered at their respective unit variable cost, *all* consumers would rank them in the same, strictly increasing, order and that this would be in terms of their quality levels. Since the utility of the lowest income person would be given by

$$U(a, q) = q[a - c(q)],$$

it follows that, for all q on offer, it must be that $\partial U/\partial q > 0$. This is equivalent to the following bound on the elasticity of unit variable costs with respect to quality (v)

$$v < \frac{a - c(q)}{c(q)}, \quad \forall q.$$

An implication of this assumption is that, if all the products were to be offered at prices equal to their respective unit variable costs, then all consumers who would choose to buy would choose to buy the top quality product. Thus the market shares of all the 'inferior' products would be zero.

Let us suppose then that, at a price equal to unit variable cost, the highest quality product would capture the entire market. We may indicate a situation like this by the two dashed lines in figure 6.6, where clearly $U(a, q_n) > U(a, q_{n-1})$. Note that on the vertical axis we are measuring the gain in utility over what could be obtained from the 'backstop' level of quality q_0. An increase in the price of good n above its unit cost is introduced by a parallel shift downwards in the utility schedule by the amount of the price-cost margin. Clearly in this case even for the consumer with the least willingness to pay for quality improvements, an increase in price will not immediately cause a switch to good $(n-1)$. Indeed, in the present example, such a switch will not occur until the price reaches $\bar{p}_n$ when the utility schedule for good n becomes the solid line. Such a move is profit increasing for firm n and indeed the best response that firm $n-1$ could make to this is to continue to set price equal to unit variable cost.

Let us imagine now that we have a very narrow range of incomes so that b is quite close to a. Would it pay the top quality firm to increase its price above $\bar{p}_n$? If it does so, firm $n-1$'s best response in a Nash equilibrium in prices will not be to increase its price above its unit cost. The resulting

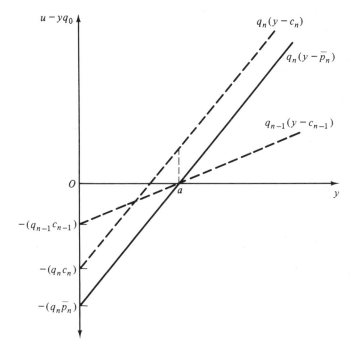

Figure 6.6

position would look something like figure 6.7. If firm n increases its price to $\hat{p}_n$ then firm $n-1$ could increase its price to $\hat{p}_{n-1}$. As a result firm n no longer supplies the entire market and the change in its profits is simply the area $(C-A)$. In the case that is illustrated here and, in general, for b relatively close to a, this will not be profitable. As a result the Nash equilibrium will in fact be

$$p_n = \bar{p}_n, \quad p_{n-1} = c_{n-1}.$$

However it should be clear from figure 6.7 that, were b to be sufficiently large, an increase in p_n above $\bar{p}_n$ would indeed be profit increasing. In such a case y_n, the critical income that divides the market into those consumers who buy good n and those who buy $n-1$ will lie between a and b.

Gabszewicz (1985, pp. 159–60) has noted that the intuition behind this result is that if incomes (or tastes) across the population are very similar then there is little to be lost in the way of consumer surplus if only the top quality is provided. At least, as long as its price is such that even the poorest consumer would buy it. Given this price, if the distribution of incomes is wider, the surplus that is enjoyed by the rich is all the greater and getting

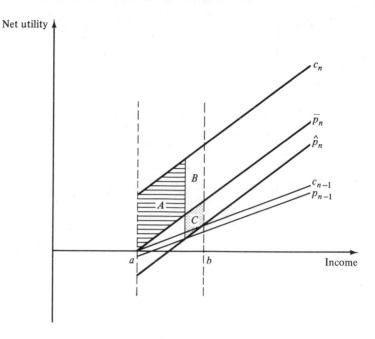

Figure 6.7

hold of this is the incentive that makes it more attractive to segment the market. Hence, in a Nash equilibrium, we have room for several firms to co-exist.

A question that arises fairly naturally at this point is why don't other firms also produce the quality n? The answer is that they would do so if there were no sunk entry costs. In such a case the Bertrand equilibrium would give each firm a zero profit. Thus the finiteness property is consistent with an arbitrarily large number of firms – all that it does is to place an upper bound to the number of *products*. However, if there is an entry cost that has to be sunk (no matter how small), no two firms will enter and choose to produce identical qualities since they know that in the resulting price equilibrium the price of this quality would only equal its unit variable cost. In order to guarantee that finiteness involves an upper bound to the number of firms that can co-exist in equilibrium we need to assume then that entry does involve a sinking of fixed costs.

As an example, let us consider the case of a *natural monopoly*. We shall proceed by obtaining the demand schedule for firm n when other products are offered at their respective unit variable cost and shall assume, for simplicity, that this is the *same for all products*. Let it be denoted by c. The price of n that would make a consumer of income y indifferent between consuming a unit of n and a unit of $n-1$ offered at c is given, from (6.4), as

$$p_n = \left[\frac{1}{r_n}\right] y + \left[1 - \frac{1}{r_n}\right] c. \tag{6.4'}$$

Let $\hat{p}_n$ be the value of p_n, given by (6.4') when $y=b$. Since this is the maximum price that the richest consumer is prepared to pay, it determines the vertical intercept of the demand schedule. This is shown in figure 6.8. Since poorer consumers are not prepared to pay as much, demand for n increases as price falls until that price is reached at which the poorest consumer (with an income of a) is just indifferent between good n and good $n-1$, available at a price of c. This price, denoted by $\bar{p}_n$, is also given by (6.4'). At this price firm n would gain the entire market and enjoy sales of $s(b-a)$. This demand schedule is the lowest of the three lines in figure 6.8.

There are three points to note about this demand schedule. First, if the lower quality product $n-1$ were offered at a price greater than c the demand schedule for product n would simply shift upwards as in the top line in the figure. Secondly, an increase in the size of the economy merely pivots the demand curve out about the point $\hat{p}_n$ as shown in the middle line. Finally, these demand schedules are linear. As we noted earlier, the sales of good n are $x_n = s(b-y_n)$.

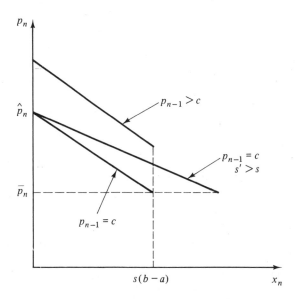

Figure 6.8

Using (6.4′)

$$y_n = r_n p_n + (1 - r_n)p_{n-1}$$

and so

$$x_n = s[b - r_n p_n + (r_n - 1)p_{n-1}],$$

which is linear in p_n as the r-terms are given constants.

Let p_n^* be the profit-maximising price. For a firm that faces a linear demand schedule and a constant unit cost this is equal to the unit cost plus half the difference between the vertical intercept and unit cost. Hence we have

$$p_n^* = c + \tfrac{1}{2}(\hat{p}_n - c).$$

However, using (6.4) when y equals b we can write this as

$$p_n^* = c + \frac{1}{2}\left[\frac{1}{r_n}(b - c)\right],$$ (6.5)

unless this is less than $\bar{p}_n$ which is given by

$$\bar{p}_n = \left[\frac{1}{r_n}\right]a + \left[1 - \frac{1}{r_n}\right]c.$$ (6.6)

In this case $\bar{p}_n$ is the profit-maximising price. Of course we know from our earlier discussion that this is just the case we had when the income distribution is sufficiently narrow in range – in fact, if $a > b + c/2$. In other words, when this last condition holds we have a corner solution in which product n is offered at $\bar{p}_n$ and all other products obtain a zero market share. $\bar{p}_n$ is the price at which those with the lowest income are indifferent between n and $n-1$ when the latter is offered at a price of c. In this case then there is only a single product and firm and we have a *natural monopoly*. However, if the range of incomes should be broader, so that $a < b + c/2$, more than one product will obtain a positive market share at a Nash equilibrium in prices. These prices will exceed unit variable cost. In particular for values of a and b such that

$$\frac{b+c}{4} < a < \frac{b+c}{2},$$

only *two* products will have a positive market share. This is a case that we shall look at in more detail in section 4.

What we have thus established is the following. If the income distribution is sufficiently small, the Bertrand-Nash equilibrium will be one in which each consumer buys one unit of the top quality product with the other products failing to win any market share at all.[6] In this case we can say that the top quality product 'covers' the market. Note that the necessary condition for such an equilibrium: $a > b + c/2$ depends in part on technology through the unit cost c.[7]

Consider the following three-stage game. Firms enter by sinking some positive set-up costs of ε. If they have entered, they must then decide on a quality to produce. Suppose this is to be given by incurring a fixed cost $f(q)$.[8] In the final stage of the game they then compete on price. If the range of the income distribution is narrow enough so that $a > (b + c)/2$, then only one firm can cover the market and earn positive profits. In other words the perfect equilibrium[9] in this game is one in which only one firm enters. However, it is important to note that, since p_n^* is independent of s or f, the result that only one firm enters is independent of the size of the market or the level of fixed costs. Changes in the value of these parameters will affect the type of qualities on offer.

6.3 The finiteness property again

Let us now return and investigate in more detail the condition that we used in the analysis above. This was that all consumers rank products in exactly the same order when they are priced at their respective unit variable costs. This will certainly be true if unit variable costs are non-increasing in quality since we have assumed that all consumers are prepared to pay some premium for quality improvements. However, whether or not it is true otherwise is a question that needs to be considered. So we shall assume that unit variable cost increases with quality.

If all products are offered for sale at their unit variable cost the utility of a consumer of income y when he buys a unit of quality q will be from (6.1)

$$U = qy - qc(q) \tag{6.7}$$

and this may be rewritten as

$$qc(q) = qy - U. \tag{6.7'}$$

In figure 6.9, we consider first the curve $qc(q)$. To any point on that there corresponds a quality level. Take for example the level q'. Suppose that a consumer with income y buys a unit of q'. Consider now the line which is drawn through the point $[q'c(q'), q']$ with slope y. This cuts the vertical axis at A. By geometry AC is equal to yq'. Since BC equals $q'c(q')$, we thus can see that AB must equal $-U[y, c(q')]$. In other words the distance that A lies below the horizontal axis indicates the utility level that a person with income y would get from buying a unit of good q' at its variable cost price.

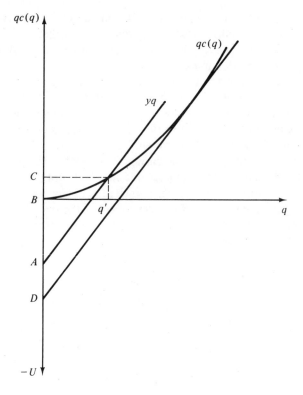

Figure 6.9

Clearly then such a person seeking to maximise utility would choose $q^*(y)$ and obtain a utility level of D. The optimal point is thus defined by the tangency condition

$$y = q^*c'(q^*) + c(q^*),\tag{6.8}$$

where the prime here denotes a derivative.

This reasoning was of course all for some specific income level. It is natural therefore to ask what qualities, if available at unit cost, would be chosen by the richest and poorest members of society. They are simply the points on the horizontal axis that correspond to the points on $qc(q)$ where the slope is b and a respectively. These are shown in figure 6.10. Assume for the moment that only qualities in the range q_0 to q' are available. Then all consumers with incomes between a and b will maximise utility by consuming q', since this gives the greatest negative intercept. Of course all those with incomes strictly greater than a would prefer to consume

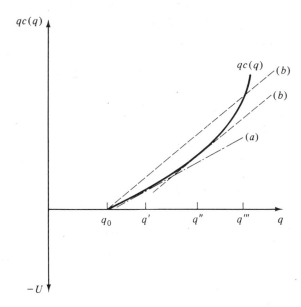

Figure 6.10

qualities above q' but these are just not available. Thus we have a situation in which all consumers, irrespective of their income, prefer q' (the highest quality available) to all other qualities and they rank qualities between q_0 and q' in the same (strictly increasing) order.

Now suppose that only qualities in the range q'' to q''' are available. Again we find that all consumers will rank qualities in the same strict, but now decreasing, order. Thus, irrespective of the level of income, the higher the quality level is above q'' the lower will be the utility obtained. In this case all consumers maximise utility by choosing q''. Qualities above q''' are not viable, given the existing income distribution, since even the richest consumers would prefer to spend their income on alternative goods to the quality one.

The final case to consider is where only qualities in the range q' to q'' are available. In this case it is clear that consumers with income b would maximise utility by consuming q'' and consumers with income a by consuming q'. Indeed, in general, the preferred quality that corresponds to each income level will be different. Thus, when qualities in the range q' to q'' are offered at unit variable cost, consumers differ as to their cost preferred choice and this is, of course, exactly what we had in the case of horizontal differentiation. In the light of our earlier comments, it therefore follows that in this case the finiteness property does not hold and hence there is no bound to the number of firms that can co-exist in an equilibrium in which each firm has a positive market share and its price exceeds its unit variable cost.

There is thus a real difference between the qualities that lie in the range (q', q'') and those in the ranges (q_0, q') and (q'', q'''). It is that in the former every consumer is able to find a distinct quality that maximises his utility whereas in the latter, everyone maximises their utility by choosing the *same* quality – respectively the highest and lowest on offer. A more general statement by Shaked and Sutton (1983) is that a necessary and sufficient condition for the finiteness property to hold in a quality interval $(q, \bar{q})$ is that the range of incomes is such that either there is no consumer for whom condition (6.8) is satisfied for some q in that interval or, if there is such a consumer, he strictly prefers not to purchase any of the quality goods so spending his income on other goods.[10] Thus finiteness requires much more than just vertical differentiation, it requires that all consumers have this common ranking.

The analysis of price competition between firms offering products of different quality that we have carried out above involved working with a simplified version of a more general model and it can be extended in a number of ways. In particular, it is important to note that the assumptions of linear utility functions, uniform income distribution, identical preferences, smooth cost functions and single-product firms may be relaxed without changing the qualitative nature of the results.[11]

6.4 Quality selection

If the number of qualities offered will not increase beyond a certain maximum, whatever the size of the market, what then is the impact of an increase in market size when goods are vertically differentiated? The answer is that market size influences the *types* of products (quality levels) that will be offered in equilibrium. This fact will turn out to be of some importance when we come to examine the impact of vertical differentiation on international trade in chapter 9. However, so that we are in a position to deal with quality selection in that context, it is useful to make a start by analysing quality selection for a given market size in this chapter. It is for this reason we now turn our attention to this issue.

The approach that we take to modelling product selection is to think of it as the first stage in a two-stage competitive game. Given the choice of a quality level, the second stage of the game involves choosing price and the equilibrium of this second stage will be a Bertrand-Nash one. This seems a fairly natural way to view the sequencing of decisions since product design is a lot more difficult to change than product price.

What we shall be solving for is *perfect equilibrium* in this two-stage game. The way that we do this is to work backwards. First we express the equilibrium price as a function of quality: $p^*(q)$. This enables us to write down the profit function for any firm as a function of quality and gives us the objective function for the first stage of the game. At this point, then, we look for a Nash equilibrium in quality levels and as a result establish a pair (p^*, q^*) which is a perfect equilibrium for the two-stage game.

We shall continue to work with the linear utility model that we used above and, in addition, assume for the sake of simplicity that there is a constant fixed cost of quality and that variable costs are zero. Hence the revenue function now becomes the firm's profit function. Furthermore we shall assume that the range of the income distribution is such that

$$\frac{b}{4} < a < \frac{b}{2}.$$

When n qualities are on offer the market share of firm k is $s(y_{k+1} - y_k)$, where s is a measure of the size of the economy. We may therefore write the revenue function for firm k as

$$sR_k = sp_k(y_{k+1} - y_k), \quad 1 < k < n. \tag{6.9}$$

Thus R is the revenue function when the economy is of size $s = 1$ and revenue is therefore proportional to the size of the economy. The revenue functions of firms 1 and n are, respectively

$$sR_1 = \begin{bmatrix} sp_1(y_2 - a), y_1 \leqslant a \\ sp_1(y_2 - y_1), y_1 > a \end{bmatrix} \tag{6.10}$$

and

$$sR_n = sp_n(b - y_n).$$

Price competition

Recall from (6.4) that the critical income that segments the market between goods k and $k - 1$ is given by

$$y_k = r_k p_k - (r_k - 1)p_{k-1}, \quad k = 1, \dots, n. \tag{6.11}$$

The profit-maximising first-order condition for the k'th good is given by $\partial R_k / \partial p_k = 0$. In the case of goods n and $n - 1$ respectively these are

$$b - y_n - r_n p_n = 0, \tag{6.12}$$

$$y_n - y_{n-1} - p_{n-1}[(r_n - 1) + r_{n-1}] = 0, \tag{6.13}$$

unless $y_{n-1} < a$, when (6.13) becomes

$$y_n - y_{n-1} - p_{n-1}(r_n - 1) = 0. \tag{6.14}$$

If we make use of the definitions of y_n and y_{n-1} we can write (6.12) and (6.13) as

$$b - 2y_n - (r_n - 1)p_{n-1} = 0, \tag{6.12'}$$

$$y_n - 2y_{n-1} - (r_n - 1)p_{n-1} - (r_{n-1} - 1)p_{n-2} = 0. \tag{6.13'}$$

Since $p_k \geqslant 0$ and $r_k > 1$, it follows that we have

$$y_{n-1} < \frac{y_n}{2} \leqslant \frac{b}{4} < a.$$

In other words, at most the two top firms can have positive market shares at a Nash equilibrium in prices. Hence we may restrict our analysis in this case to the two *natural duopolists* whom we can label 1 ('low quality') and 2 ('high quality').

In order to characterise the Nash equilibrium we need to work out the best-response functions of the two duopolists. We shall do this in income rather than price space. Thus the functions will show, for some given critical income level y_2, the best-response (profit-maximising) critical income level for firm 1 and vice versa for firm 2. Because of the intimate relationship between prices and these incomes through equation (6.11), this is equivalent to analysing prices.

Given that there is a fallback good available at zero price with quality level q_0, we know from equations (6.1) and (6.2) that

$$p_1 = \frac{y_1}{r_1}. \tag{6.15}$$

We can use this to eliminate p_1 in equations (6.12') and (6.13) and (6.14) and obtain a variant of the profit-maximising first-order conditions that sets out these best-response income levels:

for firm 2

$$y_2 = \tfrac{1}{2}[b - (v - 1)y_1]; \tag{6.16}$$

for firm 1

$$y_2 = a + (v - 1)y_1, \quad y_1 \leqslant a, \tag{6.17}$$

$$y_2 = (v + 1)y_1, \quad y_1 > a, \tag{6.18}$$

where $v = (r_1 + r_2 - 1)/r_1$.

If we graph out (6.16)–(6.18), it becomes clear that there are three possible regions in which there could be a Nash equilibrium and these are shown in figure 6.11. Which one of these is the relevant one depends on the value taken by v. In figure 6.11 the solid (discontinuous) line is the best-response locus for firm 1 and the two dashed lines indicate two possible best-response loci for firm 2. These are drawn for different values of b.

Suppose that the equilibrium is at $y_2 = (v+1)a$, $y_1 = a$, then, using (6.16) and (6.17), we have $v = (b-a)/3a$. If, on the other hand, the equilibrium is at $y_2 = va$, $y_1 = a$, we have $v = (b+a)/3a$. Thus we have three possible solutions depending on the value that v takes. If $v < (b-a)/3a$, then we are in region 3 in which both quality goods have positive market shares but there are some consumers who choose not to buy either good. However, if $v \geqslant (b-a)/3a$, then every consumer buys one or other of the quality goods since $y_1 \leqslant a$ and we are in regions 1 or 2. However, because of the restriction that $b < 4a$, it follows that if we were in region 3 we would have

$$v < \frac{b-a}{3a} < 1,$$

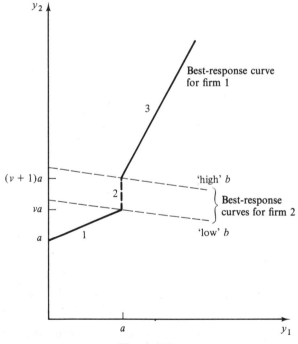

Figure 6.11

which, as a matter of definition, cannot be true. Thus the Nash equilibrium lies either in region 1 or in region 2.

In region 1, $v \geqslant (b+a)/3a$, and the critical income values are, from (6.16) and (6.17)

$$y_2 = \frac{b+a}{3}, \quad y_1 < a,$$

and the Nash equilibrium values of prices are

$$p_1 = \frac{b-2a}{3(v-1)r_1}; \quad p_2 = \frac{2b-a}{3r_2}. \tag{6.19}$$

From this we can write down the revenue functions as functions of the quality levels as

$$R_1(q_1; q_2) = \left[\frac{b-2a}{3}\right]^2 \left[\frac{1}{r_2-1}\right], \tag{6.20}$$

$$R_2(q_2; q_1) = \left[\frac{2b-a}{3}\right]^2 \left[\frac{1}{r_2}\right]. \tag{6.21}$$

On the other hand in region 2, $v \leqslant (b+a)/3a$, and the critical income values are

$$y_2 = \frac{b-a(v-1)}{2}; \quad y_1 = a.$$

The Nash equilibrium prices are

$$p_1 = \frac{a}{r_1}, \quad p_2 = \frac{b+a(v-1)}{2r_2}, \tag{6.22}$$

and the revenue functions are

$$R_1(q_1; q_2) = \frac{a[b-a(v+1)]}{2r_1}, \tag{6.23}$$

$$R_2(q_2; q_1) = \frac{[b+a(v-1)]^2}{4r_2}. \tag{6.24}$$

Quality competition

These revenue functions represent the firms' payoff functions in the first stage of the game at which they choose their optimal quality levels. This they do by maximising

$$\Pi_i(\tau_1, \tau_j) = sR_i(q_i; q_j) - F(q_i), \quad i \neq j.$$

This requires that

$$\frac{\partial R_i}{\partial q_i} = \frac{F'(q_i)}{s} = 0. \tag{6.25}$$

In order to analyse this we shall assume that $\bar{q}$ is the maximum value that q can attain given the existing technology. The first point to note is that $R_2(\cdot; \cdot) > R_1(\cdot; \cdot)$ for $q_2 > q_1$. In other words the firm producing the high quality good will earn greater revenue. This is clear since *just one* of its strategies is to charge the same price as its lower quality rival and certainly in this case its revenue will be greater. The second point is that differentiation of the revenue functions with respect to $q_2 > q_1$ shows that the revenue of both firms increases as q_2 increases.

Given these two points we are now able to show that the Nash equilibrium in the quality choice stage of the game involves the two firms choosing distinct qualities $(\bar{q}, \tilde{q})$, where $\tilde{q}$ is the optimal reply from below to $\bar{q}$. In other words it is the value of q that maximises the revenue of firm 1 when its rival chooses $\bar{q}$. The argument goes as follows. Let firm 1 choose v and firm 2 $\bar{q}$. By definition, $\tilde{q}$ is the optimal choice for firm 1 given that its rival chooses $\bar{q}$. Furthermore, since revenue for firm 1 increases with q as q gets larger than $\tilde{q}$, $\bar{q}$ is the optimal reply from above to the choice by firm 2 of $\tilde{q}$. All we need to do now is to show that firm 2 will prefer $\bar{q}$ to some q_2 that is less than or equal to $\tilde{q}$ in response to its rival's choice of $\tilde{q}$. But we know that

$$R(\bar{q}; \tilde{q}) \geqslant R(\tilde{q}; \bar{q}) \geqslant R(q_2; \bar{q}) \geqslant R(q_2; \tilde{q}).$$

However this just says that indeed $\bar{q}$ is firm 2's optimal quality choice. Thus $(\bar{q}, \tilde{q})$ is the Nash equilibrium quality pair and we find that, in common with the spatial differentiation model of chapter 2, Hotelling's principle of minimum product differentiation does not hold when vertical differentiation is present.[12]

This analysis can be illustrated using figure 6.12. Suppose that q_2 is set equal to $\bar{q}$ and that firm 1 considers choosing a value close to this. The result will be intense price competition between the two products and this will ensure that we are in region 1 of figure 6.12. As can be seen from (6.20) the profits for firm 1 will *increase* if it moves its quality level away from $\bar{q}$. This gives us the negatively sloped part of R_1. On the other hand, if firm 1 were to set its quality level close to q_0, again it would find itself facing intense price competition from the fall back good and this would ensure

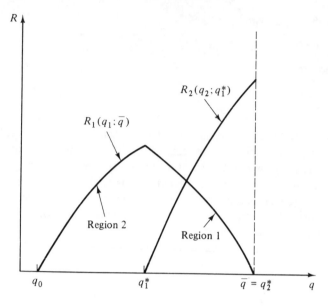

Figure 6.12

that its profits would be low and also that we should be in region 2 of figure 6.12. Provided that the gap between q_0 and $\bar{q}$ is not too great,[13] (6.23) is positively sloped. When $\tilde{q} = (b+a)/3a$, (6.20) and (6.23) are equal. Thus, from figure 6.12, we can see that q_1^* is defined by

$$(b+a)/3a = [(\bar{q} - q_0)/(\bar{q} - q_1)] \quad (= \tilde{q}).$$

This is the best response to $\bar{q}$. Furthermore, because (6.21) is increasing in the distance between the two goods, $\bar{q}$ is the best response to $\tilde{q}$.

   If we were to increase market size then this would have the effect of scaling the R functions upwards in a way that would lead to a new equilibrium quality pair $(\hat{q}_1, \hat{q}_2)$ such that $\hat{q}_1 > q_1^*$ and q_2^*. We shall in fact show this in chapter 9.

6.5 Conclusion: product differentiation and market structure

In this chapter we have concentrated on the pure vertical differentiation case. Of course in reality products are differentiated with respect to vertical and horizontal attributes and so the question of whether or not finiteness is simply a theoretical curiosum naturally arises. If one were able to show that some (possibly weaker) version of this property held in the case where vertical and horizontal attributes were combined, this would be of some importance because of the implications of the property for both the theory of industrial structure and international trade.

It should be fairly clear that the property, in the form we have used it here, does not carry over when both horizontal and vertical attributes are present. This is because if we allow for the presence of horizontal attributes then firms may set the same vertical (quality) attribute and allow only the horizontal attribute of their products to differ from that of their rivals. But this case is almost identical to the pure horizontal differentiation case where we know that finiteness will not arise. Nevertheless, as we will show in chapter 7, recent research by Shaked and Sutton (1987) indicates that a weak version of finiteness may hold when vertical and horizontal attributes are combined. Again this will be so when unit variable costs rise slowly with quality relative to consumers' willingness to pay for quality improvements.

The weak version of finiteness that Shaked and Sutton prove for the case where both attributes are present is best understood when considered in the context of the 'limit' theorems that have been used to describe horizontal markets. As we noted earlier, with pure horizontal differentiation, in the limit as the market gets large enough (or entry costs sufficiently small), an arbitrarily large number of firms, each with a very small market share, could co-exist in equilibrium. Shaked and Sutton's result is that such behaviour is not possible when vertical attributes are present and when the burden of quality improvements falls mainly on fixed costs. In such a case the market will remain concentrated irrespective of either market size or entry costs.

In conclusion let us summarise the main ideas that have come out of the vertical differentiation literature by discussing their implications for the theory of industrial structure. Clearly, the most significant aspect of this literature is the demonstration that there is a straightforward way to distinguish between those cases where product differentiation has an influence on industrial structure (the degree of industrial concentration) from those where it does not. When finiteness is present the market will remain concentrated and there can be no convergence to an atomistic competitive type of structure. The theory indeed has some predictions to make about industrial structure. Where it does not hold, product differentiation per se offers no prediction about industrial structure as in the case of pure horizontal differentiation. Our discussion therefore goes very much against the view that product differentiation is irrelevant to industrial structure.

Furthermore, it is worth drawing a distinction between the type of equilibria in vertically differentiated markets that we have described in this chapter and alternative equilibria that have been used to characterise both differentiated product markets and those with increasing returns technologies. The first thing to note is that the concentration that occurs here is not due to conditions of technology and demand such as the presence of high fixed costs relative to market size (as in the 'structure-conduct-performance' (s-c-p) paradigm) or in the more recently developed theory of contestable markets.[14] Nor is it the result of artificial entry barriers strategically erected by the incumbent firms' irreversible pre-commitments as in the more modern entry deterrence (e-d) theory that stresses conduct in seeking to explain market dominance. On the contrary, in the present case, the level of fixed costs is *endogenously* determined as part and parcel of the types of products (qualities) that firms choose to produce in equilibrium. Moreover, rather than fixed costs serving as an explanation of high concentration, here they are the *result* of large market size.[15]

A final point that is worth stressing is that in the model we have used here firms will be earning supernormal profits in equilibrium even though it is based on the assumptions of non-cooperative Bertrand behaviour and free entry. Again this is in contrast to both the s-c-p paradigm and e-d theory. These explain performance (high profits) either by the presence of some 'natural' entry barriers such as the level of fixed costs that serve to determine structure or by the entry-deterring conduct of existing firms. In the present case, structure (the number of firms) and performance are endogenously determined, a feature that is also true of contestable market theory. However the latter's assumptions of Bertrand behaviour, an absence of sunk costs and that capacity can be set up as least as quickly as firms can respond by changing prices, leads to a prediction that profits will be zero in equilibrium. In contrast to this, even with arbitrarily small sunk costs, we can still obtain an equilibrium with positive profits when goods are vertically differentiated. This fact serves to illustrate the lack of robustness that underlies contestable market theory.

7 Product differentiation and market imperfection: limit theorems

7.1 Introduction

Up to this point we have taken for granted the persistence of imperfectly competitive market equilibria. The question that we now need to pay some attention to is just how fundamental such market equilibria are. Another way of posing the question is to ask whether, in the absence of contrived barriers to entry, one might expect, in an appropriate limiting sense, such equilibria to converge to the perfectly competitive equilibrium. If the latter were to be the case we could not then consider equilibria such as Chamberlin's large-group equilibrium as fundamental. This area of limiting results is one which has been actively researched by theorists in recent years and it is the work that we want to consider now.

There have been two broad approaches to the analysis of this topic. One of these, the 'credible threats' approach, has tackled the question by trying to make barriers to entry endogenous. They then become choice variables for incumbents in a multi-stage entry game and one then looks for a perfect equilibrium in this game in which potential entrants rationally choose not to enter. This is a question to which we turn in the next chapter and it is one that pre-supposes that entry is not ultra-free. However if it is difficult to deter entry then one would expect to find market equilibria in which the number of firms in the industry reached the maximum that was consistent with economic feasibility given the relationship between technology and market size. By economic feasibility we mean that price just covers the average costs of production and the maximum number of firms that a given market can sustain consistent with this will depend on just how important economies of scale due either to technology or fixed costs are. It is consideration of this issue that has led to the second of the approaches to the question. It is this that we shall consider in the present chapter. The literature we shall examine has sought to formulate a model with differentiated goods and then look at what happens to imperfectly

135

competitive market equilibria in the limit as the fixed costs of set-up go to zero or, alternately, as the typical firm becomes small in relation to the overall market. Are such limiting equilibria characterised by zero profits and price equal to marginal cost? If they are then we may claim that in the limit the industry tends to perfect competition. In this way sufficiently large market size could replace the ultra-free entry of contestability theory as a condition necessary for a socially optimal outcome. There is a very practical reason for being interested in this and it is the following. The performance of an industry is often gauged by looking at it in relation to its domestic market. However many firms in open economies are competing in world markets which one might wish to think of as being 'very large' relative to the technologies being used.

The modern literature that deals with this issue studies market equilibria in the limit as market size goes to infinity or fixed set-up costs go to zero and for this reason the results that have been obtained can conveniently be labelled as 'limit theorems' or 'asymptotic results'. The first discussion of this goes back to the publication of Chamberlin's book in 1933 and the contributions of Robinson (1934) and Kaldor (1935). Chamberlin argued that there was a distinct monopolistically competitive equilibrium: his 'large-group' equilibrium. This is illustrated in figure 7.1.

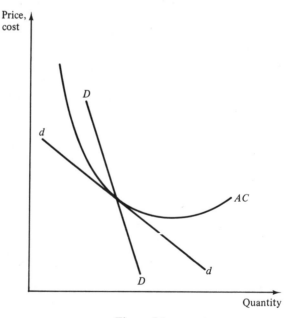

Figure 7.1

DD is the demand curve for the product that faces the representative firm if all of its rivals charge the same price as it and dd is the conjectured demand curve facing the firm if it alone changes its price. AC is the average total cost curve. The large-group equilibrium is where the DD, dd and AC curves intersect. The points to note about this are that price equals average cost so that the representative firm is earning only normal profits, that the own price elasticity of demand (on the dd curve) perceived by the firm is not infinite so that the firm is not a price-taker and that as a result price exceeds marginal cost and the average cost of production exceeds its minimum level. In Chamberlin's discussion, this equilibrium is reached from an original state, where the firm is earning above-normal profits, by the entry of new firms, each with its particular brand of the differentiated product. This result led Chamberlin to argue that in a world with many small firms one would only get perfect competition as the limit if the product were *homogeneous*. Kaldor and Robinson on the other hand argued that the limit was in fact perfect competition irrespective of whether the product was homogeneous or differentiated. Hence the discussion centres on whether the dd curve becomes perfectly elastic if the product is not homogeneous.

There are now a number of analyses of the limiting behaviour in models of Chamberlinian monopolistic competition: Dixit and Stiglitz (1979), Hart (1979, 1985a,b), Perloff and Salop (1985), Roberts (1980), Spence (1976b) and Wolinsky (1986). These models have the limiting property that, while each firm has a negligible impact on its rivals, it still possesses significant market power so that we retain monopolistic competition. However, as we alluded to in chapter 3, in some cases this is the result of special features that are assumed to characterise the underlying consumer's utility function. Hart has noted this shortcoming.

Hart's analysis of the Chamberlinian problem has also made it clear that the assumption that the industry is in the limit comprised of a very large number of very small firms is something of a red herring. The important assumption for perfect competition is in Hart's words 'not that each firm produces a small amount in absolute terms but that the output of every firm (or what a firm may *wish* to produce) be small relative to the economy as a whole'.[1] In the analysis below we shall see that as a firm's relative size declines it will usually be the case that, irrespective of whether the product market is horizontally differentiated or not, it will find itself facing an ever-increasing elasticity of demand. As the market size tends to infinity (or as relative firm size approaches zero), the own-price elasticity of demand will tend to infinity so that in the limit we have price equal to marginal cost. The first rigorous demonstration of this was by Hart (1979) in which he analysed a general equilibrium model with a horizontally differentiated sector. However, in his more recent work (1985a,b) he has shown that there are certain conditions under which the limiting equilibrium of a horizontally differentiated industry is monopolistically rather than perfectly competitive.[2] In other words there is something fundamental in the Chamberlinian large-group equilibrium. It is this result that we shall examine in the next section.

It will be recalled that in chapter 6 we showed that, in markets where goods are vertically differentiated, 'natural oligopolies' can arise. That is to say, the number of firms and the prices that they charge may be independent of both market size and fixed costs. This is another example of a fundamental imperfectly competitive equilibrium. The presence of any aspect that vertically differentiates a good appears to be important. We shall show in section 3 below that when vertical attributes are added to horizontal ones the limit properties of the market equilibrium can be very different from those where the goods possess only horizontal attributes. This demonstration makes use of the work of Shaked and Sutton (1987).

7.2 Horizontal product differentiation: limiting market equilibria

7.2.1 Imperfect competition in large economies: general equilibrium

Consider a firm selling a product to a market that is composed of a large number (r) of identical consumers. If the firm should increase its output by 1 per cent it will have to lower its price in order to be able to sell this extra output. Given that the consumers are identical, each will consume $(1/r)$ units of this extra output. For large r this will be very small indeed and the additional consumption will have hardly any effect at all on the marginal rate of substitution between this good and other goods. However the implication of this is that very little indeed will be needed by way of a reduction in price to ensure the sale of the extra output. In other words the elasticity of demand for the good will be close to infinity. The upshot of this informal argument then is to conclude that the approximate equality between price and marginal revenue (and so marginal cost) in a large economy has nothing to do with output being small but is because the slope of the demand curve is very small. That is to say firms will face a high elasticity of demand whenever they are small relative to the size of the economy.

It is this point which has proved to be of importance in looking at the limiting behaviour of monopolistically competitive market equilibria. While we want to consider this question in some detail using the model set out by Perloff and Salop (1985), it is useful to consider first the example which Hart (1979) used to illustrate the nature of the limiting equilibrium.

Let there be two goods, 1 and 2, and $(r+1)$ consumers. r of these are initially endowed with α units of good 1 alone and have a utility function $U(x_1, x_2)$ while the remaining individual has an initial endowment of β units of good 2 but a utility function defined on his consumption of good 1 given by $V(y)$. These utility functions satisfy the usual regularity conditions with the additional restriction that nowhere is the marginal rate of substitution infinite.[3] Thus the first r consumers have a taste for both goods though only endowments of the first while the last individual wants only good 1 but has an initial endowment of the second good. This then ensures that the agent with monopoly power will want to engage in trade.

If we now allow the monopolist to perfectly discriminate we know that in equilibrium he will extract an amount t^* from each of the first r individuals in exchange for (β/r) of good 2 such that the latter are indifferent between trading or not. That is t^* is defined by

$$U(a-t^*, \beta/r) - U(\alpha, 0). \tag{7.1}$$

Hence we also have

$$V^* = V(rt^*). \tag{7.2}$$

The polar opposite of this case is that of perfect competition. The r consumers give up an amount $\tilde{t}$ of their endowment of good 1 to buy good 2 whose (relative) price is denoted by p. Denote by $\text{MRS}(a, b)$ their marginal rate of substitution between goods 2 and 1 evaluated at the consumption point $x_1 = a, x_2 = b$. In equilibrium this marginal rate of substitution must be equal to the price p and there must be gains to them from the voluntary exchange. In other words we must have

$$\text{MRS}(\alpha - \tilde{t}, \beta/r) = p \tag{7.3}$$

$$U(a - \tilde{t}, \beta/r) \geqslant U(\alpha, 0). \tag{7.4}$$

The 'monopolist' therefore has an amount $r\tilde{t}$ of good 1 in equilibrium and we have

$$\tilde{t} = p\beta/r, \tag{7.5}$$

$$\tilde{V} = V(r\tilde{t}) = V(p\beta) \leqslant V^*. \tag{7.6}$$

We now want to compare these two equilibria for a large economy. The way that we do this is to see what happens in the limit as r tends to infinity. Since β is finite, β/r tends to zero as r grows so that the limiting value of $\tilde{t}$ is zero. It follows from this that the limiting value of p is therefore given by the marginal rate of substitution evaluated at the point $x_1 = \alpha$, $x_2 = 0$, i.e.

MRS$(\alpha, 0)$. From this it follows that

$$\lim \tilde{V} = \lim V(p\beta) = V[\beta \, \mathrm{MRS}(\alpha, 0)]. \tag{7.7}$$

If we can now show that this is also the limit in the monopoly case, that is, that the monopolist can obtain the same utility when $r \to \infty$ under these two cases, we shall have been able to establish that what is important is in fact the relative size of the agent with market power rather than his absolute size and, *a fortiori*, that the critical factor in what happens to imperfectly competitive equilibria in the limit is the slope of the demand curve.

It follows from (7.1) that t^* can be represented as a function of $\beta/r : f(\beta/r)$. As above, since in the limit β/r tends to zero, so does t^*. Thus we need to evaluate the limit of their ratio by l'Hôpital's rule

$$\lim[t^*/(\beta/r)] = \frac{df(0)}{d(\beta/r)} = \frac{\partial U(\alpha, 0)/\partial x_2}{\partial U(\alpha, 0)/\partial x_1} = \mathrm{MRS}(\alpha, 0). \tag{7.8}$$

This gives the result that we are looking for since by substitution of equation (7.8) in the limit of equation (7.6) we have

$$\lim V^* = \lim V(rt^*) = V\left(\lim \frac{t^*}{\beta/r}\right) = V[\beta \, \mathrm{MRS}(\alpha, 0)]. \tag{7.9}$$

What the analysis of this example has shown is that in a 'large' exchange economy a monopolist can get the same utility by behaving as a competitor as he could get by behaving as a discriminating monopolist. The conditions that characterise the two limiting equilibria are equivalent and the limiting outcome approximates Pareto optimality. Hart proves this result more generally for the case of an economy in which there is production of differentiated goods. There was no production in the economy in the example above.

Prior to Hart's paper the view generally expressed had been that the conditions that would make the equilibrium in an imperfectly competitive economy approximate the competitive equilibrium were twofold: the small relative size of traders and the existence of a large number of competing brands.[4] The upshot of Hart's analysis of the issue is to suggest that the critical factor is the size of traders relative to the economy rather than the number of goods as such. It is this point that is highlighted in the analysis of limiting behaviour in the model of a differentiated goods industry provided by Perloff and Salop (1985) and we shall now consider their argument.

7.2.2 Monopolistic competition: a partial equilibrium model

Recall from chapter 3 that a model of Chamberlinian monopolistic competition needs to have four properties. These are (1) that there are many firms producing differentiated commodities; (2) that each firm is negligible in that it can ignore its impact on, and hence the reaction of its rivals; (3) that there is sufficiently free entry to ensure that in equilibrium monopoly rents are zero; but that (4) each faces a downward-sloping demand curve so that in principle in equilibrium price could exceed marginal cost. These are all features that appear in the Perloff and Salop model and the object of the analysis is then to see in the limit just how large this wedge between price and marginal cost is.

The Perloff and Salop model is a partial equilibrium one as it analyses only the industry producing the differentiated goods. It is like a spatial model in that consumers are assumed to buy only one unit of their most preferred brand but, as in the Chamberlinian models of chapter 3, each brand actively competes with every one of the other $(n-1)$ brands on the market. For this to be so we have to assume that consumers' preferences are 'symmetric'. In other words, when plotted out in characteristics space, the fact that goods are neighbours is not taken to mean that they are closer substitutes in the consumer's eyes than goods that are further apart. They may turn out to be so but this is not necessarily the case.

A rather more formal way of stating this is the following. For every differentiated good, i, in the consumer's preference structure there is some marginal rate of substitution between it and the numeraire commodity. Denote this by θ_i. One can interpret this more informally as the value that the consumer places on brand i. In principle these θs could take a whole range of values. The assumption of symmetric preferences involves two things: the probability that θ_i equals some given value θ is given by the density function

$$g_i(\theta_i = \theta), \quad i = 1, \ldots, n \tag{7.10}$$

and that these distributions are identical and independent

$$g_i(\theta_i) = g(\theta) \text{ for } \theta \in [a, b], \tag{7.11}$$

$$\text{Prob } (\theta_1 = \theta, \ldots, \theta_n = \theta) = g(\theta)^n, \tag{7.12}$$

where $[a, b]$ is the support of the distribution. The cumulative distribution function corresponding to (7.11) is denoted by $G(\cdot)$.

The surplus obtained by the consumer from his purchase of brand i is the difference between his valuation and the price that he pays

$$s_i = \theta_i - p_i, \tag{7.13}$$

and the consumer will choose that brand whose surplus is the greatest for that will be the 'best buy'. Given θ_i, the probability that we shall observe the consumer buying brand i rather than brand j is simply the probability that θ_j is less than $(p_j - p_i + \theta_i)$. This is just $G(p_j - p_i + \theta_i)$. Thus the probability that brand i is the chosen brand is the product of these over the j's

$$\Pi_{j \neq i}[G(p_j - p_i + \theta_i)].$$

In order to work out what fraction of the consumers find that good i is their best buy we need to integrate over the density of θ_i. Since it is assumed that there are L consumers, the demand for brand i is

$$Q_i(p_1, \ldots, p_n) = L \int \Pi_{j \neq i}[G(p_j - p_i + \theta_i)]g(\theta_i)\, d\theta_i. \qquad (7.14)$$

Each brand is produced by a separate firm facing a common cost function. This has two components: a marginal cost of c and an irrecoverable fixed cost of K. The latter are thus the set-up costs. Each firm that chooses to operate will maximise its expected profits given these costs and the demand function in (7.14). Since each firm sees no direct competitors we can assume that it conjectures that

$$\partial p_j / \partial p_i = 0, \forall j \neq i,$$

so that the Bertrand-Nash equilibrium is one where

$$p_i = c - Q_1 \frac{\partial p_i}{\partial Q_i}, \quad i = 1, \ldots, n. \qquad (7.15)$$

There is of course no reason why each of these prices should be the same but for the sake of exposition we shall assume that we are dealing with a symmetric equilibrium in which each firm is charging the same price

$$p_i = p, i = 1, \ldots, n.$$

At this symmetric equilibrium let us now consider the Chamberlinian dd curve for firm i. This is just

$$Q_i(p, \ldots, p_i, \ldots, p) = L \int [G(p - p_1 + \theta_i)]^{n-1} g(\theta_i)\, d\theta_i \qquad (7.16)$$

and its slope is given by

$$\frac{\partial Q_1}{\partial p_i} = -(n-1)L \int [G(p - p_i + \theta_i)]^{n-2} g(p - p_i + \theta_i) g(\theta_i)\, d\theta_i. \qquad (7.17)$$

Since we are going to be evaluating elasticities in the neighbourhood of the symmetric industry equilibrium we shall need to know the quantity of firm i's good demanded. This is just

$$Q_i(p, \ldots, p) = L \int [G(\theta_i)]^{n-1} g(\theta_i)\, d\theta_i = \frac{L}{n}. \qquad (7.18)$$

The slope of the demand curve will of course be given by setting $p_i = p$ in equation (7.17). We can now make use of this and equations (7.15) and (7.18) to derive an expression for the equilibrium profit margin in the n firm case in terms of the own price elasticity of demand

$$\frac{p(n) - c}{p(n)} = \frac{1}{\eta(n)}. \tag{7.19}$$

In the competitive equilibrium the right-hand side of this is zero but unless the elasticity is infinite, price will be above marginal cost in the current case. Note that $\eta(n)$ can be written as $p(n)M(n)$, where

$$M(n) = -\frac{1}{Q_i}\frac{\partial Q_i}{\partial p_i} = n(n-1)\int [G(\theta_i)]^{n-2}[g(\theta_i)]^2 d\theta_i. \tag{7.20}$$

Our interest now lies in the limiting behaviour of this equilibrium. We shall look at this in three respects. First we can keep the level of fixed costs constant at K and look at what happens in the face of entry. Entry will occur until n reaches a level such that

$$\pi(n) = \frac{L}{nM(n)} - K \geqslant 0 \tag{7.21}$$

and

$$\pi(n+1) = \frac{L}{(n+1)M(n+1)} - K \leqslant 0. \tag{7.22}$$

This will be the Chamberlinian large-group equilibrium for given L and K and these two conditions merely say that those firms that are operating in the market will be making non-negative profits whereas potential entrants will anticipate non-positive profits should they enter.[5] The two other ways in which we can look at the limit is to see what happens as we let set-up costs go to zero (so that n tends to infinity) and what happens as the economy gets very large and L goes to infinity. Clearly an increase in L or a decrease in K will increase the number of firms in the Chamberlinian equilibrium.

It follows from equation (7.19) that price will tend to marginal cost as fixed costs decline if and only if $M(n)$ tends to infinity as K goes towards zero. $M(n)$ is defined in equation (7.20) and it is clear that what happens to this as n grows will depend on the characteristics of the density function. As we noted earlier this density was defined on the closed interval $[a, b]$ where b is the upper limit. b is the maximum valuation that the consumer could place on any brand and the implication of its being finite is that each brand's demand curve cuts the price axis.

Perloff and Salop show (1985, pp. 116–18) that if either b is finite or b is infinite and

$$\lim_{\theta \to \infty} [g'(\theta)/g(\theta)] = -\infty, \tag{7.23}$$

then $M(n)$ will tend to infinity as n does.[6] In other words the limiting equilibrium is one in which price is equal to marginal cost even though we are in a world of differentiated products.

To see what it is that drives these results, consider first the case of a finite b. Here the intuitive argument about what happens in the limit is straightforward. Suppose that there are an arbitrarily large number of firms offering distinct brands. Since we are considering the case of symmetric equilibrium, these all sell for the same price and so any consumer will choose that brand, i say, for which $\theta_i = b$. However, since the commodity space is densely packed with differentiated goods, there will be another brand available, j say, for which θ_j is arbitrarily close to b. But that is just to say that j will be an effective rival in the competition for the consumer's custom and it is this fact that ensures that the dd curve for brand i is approximately horizontal in the limit. Since brand i was arbitrarily chosen, the result then follows for all brands. Thus, if a firm should ever so slightly raise its price, each of its customers will choose another brand and it is this that effectively ensures that the limiting price will be at the competitive level.

Matters are less clear when b is infinite because, if we look at a consumer's most-preferred and next-best-substitute brand, there is no reason why these need be close together. In this case we need to make use of probability arguments. What constrains firms' monopoly power is not so much actual consumer behaviour as what the firms think will be the consumers' response. Thus if a firm thinks that it would suffer a dramatic loss of custom if it raised its price it would not do so. If a firm raises its price it will only keep customers whose θ's are sufficiently high. However, the firm only knows the probability density of θ and, if this is going to zero sufficiently quickly (in a way made precise in equation (7.23)), then its belief that it will *probably* lose a lot of customers is just as effective a constraint on its monopoly power.

Clearly there will be cases in which b is infinite and (7.23) is not satisfied and in which in the limit the industry does not approximate perfect competition even as the size of the economy grows (i.e. as L tends to infinity). Such cases then are monopolistically competitive in a fundamental way. Of course, from a practical point of view, one might ask about the plausibility of such cases. A necessary condition is that consumers' maximum valuations are infinite. However, since consumers' assets are likely to be finite we may reasonably want to assume this case away.

Note that when K is sufficiently small (or L sufficiently large) the free-entry conditions (7.21) and (7.22) can be replaced by the zero-profit condition.[7] This can be re-arranged to give the following relationship between the relative size of the firm and the level of fixed costs and elasticity

$$\frac{n}{L} = \frac{1}{KM(n)}.$$

As the level of fixed costs goes to zero, n becomes unbounded and each firm's market share (L/n) will go to zero. However, it does not necessarily follow that price will be driven down to the level of marginal cost. This will depend on what happens to $M(n)$. What about the effect of increased market size? When b, the maximum valuation, satisfies either of the two conditions mentioned earlier, $M(n)$ is increasing in n and, in the limit, market share goes to zero and price goes to marginal cost. If these conditions are not satisfied, neither of these limiting conditions may obtain. As an example we might consider the negative exponential distribution for θ:

$$g(\theta) = \lambda e^{-\lambda\theta}, \theta \in [0, \infty).$$

Here $g'(\theta)/g(\theta)$ equals $-\lambda (> -\infty)$ irrespective of θ and the limiting market share would be $(K/\lambda) > 0$. Thus we have to conclude that entry competition, whether through reductions in fixed cost or increases in the number of consumers, does not guarantee a limiting scenario of perfect competition. However, in order to get market power in the limit it was necessary for some consumers to have an infinite valuation of the brand and this is something we discounted in our earlier remarks. Thus our analysis so far is consistent with Hart's contention that monopoly power will disappear even under product differentiation as long as firms are insignificant relative to the size of the market in which they operate.

Before concluding this subsection we should give a brief mention to three other contributions to the discussion of the relationship between market size and the degree of competition: those of Salop (1979), Novshek (1980) and Eaton and Wooders (1985). These are papers in which product differentiation is modelled according to the Hotelling, spatial-competition, paradigm.

In his paper, Salop (1979) was not concerned with asymptotic results as such. However, from our discussion of his model in chapter 2.5 it is clear that, other things remaining equal, as long as the ratio (F/L)[8] is sufficiently small, we shall have a competitive equilibrium with price tending to marginal cost in the limit. This limiting price will equal v $(< \infty)$, the maximum price that consumers are prepared to pay for their ideal brand.

Salop's paper only looks at symmetric Nash equilibria for the case where firms face no costs of relocation. For this reason price is the only decision variable. Although Novshek uses the same kind of model to Salop – a circular market and decreasing average total cost, his paper is different in that he considers equilibria in price *and* location. These are analysed on the assumption that rival firms will only react if they find themselves being undercut at their own locations. We referred to this as 'modified zero conjectural variations' in chapter 2.

Recall that Novshek's model is one of a uniform market in which the buyers have linear demand curves and in which the production technology is characterised by a cost function with a fixed cost of F and a constant marginal cost. The limit result that Novshek shows is that, if fixed costs are sufficiently small given the other parameters that describe the market, a free-entry equilibrium exists and is approximately competitive in that all consumers are able to buy the good at delivered prices approximately equal to the marginal cost of production.

It is important to note that these results do not necessarily imply that in very large markets pure profit will approach zero or that such markets will be socially optimal. This point has been stressed in the paper by Eaton and Wooders (1985). They consider limiting behaviour in a more complex model of entry. In their model firms, once they enter, are locked into a location. However, the decision to enter is a 'sophisticated' one because entrants take account of post-entry price competition and the effects that this would have on the profits from entry. Only if these are positive in the resulting Nash equilibrium will they enter.

The model is one in which consumers are uniformly distributed with density D along the real line. Each has an inelastic demand for one unit of the good. The resource costs involved in satisfying consumers needs are threefold. There is, first of all, a location-specific sunk cost of K per period. The cost of production itself rises proportionately to square of output. Hence the total cost of producing an output q is

$$c(q) = K + aq^2.$$

If a is zero then we have the Novshek/Salop case of constant marginal costs but decreasing average costs. Where $a > 0$ we have a U-shaped average cost curve. In fact in the analysis of limiting behaviour it is important to distinguish between these two cases.

The free-entry equilibria in this model are asymmetric both in location and price. Thus, if a firm enters at some point on the line, its delivered price schedule will be symmetric about and increasing from the point of entry. However, firms are no longer charging the same price. Eaton and Wooders' objectives are twofold: to compare the optimal number of brands with the free-entry market equilibrium number and to look at the limiting behaviour of the latter, in particular to show that pure profit might persist in the limit. They have no general answer to the former question. In small economies with large sunk costs there will be an *excessive* number of brands and those firms in operation may earn substantial pure profit. As these sunk costs become smaller one needs to distinguish between the two cost cases. With constant marginal costs, excessive diversity remains the case. However the question of its limiting competitiveness is a little complex. As we let either K go to zero or D go to infinity the (common) price tends to marginal cost. However the ratio of the equilibrium distance between firms (L^e) and the socially optimal distance[9] (L^*) is bounded *away* from both zero *and* one.[10] Hence while 'competitive' in the price sense it does not replicate the social optimum nor does it imply zero profit. Nevertheless by comparing the resource costs per head in the market equilibrium as D gets large Eaton and Wooders show that the magnitude of the inefficiency due to excessive brands becomes vanishingly small. This is probably what one might have expected since the source of the inefficiency is the product specific fixed costs and in per capita terms they are going to zero in the limit. Eaton and Wooders refer to this case as being *approximately competitive* in the limit.

The limiting behaviour of the U-shaped cost function case is clearer. As we mentioned above, when K is sufficiently large there will be an excessive number of brands. As K declines it is possible for there to be either too many or too few brands in the free-entry equilibrium. However things clear up in the limit as either K goes to zero or D goes to infinity; market imperfections disappear, firms earn no profit and the (unique) free-entry equilibrium is socially optimal.

7.2.3 Conditions for imperfect competition in large markets

We saw in the previous section in our discussion of the Perloff and Salop model that the presence of an infinite number of firms in the market did not guarantee perfect competition. The condition that was needed to get this imperfectly competitive limiting equilibrium was, of course, that some consumers placed an infinite value on the differentiated brands. That is, the marginal rate of substitution between the numeraire and the branded good was infinity. However we suggested that, because of the finiteness of consumers' resources, this was probably a rather unlikely scenario. Hence the question that arises is whether or not there are reasonable conditions under which the equilibrium in a large market remains imperfectly competitive.

In chapter 3 we looked at a representative consumer model that was based on that of Dixit and Stiglitz. In it the market remained mono-polistically competitive as the ratio of fixed cost to consumers' expenditure went to zero (and hence the number of firms went off to infinity). This occurred even though in the limit each firm was negligible in the sense that the amount spent on each brand as a proportion of total expenditure (and hence the per capita consumption of each brand) approached zero. Intuitively one might have expected that perfect competition would have been the result. The reason for thinking this is the following.[11] Since we have assumed by using the idea of a representative consumer that each individual is identical, the price at which a brand sells is given by the marginal rate of substitution between the brand and the numeraire, evaluated at the per capita consumption bundle. Suppose now that one firm doubles the quantity supplied of the brand it produces. The per capita consumption won't change by very much because every consumer buys it and the number of consumers is very large. As long as the marginal rate of substitution is a continuous function of per capita consumption there will be little or no impact on the price of the brand. However, this is just another way of saying that the firm's demand curve will be approximately perfectly elastic.

The implication of this argument is that in order to obtain monopolistic competition rather than perfect competition it must be that we have implicitly assumed that the marginal rate of substitution is a *discontinuous* function of per capita consumption at the equilibrium bundle. This will induce the change in the equilibrium price that is needed if a firm is to believe that its actions will have a significant impact. How then has this come about? In fact the answer lies in the rather open-ended specification of the model and, in particular, in the incomplete specification of the commodity space. In the limit we have two things going on: an infinite number of brands will enter, each of them introducing a new dimension, and the per capita consumption of every brand goes to zero. Thus we need to think what is likely to be happening on the 'numeraire axis', as it were, since this is where the consumer is going to be located in the limiting equilibrium. Figure 7.2 tries to illustrate the problem. It is drawn for only three dimensions: the numeraire, x_0, and two branded commodities, x_1 and x_2, but one can think of this as part of a much higher-dimensional picture.

If we imagine that initially there is only the one differentiated good we may find the consumer in equilibrium at point A on the indifference surface EFG. A is 'close' to the limiting equilibrium of $x_1 = 0$. The marginal rate of substitution is indicated by the slope of the line CD. Now bring in the second differentiated commodity. Since A was close to the limiting equilibrium the amount of x_1 demanded changes by virtually nothing but

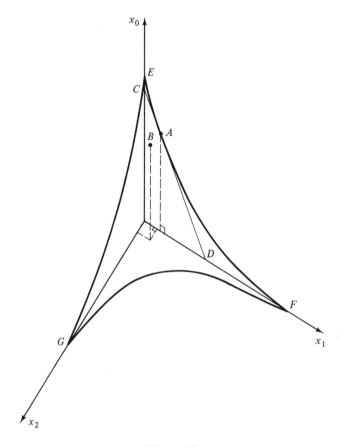

Figure 7.2

the new equilibrium position is at point B. If we now evaluate the marginal rate of substitution between the numeraire and commodity 1 at B we will find that it has changed discretely. In other words there will be a discrete change in the equilibrium price of the brand even though per capita consumption has virtually remained the same. It is this that creates the problem and it is the reason why both the model of chapter 3 and the Dixit and Stiglitz model generate monopolistic competition in the limit.

Hart's argument has been that this continual redefinition of the *preference* space as new brands appear is not sufficiently rigorous. Instead he restricts the consumer to having preferences defined over a finite number, m ($<n$), of the brands. He still allows the number of potential brands to increase without limit but places this restriction on his

consumers.[12] Over these brands preferences are symmetric. The fact that consumers are interested in only a small fraction of the potential brands as n gets large is actually a crucial ingredient in Hart's analysis. Because consumers tastes have been confined to a finite subset of the available brands it now makes sense to think of consumers being heterogeneous and so to think about there being a density function describing the number of consumers who have a taste for any particular brand. Any consumer's utility function is symmetric in the m brands for which he or she has a taste. However, whether these brands are 'neighbours' or not is a random event. Specifically he assumes that for each consumer every combination of these m brands is equally likely to be desired by the consumer so that the fact that a consumer likes brand 1 provides no information about whether the consumer has a taste for brand 2 or brand 52. Hence we have no neighbouring goods and so can assume that the impact of a change in any one firm's actions will be evenly spread over all n firms. When n is very large this will therefore be negligible. The assumption that consumers don't possess a natural ranking of the brands that they like is a strong one and requires that each brand has its own peculiar distinctiveness. Hart suggests as examples chocolate-covered bars, breakfast cereals, soap powders and restaurants. In any event, if we make this assumption we have a model that satisfies the second in our list of ingredients.

In Hart's model any particular consumer i is characterised by the partitioned vector (i, v), where

$$i = (i_1, \ldots, i_m)$$

and

$$v = (v_1, \ldots, v_m).$$

The elements of i are just the labels of the m brands for which the consumer has a taste while v contains the valuations placed by the consumer on each brand. The typical consumer is taken to have a utility function

$$U(x_{i_1}, \ldots, x_{i_m}, x_0, v), \tag{7.24}$$

where x_0 is the consumption of the numeraire commodity.

As in the Perloff and Salop model the valuations are probabilistic and each is assumed to be independently and identically distributed. The distribution function that describes this, $H(v)$, is continuous on the support interval $[v^-, v^+]$. Hence valuations are bounded and finite.

Given that there are n commodities, there are $\binom{n}{m}$ ways of getting m items from a list of n. We might call i a 'taste combination'. Then, there are $\binom{n}{m}$ possible taste combinations and these are taken to be equally probable.

Hence the density function that describes them is uniform with parameter $\binom{n}{m}^{-1}$.

Since Hart wants to concentrate on what happens in the limit he takes the number of potential brands, n, to be very large. However, because of the presence of fixed costs and limited resource endowments it may not be possible for the economy to sustain a market with n firms. Indeed Hart makes an assumption that ensures this will be the case. The economy's entire endowment of the numeraire is assumed to be kn. Each firm faces a fixed cost of $f > k$. If all n potential firms were to operate, the economy would need an endowment of fn. Hence at most, only a fraction $\delta < 1$ can operate. Note that while δ has an upper limit of (k/f), it is quite likely that in equilibrium it will be less than this. This has one important implication and that is that it may well happen that, for certain consumers, only a subset (and possibly none) of the brands for which they have a taste may be produced. δ in fact becomes the probability that any brand is being produced and the probability that, out of the m brands that a consumer likes, only r are being produced is given by the binomial probability

$$\binom{m}{r} \delta^r (1-\delta)^{m-r}. \tag{7.25}$$

The model in Hart (1985a) has all these elements and is quite generally specified. In Hart (1985b) a more explicit model is considered. It is around this latter model that we shall build our discussion for it contains all the elements that are necessary for the points that we want to make. The simplification comes in the form of the utility function (7.24). It is additively separable in the branded goods and numeraire. Furthermore the m branded goods are all perfect substitutes for one another, the marginal rate of substitution between j and i being given by

$$\text{MRS}_{ji} = \frac{v_i}{v_j}, \quad \text{a constant.}$$

This specification has the useful simplifying feature that the consumer only buys a single brand. This is the consumer's 'best buy', the one for which (v_j/p_j) is greatest (p_j is the good's price). Recall that this was also a feature of the Perloff and Salop model. Given this, the quantity of the best buy that the consumer will buy will be that which maximises the surplus over expenditure. This we can write as

$$x_j = \frac{v_j^{\eta-1}}{p_j^{\eta}}, \tag{7.26}$$

where $\eta = (1-\alpha)^{-1}$ is the own price elasticity of demand.[13] If good j sells for p and all other goods for p^*, then x_j will be given by (7.26) as long as

$$v_j/p \geqslant v_i/p^*, \quad i \neq j,$$

and will be zero otherwise.

We now consider the nature of the demand function for a particular brand, brand h say, which sells at p, all other brands selling at p^*. Consider those who have a taste for brand h and for whom $r \leqslant m-1$ brands that they like are also available. The number of such people is the product of the number of people who like brand h and the probability that r other brands they like are also being produced. There are kn consumers in the economy and n potential brands. If each only liked *one* brand then k would be the number of potential consumers per brand. However, since each consumer likes m brands, the number of potential consumers is km. The probability that the other r brands are being produced is given by (7.25) so that the number who like brand k and find that just r of the other brands for which they have a taste are available is just

$$km \binom{r}{m-1} \delta^r (1-\delta)^{m-r-1}. \tag{7.25'}$$

Now, consider those in this group who have a specific valuation v_h that is equal to v. The number of those who find that brand h is a best buy is the number for which

$$\frac{v_b}{p^*} \leqslant \frac{v}{p}, \quad b \neq n.$$

There are $H[p^*v/p]^r$ of these and each demands an amount that is given by (7.26). Since this was for a specific value for v_h we need to integrate over the range of v. Hence we have it that the demand from any consumer who finds that brand h is their best buy and that another r of their preferred brands are available is

$$X(r) \equiv \int_{v^-}^{v^+} \left[\frac{v^{\eta-1}}{p^{\eta}} \right] H \left[\frac{p^* v}{p} \right]^r h(v) \, dv. \tag{7.27}$$

The product of (7.25') and (7.27) gives the quantity demanded for some given number r. To get the market demand we need to sum over all values that r can take. Doing this gives us the total demand for the brand as

$$D(p, p^*, \delta) = \sum_{r=0}^{m-1} [X(r) km \binom{m-1}{r} \delta^r (1-\delta)^{m-r-1}]. \tag{7.28}$$

This is a fairly intimidating expression but it is a differentiable function with some useful properties. Denoting by an appropriate subscript partial differentiation with respect to some variable we have

$D_p < 0,$

$D_{p^*} > 0,$

$D_\delta < 0$

and

$|D_p(p^*, p^*, \delta)| > |D_{p^*}(p^*, p^*, \delta)|.$

A final property of this demand function is that the aggregate demand for all brands is higher the more brands are actually being produced – the greater is δ. The reason is that as more brands become available it is more likely that any consumer will find that his most highly valued brand will be amongst these. Thus the average valuation placed on all the brands on the market will increase and as a consequence so will aggregate demand.

A symmetric monopolistically competitive equilibrium will be characterised by each firm maximising its profits but for each firm price will only equal average cost. If such an equilibrium exists for this model (and that we have not yet shown), then a good's own price elasticity of demand is increasing in δ. This merely reflects the effect of increasing competition. Furthermore, the equilibrium price is decreasing in δ as are profits. By the resource constraint condition, $fn > kn$, profits $\Pi(\delta)$ when δ is unity are negative. If we make the additional assumption that $\Pi(0) > 0$ so that it always pays at least one firm to set up, then Hart establishes that at most there is one equilibrium. Unfortunately to show that this is unique it seems necessary to impose fairly stringent conditions. Two alternatives that Hart offers are:
(1) that valuations are uniformly distributed on the closed interval $[0, v^+]$ and
(2) that the consumer likes only two brands and that $dH(v)$ is non-increasing in the closed interval $[0, v^+]$.
It would obviously be of great value to establish other (less stringent) conditions but so far this does not seem to have been possible.

If we accept for the moment that an equilibrium exists then what of its comparative static properties? A rise in fixed cost reduces aggregate output (and the fraction of operating firms) and causes price to rise. An increase in the number of brands for which the consumer has a taste reduces the equilibrium price because there are more likely to be suitable substitutes in existence for any consumer and this will increase price elasticity.

If we recall the assumption on the uniform distribution of v, we can see intuitively how it is that this helps us to get the result that the limiting equilibrium price exceeds marginal cost. Consider the symmetric equilibrium where $p_i = p^*$. A consumer will be indifferent between two brands, 1 and 2 say, for which he has a taste only if v_1 equals v_2. But, that this is true for a consumer is rather unlikely give the 'wide' and uniform distribution of possible values of v. Because of this if firm 1 were to raise its price a fraction above p^* its customers would still find that $(v_1/p_1) > (v_2/p^*)$ and so would not automatically desert it. Hence in the equilibrium we can have

$$p^* > C'[D(p^*, p^*, \delta)].$$

This reasoning might lead one to suspect that the more concentrated the distribution of v the closer one would get to a horizontal dd curve just because it would be increasingly likely that consumers would be almost indifferent between brands and so abandon a particular firm in droves if it were to raise its price. However, this is still not sufficient because, as we know, δ has to be strictly less than one. From this it follows that for some consumers the branded good whose price has risen may be the *only one* in their taste set that is being produced. In fact for precisely $km(1 - \delta)^{m-1}$ of them this is true.[14] Now suppose that we imagine that we are at a monopolistic competition equilibrium and that we have a concentrated distribution of the v's. By the reasoning above, any firm that raises its price will not lose all its customers. It may therefore pay a firm to deviate from the assumed equilibrium so contradicting the assumption that we were in equilibrium at all. In other words, when we have a highly concentrated distribution of the v's, a monopolistically competitive equilibrium may fail to exist.

In fact, we can see in this problem of existence the conditions that we need to obtain perfect competition in the limit. Not only do we need to have the consumer indifferent between the brands that he likes, we also need to have m sufficiently large so that, even when $\delta < 1$, there is some guarantee that there are alternative acceptable brands available to the consumer. Indeed there is a proposition to the effect that as m goes to infinity, the monopolistic competition price approaches minimum average cost. That is, we get a limiting result of perfect competition. The condition is of course that the consumer has a taste for *every* brand. This was a feature of the Perloff and Salop model. If you will recall, in that model finite valuations on the brands led to perfect competition in the limit. It is comforting that our earlier conclusions have been confirmed by rather more rigorous reasoning.

In conclusion then, we have seen that under horizontal product differentiation we can obtain perfect competition in the limit when consumers have a taste for all potential brands and when the valuation that they place on each of these is finite. In that limiting equilibrium, price equals marginal cost, profits are zero and the size of the firm is negligible relative to that of the market. An important element in Hart's contribution to this literature has been to show that to get this conclusion it is not necessary to have the entry of an infinite number of firms. The critical factor is that there are an infinite number of brands potentially available and for which the consumers have a taste. This would seem to make a lot of sense for it really opens up to possibility for consumers' indifference between brands to effectively influence each firm's conjectures about the effects of its actions.

7.3 Vertical product differentiation and industrial structure

So far in this chapter we have assumed that products are horizontally differentiated. In our analysis of these we have seen that, on the whole in such cases, the number of firms in the free-entry equilibrium increases without bound as the size of fixed set-up costs goes to zero or as the size of the market becomes very large. In addition the limiting price approached marginal cost.

Recall however that the point of our discussion in chapter 6 was to indicate that matters may not be the same in markets in which the goods are differentiated vertically. The analysis we did was for the case of pure vertical differentiation: where the good in question could be classified entirely by a quality index, q. The particular result that we showed was that if the consumers' willingness to pay for quality rose much more rapidly than the unit variable cost of providing that quality – as it might do were quality improvement to be incorporated in a product mainly by way of increased fixed cost – then the number of firms that could operate in the market would be independent of the size of both the market and of fixed costs. Indeed, in the free-entry equilibrium that number would not rise beyond a maximum that was determined by income distribution. In that equilibrium, some firms will be able to charge a price that exceeds marginal cost and will also earn positive profits. This phenomenon was referred to as the 'finiteness property' of vertically differentiated markets.

In this section our aim is to show that a weaker version of the finiteness property can arise in the case where horizontal product attributes are also present. As before, the condition that needs to be met is that the unit cost of quality rises slowly relative to consumers' willingness to pay for such improvements. The analysis we carry out follows that of Shaked and Sutton (1987).

Products will be described by a vertical characteristic, q, and a horizontal characteristic, h. It seems natural to use the spatial model for the horizontal characteristic and so we let h^* be the ideal value of this attribute for some particular consumer. A good can thus be characterised by the pair (q, d), where $d = |h - h^*|$ is a measure of how far the good is in the horizontal dimension from the consumer's ideal. We consider a consumer with income Y who buys one unit of the good at a price p. The utility received by a consumer with income Y who buys one unit of the good at a price p and spends $Y - p (= y)$ on other goods can be written as

$$U(q, d, y). \tag{7.29}$$

Two assumptions that we make about U in addition to its having the necessary differentiability are:

(a) Utility is increasing in quality and decreasing in the distance that the consumer is from the ideal. Hence

$$\frac{\partial U}{\partial q} > 0, \frac{\partial U}{\partial d} < 0,$$

(b) The marginal utility from quality increases with income. This will ensure that richer consumers will be willing to pay more for any given quality improvement. Formally this is

$$\frac{\partial}{\partial y} \left(\frac{\partial U}{\partial q} \right) > 0.$$

To illustrate the argument in fact we use the following example of a utility function that satisfies assumptions (a) and (b)

$$U = q(Y - p) + [a - b(h - h^*)^2]. \tag{7.30}$$

It is also necessary to make some assumptions about the distribution of income and the nature of the production technology. On the former we assume a distribution $f(Y)$ on the finite closed interval $[Y^-, Y^+]$. On the latter, firms have two items of cost: a quality-dependent fixed cost of set-up, $f(q)$, which one might think of as 'design' cost, and a quality-dependent unit production cost reflecting elements such as specification and quality assurance costs, $c(q)$. On these we impose conditions that ensure that the main burden of the cost of quality improvement falls on fixed costs. These are

$$Y^+ > c(q), \quad \text{for all } q \tag{7.31}$$

and

$$0 < \frac{\partial \log f(q)}{\partial q} \leqslant \beta < \infty. \tag{7.32}$$

The first of these conditions is designed to ensure that the richest members of society can afford to buy the highest quality of good that is available at a price fractionally above its unit production cost and still be better off. There thus exists a price that covers production costs and makes both the firm a profit and the richest consumer better off.

However, note that, while (7.31) puts an upper bound on the unit production costs, there is no reason why fixed costs should not increase without bound since (7.32) only places a restriction on the rate at which they increase with quality. This is the sense in which we mean that the main burden of increased quality falls on fixed costs.

The object of setting up this example is to show that in a free-entry equilibrium in which firms compete on price at least one firm will have a strictly positive market share, μ $(0 < \mu < 1)$. This share does not depend on the size of the economy. What determines it are the nature of technology and preferences.

In order to characterise these conditions, suppose for the sake of argument that there are n products in the market and that the current top quality is q^+. What we need then are simply conditions that say that there exist strictly positive values for the variables Δ, m and μ such that, if a firm incurs the fixed cost $f(q^+ + \Delta)$, it can obtain a product of quality $(q^+ + \Delta)$ and get at least μS customers at a price of $[c(q^+ + \Delta) + m]$ where S is the size of the economy and m is the markup over unit variable cost. In other words we need to ensure that there is always some (finite) increase in fixed (R&D) costs that enables the firm to produce a quality superior enough to guarantee that, if it offers it along with the horizontal attribute h, it can capture a fraction μ of the market *and* make a positive gross profit.

Consider a consumer of income Y and buying the top quality good that is currently available, q^+. The utility obtained is

$$U = q^+(Y - p(q^+)) + K,$$

where K is a constant. If this consumer were now to purchase the new higher quality good offered at the level $q^+ + \Delta$ and at a price equal to $[c(q^+ + \Delta) + m]$, the utility obtained would be

$$U' = (q^+ + \Delta)[Y - c(q^+ + \Delta) - m] + K.$$

Given (7.31) it is true that for consumers whose income is Y^+ there is certainly a small enough m and a large enough Δ to make U' larger than U, and so to make these consumers prepared to switch from q^+ to $q^+ + \Delta$ (for any h). Thus, for example, if U is given by (7.30) and if (7.31) is satisfied then there exist strictly positive values of Δ, m and μ such that a firm offering the product $(q^+ + \Delta)$ (and any h) at a price $[c(q^+ + \Delta) + m]$ can obtain a market of size μS. In order to be able to satisfy this condition we require it to be the case that, when we produce a marginally higher quality good, the evaluation placed by some consumers on this enhancement should sufficiently exceed the new good's actual cost of production. But, to produce a higher quality good will involve spending more resources. The condition is that these must be largely in the form of once and for all development costs.

So much then for the condition that is needed for such product enhancement to be profitable. The question we now need to consider is whether this condition still holds in the free-entry equilibrium in which no *potential* entrant could expect to earn positive profits. In fact we shall indeed show that in such an equilibrium at least one firm will have a strictly positive share. More formally we wish to prove that there exists some $\epsilon > 0$ such that, for at least one firm, $\mu \geqslant \epsilon$ at such an equilibrium and that this does not depend on the total size of the market. It is thus a limit result.

The proof goes as follows. Consider the following value of ϵ

$$\epsilon < \frac{\mu m}{Y^+ e^{\beta \Delta}}. \tag{7.33}$$

What we now need to show is that a state in which *none* of the firms has a share greater than ϵ cannot be a free-entry equilibrium.

Consider the good q^+ and suppose that its share of the market is $\mu^+ \leqslant \epsilon$. The revenue from this share cannot be sufficient to meet the fixed costs of $f(q^+)$. It therefore follows that

$$f(q^+) \geqslant (\epsilon S) Y^+, \tag{7.34}$$

where the term on the right-hand side is greater than or equal to the revenue that the producer of the good actually gets.[15]

By assumption, an entrant offering $(q^+ + \Delta)$ can capture μS of the market at a Nash equilibrium price of $[c(q^+ + \Delta) + m]$ so that its revenue net of variable costs is at least as large as $(\mu S)m$. Its fixed costs are $f(q^+ + \Delta)$. But from (7.32) we have

$$f(q^+ + \Delta) \leqslant e^{\beta \Delta} f(q^+).$$

Thus the entrant could anticipate a profit of

$$\begin{aligned} \Pi &= (\mu S)m - f(q^+ + \Delta) \\ &\geqslant (\mu S)m - e^{\beta \Delta} f(q^+). \end{aligned} \tag{7.35}$$

But, by (7.34), this can be written as

$$\Pi \geqslant (\mu S)m - e^{\beta\Delta}(\epsilon S)Y^+$$
$$= S[\mu m - \epsilon e^{\beta\Delta}Y^+]$$
$$\geqslant e^{\beta\Delta}Y^+ S\left[\frac{\mu m}{Y^+ e^{\beta\Delta}} - \epsilon\right]. \qquad (7.36)$$

However, by (7.33), the term in square brackets is strictly positive as is the first term on the right-hand side. It then follows that a consequence of our original assumption is that $\Pi > 0$: expected profits are *strictly* positive so that we cannot have a free-entry equilibrium if we find that *none* of the firms has a share greater than $\epsilon > 0$. From this we conclude that in a free-entry equilibrium *at least one* of the firms must have a strictly positive market share and as a consequence strictly positive profits.

This then is Shaked and Sutton's result and they show that this result does not depend on firms being single-product firms or on the nature of the anticipated post-entry equilibrium (Bertrand or Cournot). The result thus gives us conditions under which markets in which the goods have vertical attributes will remain non-atomistic[16] even as their size approaches infinity. It is an important result because what it does is show that while some kinds of product differentiation have no fundamental influence on market structure there are others that do. When vertical attributes are present and the interplay between demand and technology results in unit variable costs increasing slowly as quality improves relative to consumers' willingness to pay for this then, irrespective of the size either of the market or of fixed costs, the market will remain essentially imperfectly competitive. In the opposite case, as when horizontal attributes are present, product differentiation per se offers no prediction about what the industrial structure will be. Thus our analysis in this chapter has served to illustrate the flaw in the traditionally accepted view that argues that product differentiation is indeed irrelevant to industrial structure.

This conclusion that vertical attributes matter is of some empirical relevance. Under pure horizontal differentiation, the results of the limit theorems are of more or less theoretical interest. We say this because, even though monopolistically competitive equilibria are theoretically fundamental, the welfare costs of very large horizontally differentiated monopolistically competitive markets are likely to be fairly small. Hence, there is no significant policy conclusion to be drawn. However, when vertical attributes are present one may, even in very large markets, get only a *few* firms. In other words, we can get 'real monopoly power' and this will have significant welfare costs and clear policy implications.

8 Product differentiation and the entry process

8.1 Introduction

In this chapter we focus once again on the Hotelling-type of spatial model and use it to consider some predictions about the effects of product differentiation. We shall deal with two aspects thought to be characteristic of differentiated product markets. The first of these is the question of whether or not there exist pure profits in a free-entry equilibrium. The second is the question of whether or not it is optimal to use the introduction of new products (brand proliferation) as an entry-deterring device.[1] These are issues that have been examined by a number of authors: Archibald and Rosenbluth (1975), Bonnano (1987), Eaton and Lipsey (1976, 1978, 1980), Hay (1976), Judd (1985), Lane (1980) and Schmalensee (1978).

8.2 The existence of pure profit in free-entry equilibrium

To motivate the discussion in this section let us start by considering a market, entry into which involves the non-recoverable (sunk) cost of F. Suppose also that in the oligopoly equilibrium each firm in the market earns a profit of $\pi(n)$, where n is the number of firms in the market. (Since a firm is free to close down, $\pi(n) > 0$, for all n.) Now assume that $\pi(n)$ decreases with n (as would be the case in standard Cournot-type oligopoly models). It is then a matter of definition that the maximum number of firms that can be profitably accommodated in the industry, N, is given by

$$\pi(N) \geqslant F > \pi(N+1).$$

This suggests that free-entry equilibrium may be characterised by positive profit since, with positive sunk costs, the entry of an additional firm may turn a positive profit for all firms into a loss for all (though, the amount of profit may be thought of as negligible for small F). Strictly speaking it is only under product homogeneity or Chamberlinian product differentiation that entry affects the profit of each existing firm in a symmetric way, so that $\pi(N)$ and $\pi(N+1)$ can be used, respectively, to represent the profit of any firm before and after the entry of an additional firm. Under Hotelling-type competition, assuming that the location of existing firms is fixed, even if prior to entry we thought of a symmetric equilibrium with each firm receiving $\pi(N)$, entry will affect asymmetrically the demands and profits of existing firms: firms producing goods neighbouring that of the entrant will face drastic reductions in demand and profits whilst other firms will be affected in a less severe way. Assuming that the anticipated post-entry profit of the entrant is at most equal to that of the firms producing neighbouring goods, this implies that, in this case, quite *large* profits earned by existing firms could be providing insufficient incentives to outside firms to enter the market. The suggestion is therefore that the existence of 'localised' competition between firms will magnify the effect that positive sunk costs have on the ability of firms to earn profits in a free-entry equilibrium. Intuitively, this is because, with localised competition, there will be intense competition between existing firms and new entrants if the former do not relocate to accommodate the latter. If the existing firms in the industry have incurred location-specific sunk costs so that they are relatively immobile, the anticipation by potential entrants that they are likely to face such competition may make entry particularly unattractive.

Let us now look at this argument in rather more detail. Consider first a linear market in which firms are located at a distance d from each other and where consumers are distributed uniformly over its length. Assume also a constant transportation cost of c, a constant marginal production cost of m and a fixed cost of F (where F is taken to be a location-specific sunk cost).[2] What we now want to do is to examine the price and location decisions of a new firm (which we shall call firm 3) that is contemplating locating between two existing firms (called 1 and 2). It is assumed that the location of the latter is fixed (an assumption that we shall re-examine later). This is illustrated in figure 8.1.

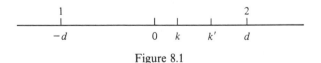

Figure 8.1

Following Eaton and Lipsey (1978), we let

$$V = g(p, v, x)$$

indicate the price that any firm expects a neighbouring firm to charge dependent on its own price, p, the price currently being charged by the neighbouring firm, v, and the distance between the two firms, x. Letting an i subscript denote partial differentiation with respect to the i'th argument of g, it is assumed that

$$0 \leqslant g_1 \leqslant 1, \quad g_3 \leqslant 0 \quad \text{and} \quad g_{33} \leqslant 0$$

and mill-price undercutting is ruled out.[3] Firm 3 is contemplating locating at k, i.e., at distance $(d-k)$ from firm 2. Let k' be the point at which it anticipates its delivered price will equal that of firm 2. In other words, it is anticipated that at k' the following condition will hold

$$p + c(k' - k) = g(p, v, d - k) + c(s - k'). \tag{8.1}$$

Solving for k' yields

$$k' = (1/2c)[g(p, v, d - k) + c(d + k) - p]. \tag{8.2}$$

Substituting (8.2) into the right-hand side of (8.1) and solving, we find that the anticipated delivered price at k', $P_2 = p + c(k' - k)$, is given by

$$P_2 = (1/2)[p + g(p, v, d - k) + c(d - k)], \tag{8.3}$$

where the subscript '2' indicates that this is the anticipated delivered price at the market boundary with firm 2. If we now represent the demand by an individual consumer located at a distance z from the origin as a function, f, of the delivered price

$$f[p + c(z - k)],$$

then the aggregate demand from consumers between k and k' that firm 3 expects is simply

$$\int_k^{k'} f[p + c(z - k)] dz. \tag{8.4}$$

If we let $u = p + c(z - k)$, so that $du = cdz$, equation (8.4) becomes

$$\frac{1}{c} \int_p^{P_{k'}} f(u) du = \frac{1}{c} [F(P_{k'}) - F(p)], \tag{8.5}$$

where F is the indefinite integral of f. In exactly the same fashion, we can obtain the anticipated delivered price, P_1, at the boundary with firm 1 and thus the expected demand to the left of k for firm 3. Then, combining this with (8.5) gives firm 3's demand function

$$Q(k, p) = \frac{1}{c} [F(P_1) + F(P_2) - 2F(p)]. \tag{8.6}$$

Now note that, with constant marginal cost, firm 3 will wish to maximise sales for any given price $p > m$. This will maximise its profits. The required conditions to maximise sales are that

$$\frac{\partial Q}{\partial k} = 0 \quad \text{and} \quad \frac{\partial^2 Q}{\partial k^2} < 0. \tag{8.7}$$

Taking (8.6) and (8.7) together implies that to maximise sales at any given price, k should be set to zero. In other words, the optimal location is mid way between the existing firms.

Now go back to (8.3) and note that, when k is zero, firm 3 anticipates that

$$P_1 = P_2 = P = 1/2[\, p + g(p, v, d) + cd\,], \tag{8.8}$$

so that, from (8.6), its expected demand is

$$Q(0, p) = \frac{2}{c}[F(P) - F(p)] \tag{8.9}$$

and its expected profit is

$$\pi = (p - m)Q - F. \tag{8.10}$$

Using (8.8)–(8.10) along with the profit maximisation condition

$$\frac{\partial \pi}{\partial p} = 0, \tag{8.11}$$

Eaton and Lipsey (1978) show[4] that there exists at least one value of p, p^*, that satisfies (8.11). In other words, if every firm charged this price and located at a distance d from any other, no firm would wish to move or alter its price. They term this the fixed-numbers (no-free-entry) equilibrium. It is defined as a state such that 'no firm can find a combination of location and price that offers it a larger anticipated gross profit than that obtained with its present combination of location and price' (*ibid.*, p. 458).

An important feature of this equilibrium is that p^* is independent of the fixed cost F. Thus there will be values of F for which, at a fixed-numbers equilibrium, all the firms earn strictly positive profits. The crucial question is, could these profits persist once the assumption of fixed-numbers is removed; that is, once we allow for free entry?

To deal with this question we use equations (8.8) and (8.9) to write the demand function of an existing firm at a fixed-numbers equilibrium (that is, its demand were it to charge a price p when all other firms charge p^*) as follows

$$Q = \frac{2}{c} \left\{ F \left[\frac{p}{2} + \frac{g(p, p^*, d)}{2} + \frac{cd}{2} \right] - F(p) \right\},$$

where

$$g(p, p^*, d) - cd < p < g(p, p^*, d) + cd$$

as otherwise the no-mill-price-undercutting assumption would be violated. Now allow free entry. A potential entrant's anticipated demand function, Q^N, when he contemplates locating mid way between two existing firms both of which charge p^* is

$$Q^N = \frac{2}{c} \left\{ F \left[\frac{p}{2} + \frac{g(p, p^*, d/2)}{2} + \frac{cd}{4} \right] - F(p) \right\},$$

where again, no-mill-price-undercutting implies that

$$g \left(p, p^*, \frac{d}{2} \right) + \frac{cd}{2} > p > g \left(p, p^*, \frac{d}{2} \right) - \frac{cd}{4}.$$

Since[5]

$$\frac{p}{2} + \frac{g(p, p^*, d)}{2} + \frac{cd}{2} > \frac{p}{2} + \frac{g(p, p^*, d/2)}{2} + \frac{cd}{4},$$

and, since $F(p)$ both increases with g and with distance for a given p, a comparison between Q and Q^N reveals that

$$Q > Q^N.$$

In other words, the entrant's anticipated demand curve lies to the *left* of the demand curve that existing firms face. Hence, even if the latter make pure profits (so that the demand curve they face lies above their long-run average total cost at p^*), if the entrant's anticipated demand curve lies wholly below this average cost curve, as in figure 8.2, entry will not take place.

Eaton and Lipsey have indicated by means of an example that the pure profit earned by existing firms may be as high as twice the normal rate of return on capital without attracting entry. Furthermore, the result has also been shown to hold in alternative models such as that of a circular market (Schmalensee, 1978) and in the Lancaster-type (multi-characteristic product-space) framework (Archibald and Rosenbluth, 1975).

It is important to note that the shift in demand that makes potential entrants' anticipated demand smaller than that of existing firms is not peculiar to the location models used in this section. What localisation

Figure 8.2

does is to magnify the shift by producing a 'crowding effect'. Under Chamberlinian symmetric preferences, which gives rise to multi-brand competition, a new firm entering the market will expect to pick up some sales from *all* existing firms. Thus its entry will only produce small shifts in the demand curve facing any one of the existing firms.

8.3 Brand proliferation and entry deterrence

8.3.1 The strategy of brand proliferation

It should be clear that the result that we have obtained above relies on the assumption that firms have to incur sunk costs and that this makes them relatively immobile. Whilst we assumed that *all* fixed costs are sunk, this is not essential for the result to hold. The point is that, for as long as *some* costs are sunk, an entry barrier is created and the effect of this is magnified by localised competition. Another implication of localisation when combined with the existence of some sunk costs should be fairly evident from the discussion of the previous section. This is that firms may employ the strategy of product introduction to fill up the characteristics space and use this as an entry-deterring device. We shall discuss this using the circular-market model employed by Schmalensee (1978) in his study of the US ready-to-eat breakfast cereal industry.[6]

Schmalensee considers the case of n firms, each producing a single brand and located at a distance of $1/n$ apart around the unit circumference circle (the latter assumption is important and we return to it below). He assumes that a firm's demand function takes the form

$$Q(p, n) = a(p)b(n); \quad a'(p), \ b'(n) < 0. \tag{8.12}$$

In other words, as in Eaton and Lipsey, demand is decreasing in price and the number of firms. Assuming again a constant marginal cost m and a fixed cost F, profits are

$$\pi(p, n) = (p - m)Q - F = A(p)b(n) - F, \tag{8.13}$$

where

$$A(p) = (a(p))(p - m). \tag{8.14}$$

For a given p, let $\bar{n}$ be the solution to the equation

$$\pi(p, n) = 0$$

so that, $\pi(p, n) \geqslant 0$, for $n \leqslant \bar{n}$. A price-matching potential entrant who is contemplating location mid-way between two existing firms, both of which are charging a price of p, will anticipate a profit of $\pi(p, 2n)$. This is because the distance between it and its two neighbours will be half of that between existing firms (who are assumed completely immobile). There are two interesting implications to note:

(i) First, it is worth noting that, for as long as $\bar{n}/2 < n < \bar{n}$, all existing firms can earn positive profit (since $n < \bar{n}$ and π is decreasing in n) whilst entry is unattractive to potential entrants (since $2n > \bar{n}$). That is, as in the Eaton and Lipsey (1978) model examined in the previous section, there exists the possibility of positive pure profit in equilibrium under conditions of free entry.

(ii) This gives rise to another possibility. That of brand proliferation serving as an optimal strategy for entry deterrence. To see this assume that existing firms collude and maximise their joint profits with respect to both price and the number of brands on offer.[7] That is, they

$$\underset{n,p}{\text{Max}}[n\pi(p, n)] = \underset{n,p}{\text{max}}[nA(p)b(n) - nF] \tag{8.15}$$

subject to

$$\pi(p, 2n) = A(p)b(2n) - F \leqslant 0. \tag{8.16}$$

Let the *unconstrained* maximisation of (8.15) have a solution indicated by (n^m, p^m). There are now two cases. Either in the post-entry equilibrium anticipated by a potential entrant

$$\pi(p, 2n^m) \leqslant 0, \tag{8.17}$$

in which case optimal number of brands n^* is

$$n^* = n^m$$

(that is, entry is blockaded), *or else*, (8.17) does not hold. In the latter case the number of brands that will deter entry will be greater than n^m. Now, given that n^m does not deter entry so that $\pi(p, 2n^m) > 0$, there will exist some k, where k is an integer greater than or equal to unity, that satisfies

$$\pi(p, 2^k n^m) > 0 > \pi(p, 2^{k+1} n^m). \tag{8.18}$$

This then says that $(2^k n^m)$ is the maximum number of brands consistent with positive profit in equilibrium (hence, it can be thought of as the equilibrium number of brands if no entry deterrence is practised). Now, let existing firms produce a number of brands n^d such that

$$2^k n^m \leqslant 2n^d < 2^{k+1} n^m \tag{8.19}$$

and for which

$$\pi(p, 2n^d) = 0. \tag{8.20}$$

Clearly n^d is the value of n that maximises (8.15) subject to (8.16); that is the entry-deterring value of n. Now, if $n = n^d$, entry is deterred (since entrants anticipate earning $\pi(p, 2n^d)$) and profit per existing brand will be (given that $p = p^d$ maximises (8.15) subject to (8.16))

$$\pi(p^d, n^d)$$

If, on the other hand, entry is allowed, profit per brand will be

$$\pi(p, 2^k n^m)$$

which is less than $\pi(p^d, n^d)$ since, from the second inequality (8.19), $n^d < 2^k n^m$ and an increase in the number of firms must reduce profit (in the absence of collusion between existing firms and new entrants). That is brand proliferation, involving the production of a number of brands that deters entry, $n^d > n^m$, is the optimal strategy of the existing joint-profit-maximising firms. Clearly, what generates this result is the assumption that, because of the sunk nature of location costs, entrants consider the location of existing brands as fixed and that, given this, the anticipated profits of a potential entrant depend upon $2n$ brands whilst those of the existing firms depends only upon n brands.

8.3.2 Is brand proliferation the best credible entry-deterrence strategy?

We need to turn now to a more careful examination of some assumptions in the above analysis. First, we consider the assumption that firms do not relocate in the event of entry. The obvious question to ask is whether the threat not to relocate is a *credible* threat to potential entrants (that is, a threat that existing firms will have an ex-post incentive to fulfil)?

In order to determine the conditions under which this will be the case suppose that a fraction $\lambda, 0 < \lambda \leqslant 1$, of the fixed cost is sunk in location-specific investments (e.g. marketing a product with specific characteristics) and has to be re-incurred in the event of relocation. It follows then that $(1 - \lambda)F$ of these costs are recoverable on exit. Furthermore, assume for the moment that an existing brand will, in the event of entry, either relocate or stay where it is (i.e. it doesn't exit the market). With n such that $\bar{n}/2 < n < \bar{n}, n \geqslant 2$, it is assumed that, if existing firms relocate, a potential entrant would be able to enter without making any losses. The question is, will it pay them to relocate?

Since the existing firms are assumed to act collusively it is convenient to think of them as a multi-product monopolist. Let the capitalised value of the stream of revenues over variable costs *per brand* of this multi-product monopolist be R^l if no brands are relocated and R^s in the new symmetric equilibrium if they do relocate. Clearly $R^s > R^l$. (The assumption that it pays to enter were the monopolist to relocate his brands means that $R^s > \lambda F$). By relocating a brand the monopolist recovers $(1 - \lambda)F$, so his commitment to the present location is $R^l - (1 - \lambda)F$. This we assume to be positive. On the event of entry, on the other hand, by not relocating the firm foregoes a stream of $R^s - \lambda F$. Thus it does not pay to relocate if

$$R^l - (1 - \lambda)F > R^s - \lambda F$$

or if

$$F(2\lambda - 1) > R^s - R^l. \tag{8.2}$$

This is more likely to hold the larger is F and, for a given F, the closer λ is to unity. Notice that, with all fixed costs sunk, (8.21) reduces to the condition $F > R^s - R^l$. For, as long as (8.21) holds, the potential entrant will regard the present location of existing firms as fixed.

Now given that (8.21) holds, the prospective entrant's present value of expected profit stream is $R^e - \lambda F$, where R^e cannot exceed R^l.[8] Thus, it is sufficient for entry to be deterred that (8.21) holds *and*

$$R^l - \lambda F < 0$$

holds. With $\lambda = 1$ this says that, for credible entry deterrence, F must be such that $F \geqslant \max[R^l, R^s - R^l]$.

8.4 Exit costs

The analysis in the last section implicitly assumed that establishing a brand involves an irreversible decision, or, that the costs of exit are prohibitively high. Under this assumption the only alternatives facing the monopolist, were entry to take place, are to maintain the locations of existing brands unchanged or else relocate and produce the same number again in competition with the entrant. However, as Judd (1985) has noted, in practice exit costs may be very low, and then it may pay the monopolist to *withdraw* some of his brands from the market in the event of entry.

Judd constructs examples in which the strategy of proliferating brands so as to deter entry is not an equilibrium in the relevant four-stage entry game. This is a game in which in stage 1 the incumbent decides how many brands to produce, in stage 2 an entrant decides whether or not and where to enter, in stage 3 the two firms simultaneously make their exit choices and in stage 4 they finally compete for custom in the market. The main point raised by his analysis is that one must pay careful attention to the fact that a multi-product firm's optimal response to entry must take into account the effect that such entry has on *all* its products rather than just on the ones directly competing with that introduced by the entrant. If the firm produces a range of substitute products (e.g. along the circular market) then entry will lead to a loss of sales and profits on the goods neighbouring the entrant *and*, if the firm responds by lowering the price of these products, on the goods neighbouring the latter two. This effect will be stronger the more crowded the existing goods are. In such a case, the existing firm may find it best to *remove* from the market one of the goods that is closest to the entrant, thus easing competition with him, and so reducing the detrimental effects of this competition on the rest of its product range. The incentive to do so will be greatest when *exit costs* are low (as one may reasonably assume them to be).

In order to make this argument clearer it may be helpful to use one of Judd's examples. A constant unit variable, and hence marginal, cost is assumed. Suppose that the entrant locates next to one of the brands of the existing firm and that there is Bertrand competition post entry. Denote by i the brand facing direct competition from the entrant and by l and j the brands neighbouring it. In the event of entry, profits on i drop to zero.

Simultaneously, the drop in the price of i depresses profits on l and j. If, on the other hand, the incumbent removes or relocates brand i the price of i will rise and so will the profits earned on l and j. In this case of intense post-entry competition, it is unlikely that (8.15) will hold. Furthermore, if it is also the case that by removing i the incumbent can, in the post-entry equilibrium, earn more profits net of exit costs than he could by maintaining i but relocating it (so incurring relocation costs of $R^s - \lambda F$ per brand), then it will be best to remove i and, knowing this, it is optimal for the entrant to enter. This in turn implies that using brand proliferation to deter entry will not be a perfect-foresight equilibrium in the four-stage game described above. As this example implies, the circumstances where removal of a brand is preferred to relocation are likely to arise when exit costs are low, brands are close substitutes and entry results in intense head-to-head competition.[9]

8.5 Product specification as an alternative entry-deterrence strategy

Another of the assumptions of Schmalensee's analysis that requires re-examination is that brands are located symmetrically at distances $1/n$ apart and that, on entry, new firms charge the same price as that of existing brands. Because of these assumptions the issues of location choice and price competition are not explicitly treated. However, with location choice endogenous and assuming that entry is not blockaded, it may pay the incumbent monopolist to deter entry by strategically locating brands in product space rather than by introducing an excessive number of brands. This result has been shown recently by Bonanno (1987) and has also been highlighted by Neven (1987).

Bonanno uses a version of the Hotelling model that we discussed in chapter 2 in which firms locate on a linear market of unit length. To do so they must incur a positive sunk entry cost of K.[10] He considers the perfect equilibrium of the following three-stage game. In stage 1 a monopolist decides on how many 'stores' to open and at what locations; in stage 2 an entrant decides whether and where to enter and in stage 3 firms engage in Bertrand-Nash competition. He shows that for a range of values of the sunk entry cost (not high enough to blockade entry but not too low either), whilst entry deterrence is optimal for the incumbent, product proliferation is not the best means of achieving it. For the range of values of sunk costs that he considers, a *protected* monopolist would open two stores at locations $\frac{1}{4}$ and $\frac{3}{4}$. However, if we allow for entry, an entrant would then find it profitable to enter and locate at one end point of the market as he will then be facing competition from just one store. To deter entry the monopolist can either introduce a number n ($\geqslant 3$) of stores *or* else locate its two stores more towards the extremes of the market. The latter is more profitable because, even though it involves sub-optimal locations, the loss of profits due to this is less than the extra cost of K required to introduce another store. On the other hand, for even smaller values of K, the product specification strategy fails to deter entry and, to achieve that, the monopolist will have to resort to product proliferation.

Neven's analysis of the problem involves numerical simulation of the effect of allowing sequential entry in a Hotelling model on the resulting product location pattern. He considers two scenarios: one in which the eventual number of entrants is exogenous and known and the other, a simultaneous location equilibrium, in which the number of entrants is endogenously determined by the level of fixed costs.

In the first of these, the equilibrium pattern of firm/product locations becomes ever more symmetric as the number increases. A feature of the simulation results is that 'early' entrants select their locations to ensure that 'later' entrants locate closer to the boundary of the market. While equilibrium prices and profits fall with entry, there remains an advantage to 'pioneering' brands: profits are systematically related to the order of entry with the first entrant earning more than the second, the second more than the third, and so on.

In the second scenario, Neven's purpose is to examine the role of location as a strategic variable in entry deterrence. He does this by exploring the effect of reducing brand-specific fixed cost on the equilibrium number of firms/products and their locations. (Relocation is costless after entry.) For any given number of firms, there is a level of fixed costs above which their choice of location is unaffected by the prospect of entry and corresponds to those they would choose under the first scenario. He then finds that, if fixed costs are reduced below this, these firms will relocate more towards the centre of the market and the equilibrium is one in which he finds an increasing density of firms towards the centre.

8.6 Market preemption in expanding markets

Whilst above we described situations where entry deterrence via brand proliferation may be used to ensure that existing firms with first-mover advantages earn positive profits in a static market, brand proliferation may also be used, to the same effect, to preempt the entry of rivals where the latter is made possible by exogenous market growth. This is the last issue we shall look at in this chapter. It is an aspect that has been analysed by Eaton and Lipsey (1979).

To summarise their argument, assume that an increase in consumer density, anticipated by all firms currently inside or outside the market, is to take place at some future date T_2. This increase is assumed to be such that existing market gaps will then be insufficient to deter entry (that is, given present locations, prospective entrants' demand curves will become such, at T_2, as to enable them to enter profitably the market). Under free competition, entry into the market will occur at a date T_1 ($< T_2$) such that 'the present discounted value of losses from T_1 to T_2 exactly equal the present discounted value of the profits to be earned from T_2 onwards' (Eaton and Lipsey, 1979, p. 84).

Now, assume that in the market there is currently only one firm and consider this firm's response. If it does not preempt entry by building additional plants just before T_1, new firms will enter at T_1 and the stream of profits and sales from its current plant will fall abruptly at T_1. Let post-entry industry profits be π^E and the profits of the existing monopolist (post-entry) be π_m^E. The assumption that entry takes place at T_1 with T_1 defined as above implies that $\pi^E = \pi_m^E$ (entrants earn zero profits). If, on the other hand, the monopolist preempts potential entrants and establishes the plants just before T_1 it can anticipate earning monopoly profits of π_m. Its incentive to preempt is $\pi_m - \pi_m^E$ which must be positive in the absence of collusion with new firms. Thus preemption is the optimal strategy, even though the new capacity remains unused until T_2.

9 The gains from trade under product differentiation

9.1 Introduction

In addition to its impact on the economics of industrial organisation, the theory that we have looked at in the previous eight chapters has had important implications for international economics. Until recently, the theory of international trade has used either the perfect competition or the pure monopoly model. However, the last few years have seen efforts to base it on a model of imperfect competition. Thus a suitable way of closing this study of the economic theory of product differentiation seemed to be to use this last chapter to give the reader a flavour of this important and rapidly growing literature dealing with international trade under imperfect competition. This is not a book about international trade and so inevitably our treatment will be a little selective. However, what we shall endeavour to do is to highlight the different routes through which trade under product differentiation may increase potential social welfare. In other words, our concern will be to discuss the *gains* from trade rather than the positive theory of trade (the latter dealing with the volume, composition and pattern of trade), or the theory of trade policy. The reader who is interested in a thorough discussion of these other topics should refer to Helpman and Krugman (1985), Kierzkowski (1984) or, for a very useful informal survey, to Venables (1985).

There are a number of ways or mechanisms through which trade under imperfect competition may lead to an increase in welfare. It may do so by increasing market size, so making markets more competitive. Another possibility is that it may enable firms to exploit more fully economies of scale in production or marketing. A third possibility is that it may result in an increase in the number of product varieties that are available. Equally plausible is the possibility that it may increase firms' marginal returns from R&D thus providing the incentive to introduce superior quality products. In what follows we shall use the models of product differentiation that we discussed in chapters 3 and 6 to provide simple analytical explanations of how these mechanisms may operate. The study of the welfare-improving effects of trade does not only deal with the case of differentiated products; Venables (1985, pp. 17–23) has also examined them for the case of *homogeneous* imperfectly competitive markets. Here, with free entry, trade has a pro-competitive effect that leads to a reduction in equilibrium price-cost margins. This benefits consumers, whilst the zero-profit condition implies that producers are unaffected. This mechanism is in contrast to that which we describe below when we show the way in which trade improves welfare in vertically differentiated markets.

9.2 The gains from trade under horizontal product differentiation

In this section we shall use a slightly modified version of the model of imperfect competition that was developed in section 2 of chapter 3 to show that, under horizontal product differentiation, a country's welfare may be increased when such products are introduced by trade, even though there may not be international differences in tastes, technology or factor endowments. The only difference between the present model and the model in chapter 3 is that here we introduce factors of production.

We consider a two-sector economy. The first sector is a perfectly competitive one in which a homogeneous numeraire commodity is being produced under constant returns to scale. The second is a monopolistically competitive sector composed of n firms, each producing a distinct brand, the output of which is denoted by x_i, $i = 1, \ldots, n$. There is a population of L consumers-workers whose (wage) income is denoted by w. So aggregate expenditure is wL. We assume that only one factor, labour, is used. The labour input requirement for producing the differentiated product i is

$$l_i = F + \beta x_i; \quad \beta > 0, \tag{9.1}$$

where F is the fixed labour input. Thus, marginal cost is equal to $w\beta$ for all differentiated products.

The representative consumer's preferences for the differentiated products are described by the homothetic sub-utility function

$$V = \left[\sum_{i=1}^{n} x_i^{\sigma - 1/\sigma} \right]^{\sigma/\sigma - 1}, \tag{9.2}$$

where $1 < \sigma < \infty$ (σ being the elasticity of substitution between any two of the industry's products). As noted in chapter 3, we can think of a consumer as first maximising $U = x_0^{1-s} V^s$, subject to $x_0 + qV = w$, where q is the 'price index' corresponding to V (which implies that $qV=sw$, $0<s<1$), and then maximising (9.2) subject to[1]

$$sw=y=\sum_{i=1}^{n} p_i x_i.$$

This second maximisation problem we found gave rise to the following demand equations

$$x_i=\frac{Y}{p_1^{\sigma} A}, \quad i-1,\ldots,n, \tag{9.3}$$

where $Y=yL$ and $A=\Sigma_{i=1}^{n} p_i^{1-\sigma}$. Thus, in a symmetric situation, with $p_i=p$, and $x_i=x$, the elasticity of demand will be

$$\eta=\sigma-\left(\frac{\sigma-1}{n}\right)$$

or, under monopolistic competition (see chapter 3, section 3)[2]

$$\eta=\sigma. \tag{9.4}$$

Using (9.4) and the first-order profit-maximisation condition that

$$p\left(1-\frac{1}{\eta}\right)=w\beta,$$

gives

$$p^*=w\beta\left(\frac{\sigma}{\sigma-1}\right) \tag{9.5}$$

as the monopolistically competitive equilibrium price. From the demand function (9.3), and in a symmetric equilibrium, $x=Y/np$, or $x=[sL(\sigma-1)/\sigma n\beta]$. If we now use the zero-profit equilibrium condition that

$$(p-w\beta)x=wF,$$

we obtain the monopolistically competitive equilibrium level of n as

$$n^*=\frac{sL}{\sigma F}. \tag{9.6}$$

Substituting back, it follows that

$$x^*=\frac{(\sigma-1)F}{\beta}. \tag{9.7}$$

Now, in a symmetric equilibrium, the utility function of the representative consumer can be written as

$$V = n^{1/\sigma - 1} x = \left(\frac{sL}{\sigma F}\right)^{1/\sigma - 1} \left(\frac{\sigma - 1}{\beta}\right) F. \qquad (9.8)$$

Suppose now that the economy that we have just described above refers to the world economy and that the domestic economy is a scaled replica of it. In other words, the domestic economy has a fraction λ, $0 < \lambda < 1$, of the world labour endowment. Furthermore assume that transport costs are zero and that there are no taxes on trade. From (9.7), the output per product in the domestic economy under autarky is the same as in the integrated (world) economy (though output per capita $(x/\lambda L)$ is greater under autarky than under free trade (x/L)). From (9.6), the number of product varieties offered under autarky, n_H, is given by

$$n_H = \frac{\lambda s L}{\sigma F},$$

and this is smaller than the number, n^*, under free trade. Using (9.8) this leads to the conclusion that the utility of all consumers is less under autarky than it is under free trade

$$V(n_H) < V(n^*).$$

The gain from free trade arises because of the fact that in the world economy each consumer gets a larger number of product varieties and a proportionately smaller amount of each variety (than under autarky) – with convex preferences each consumer prefers this. The important point is that gains from trade are seen to arise in the absence of international differences in tastes, technology or factor endowments (we may take $L_H = \frac{1}{2}L$). There is one caveat however: the homotheticity of the sub-utility function V guarantees that the ratio of consumer surplus to revenue is the same for all differentiated products and is independent of the quantity consumed. This implies that trade has an unambiguously beneficial effect as it leads to an increase in the number of product varieties. If, say imported goods have a lower consumer surplus to revenue ratio than domestically produced goods (which, with iso-elastic demands, is equivalent to having a higher elasticity of demand) then, as Venables (1985, p. 24) notes, 'trade will generally lead to the replacement of some domestic product types by imports, and may then reduce welfare'.

9.3 The gains from trade in vertically differentiated products

9.3.1 The short-run (impact) effect of trade

It was shown in chapter 6 that, in markets where products are vertically differentiated and where improvements in product qualities are not associated with large increases in unit variable costs (relative to consumers willingness to pay for such improvements), there will be an upper bound to the Bertrand–Nash equilibrium number of firms. Further it was shown that this upper bound is independent of the size of the market:[3] changes in the latter raise proportionately the sales and profits faced by all firms but do not alter equilibrium prices, or the equilibrium number of firms.

Thus the introduction of trade between two economies containing such 'natural oligopolies' will normally lead to a reduction in the total number of products offered in the new joint market. If the economies are *identical* in all respects, except perhaps size, then trade between them will lead to the elimination of products up to the point where the world economy produces the same number of products as each of the previously isolated economies.

The effect on the number of products of trade between *different* economies has been examined by Gabszewicz, Shaked, Sutton and Thisse (1981b). They show that, when two economies differing in terms of their income distribution are joined up by trade, the effect will be the elimination of some products provided the income distributions are not too dissimilar. In particular they show that, 'given two separate economies, in each of which incomes are distributed uniformly over some range $[a_i, b_i]$, $2a_i < b_i < 4a_i$, suppose each of these economies initially supports two goods and that all four goods are distinct. Then if $b_1 > b_2$, $a_1 > a_2$ and $b_1 < 2b_2$, $a_1 < 2a_2$, the combined economy supports, at most, 3 goods.' The combined income distribution that they consider is as shown in figure 9.1. Furthermore, the conditions that they postulate to hold on the income distribution imply that

$$\frac{a_1}{2} < a_2 < a_1 < \frac{b_1}{2} < b_2 < b_1. \qquad (9.9)$$

Assume now, for simplicity, that costs are zero. Then, given (9.9), the necessary conditions for profit (revenue) maximisation, $\partial R_k / \partial p_k = 0$, indicate that in equilibrium the following inequalities must hold[4]

$$y_n < \frac{b_1}{2}; \quad y_{n-1} < a_1; \quad y_{n-2} \lessgtr a_2,$$

where y_k is the income of the consumer who is indifferent between a good

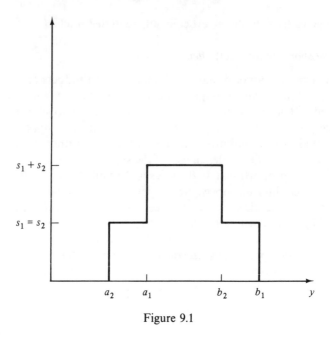

Figure 9.1

of quality q_k, offered at p_k, and that of quality q_{k-1} offered at p_{k-1}, $k=1,\ldots,n$ (see chapter 6 for details). Since y_{n-2} (the income of the consumer who is indifferent between the third- and fourth-from-top qualities) is less than or equal to a_2 (the minimum income of the combined economy), the combined economy can support at most three goods. In other words, the minimum quality previously produced is eliminated by trade.

The effect on consumers' welfare following the *elimination* of some products due to the introduction of trade is positive because of the reduction in the prices of the remaining products. It is this that actually drives the lower quality products out of the combined market. We can illustrate this effect by using the example of two economies, each supporting two qualities before trade, where trade results in the elimination of the previously lowest quality product. We assume that in the before-trade equilibrium all consumers in both economies consume one or other of the quality goods with consumers of minimum income in both countries being indifferent between consuming the low quality product offered and spending all their income on the outside good. This last good gives a utility of $q_0 y$ when income is equal to y. Let the qualities offered before trade be $q_4 > q_3 > q_2 > q_1$, with q_1 eliminated in post-trade equi-

librium. All we need to show is that the elimination of q_1 implies
a reduction in the price of q_2 that makes even consumers of income a_2 (the
lowest income in the combined economy) better off than before. Since
consumers of income $y > a_2$ can do at least as well as those of income a_2,
all consumers with income higher than a_2 must then also gain from the
change (that is, p_3 and p_4 must be also reduced).

To see that this must be the case just note that in the combined
economy, for q_1 to be eliminated, consumers must prefer q_2 to q_1 (or be at
most indifferent between them) even when the latter is offered at its unit
variable cost. Since it is assumed that this is zero for all goods, the price of
q_2, p_2^*, must, in equilibrium, be such that

$$p_2^* \leqslant \bar{p}_2,$$

where $\bar{p}_2$ is defined by[5]

$$q_1 a_2 = (a_2 - p_2) q_2. \tag{9.10}$$

In other words, consumers of income a_2 must be at most indifferent
between q_2 and q_1 when the latter is offered at a zero price. Since their
utility score before trade was $q_0 a_2$ and is now at least $q_1 a_2$, their (and thus
all other consumers') welfare in the post-trade equilibrium is increased.

It is worthwhile stressing that the improvement in consumers' welfare
following trade in the above example is purely due to the reduction in
prices in the process of competition through which lower quality products
are *eliminated* from the market. Another mechanism has often been
stressed. This can be easily described in terms of the above example by
assuming that firms operate on declining unit cost curves. Then the
rationalisation of production following the elimination of some firms will
enable surviving firms to reduce both costs and prices.

This latter mechanism can also be seen to operate when trade results in
the joining up of economies with *contestable markets*. In the latter the
condition of entry is such that incumbent firms do not make any profits,
that is, prices are equal to unit costs. Thus if, for example, a single firm
is supported by each market in the pre-trade equilibrium (natural
monopoly), the combined post-trade economy will also be supplied by
a single firm at a much lower price. However, the location of this firm and
the pattern of trade are here indeterminate when firms face identical costs.

9.3.2 The gains from trade in the long run

Whilst the impact (or short-run) effect of trade on consumers' welfare in
the case of natural oligopolies is positive due to the elimination of some
low-quality products and the reduction in the prices of the 'surviving'

products, there will be an additional positive long-run effect. This arises as the firms that 'survive' will then *increase the quality* of their products, since in the combined economy with fewer firms present, they enjoy 'greater marginal returns to (R&D) expenditure on quality improvements'.[6] This contrasts sharply with the case of horizontal product differentiation examined in the previous section where the post-trade increase in welfare was due to an increase in the number of product varieties. What this long-run effect implies is that with natural oligopolies it is exactly *due to the reduction in the number of products* that we get a positive welfare effect.

The way that we shall examine this long-run effect is by considering the example of the joining through trade of two economies whose populations are assumed to be identical in incomes and tastes; they differ only in their respective sizes. With each of the economies supporting two qualities before trade (as we are going to assume), the combined economy will also support at most two. First, we wish to show that the 'quality pair available in the combined economy dominates pairwise that which is available in either of the separated economies'.[7] Second we will show that, under certain restrictions, the welfare of all consumers is increased in the combined economy.

The first result is established by proving that in a single economy of size s supporting two products, the equilibrium quality pair (q_1, q_2) is increasing in s. The equilibrium quality pair for given s was obtained in chapter 6 (section 4). As noted there, it must generally satisfy the first-order conditions

$$\frac{\partial R_i}{\partial q_i} = \frac{F'(qi)}{s}, \quad i = 1, 2, \tag{9.11}$$

where $R_i(q_i; q_j)$; $i = 1, 2, i \neq j$, is the revenue of firm i when it produces quality q_i and its rival produces quality q_j at a Nash equilibrium in prices, and $F(q_i), F'(q_i) > 0$, is the R&D expenditure required to make possible the production of q_i. Figure 9.2 illustrates the revenue functions that we looked at in chapter 6.

Note that the case indicated in figure 9.2 will hold for as long as s is sufficiently large. Then, as in the case where $F = 0$ which was examined in chapter 6, the equilibrium low-quality choice is given by the corner solution: that is, q_1^* satisfies the equation[8]

$$v = \frac{q_2^* - q_0}{q_2^* - q_1^*} = \frac{b + a}{3a}.$$

This may be rewritten as follows

$$q_1^* = q_2^* \left(\frac{b - 2a}{b + a} \right) + q_0 \left(\frac{3a}{b + a} \right). \tag{9.12}$$

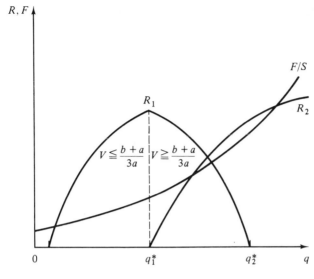

Figure 9.2

Equation (9.12) gives q_1^* as an increasing linear function of q_2^*.

Assuming that s is indeed sufficiently large so that the equilibrium pair (q_1^*, q_2^*) always satisfies equation (9.12), let us now turn to the first-order condition for profit maximisation for the high-quality good. From (9.11) this is

$$\frac{\partial R_2}{\partial q_2^*} = \frac{F'(q_2^*)}{s},$$ (9.13)

where, as noted in chapter 6, it is assumed that

$$F''(q_i) > 0.$$ (9.14)

From (9.13) and (9.14), an increase in s will increase the equilibrium quality of the higher quality product if the second partial derivative of R_2 with respect to q_2 is either negative or, if positive, always smaller than $F''(q_2)$. Our revenue function satisfies this condition provided that F is 'sufficiently convex'.[9] Given this, q_2 is increasing in s and therefore, from (9.12), the equilibrium quality of the low quality product is also increasing in s.

Having established conditions that guarantee an increase in the equilibrium values of q_2 and q_1 as s increases, we must now show that this will lead to an increase in the welfare of all consumers. To do so, first note that since q_2^* and q_1^* satisfy (9.12) (i.e., move, as s increases, so as to maintain the equality $v = (b + a/3a)$), y_2, the marginal income of the consumer who is indifferent between q_1 and q_2, remains unchanged. This is because from section 4 of chapter 6, when $v=(b+a/3a)$, we have $y_1=a$ and $y_2=1/2[b-a(v-1)]$. Thus, the firms' market shares $[(b-y_2)$ and $(y_2-a)]$ remain constant though, when $v=(b+a/3a)$, since p_1 and p_2 are given by equation (6.19) and hence are

$$p_1 = a\left(\frac{q_1 - q_0}{q_1}\right) \quad \text{and} \quad p_2 = \left(\frac{2b-a}{3}\right)\left(\frac{q_2 - q_1}{q_2}\right), \tag{9.15}$$

prices are increased. p_2 increases because, from (9.12)

$$\frac{dq_1}{dq_2} = \frac{b-2a}{b+2} < 1.$$

Thus, q_1^* does not increase as much as q_2^*.

Despite the fact that prices go up, the increase in qualities compensates for that, so the end result is that there is an increase in the welfare of every consumer. To establish this, first consider consumers of income y, $a \leqslant y \leqslant y_2$ consuming q_1 and obtaining a utility of

$$q_1(y-p_1)=q_1(y-a)+q_0 a. \tag{9.16}$$

In writing this we have taken account of the first of equations (9.15). Since this is increasing in q_1, all consumers of income $y>a$ have their utility increased, whilst those of income $y=a$ get the same utility. Next consider consumers of income y, $y_2 < y \leqslant b$ consuming q_2. They obtain utility of

$$q_2(y-p_2)=q_2(y-y_2)+q_2(y_2-p_2). \tag{9.17}$$

The first term on the right-hand side of (9.17) is increasing in q_2 (and hence in s) whilst the second term is just the utility of a consumer of income y_2 when he consumes q_2 and thus it is just equal to $q_1(y_2-p_1)$. However, this is increasing in q_1, and hence in s. So $q_2(y-p_2)$ is increasing in s. Thus the welfare of consumers of every income has been increased.

9.4 Conclusion

This concluding chapter has shown how it is that trade can lead to welfare gains for an economy when there is product differentiation even though the trading economies involved do not differ in terms of their tastes, technology or factor endowments. Under horizontal differentiation of the Chamberlinian type, this is the result of the increased variety of goods that is brought about by trade. This assumes of course that there are no adverse product-selection effects such as may arise when imported goods have a lower consumers' surplus to revenue ratio than domestic ones. When there is vertical differentiation, trade will increase welfare in the short run if it leads to the elimination of some low-quality goods because of the reduction in the prices of the higher quality goods that are available. In the long run, welfare will increase as trade increases market size and this increases the marginal return to a firm's R&D. This will then give it the incentive to introduce products of superior quality.

Notes

1 Introduction

1 Reference should be made to the work of Duncan Ironmonger (1972). This work, which is quite close in conception to Lancaster, was actually based on his Ph.D. thesis submitted to the University of Cambridge in the early 1960s.

2 Although we shall have a few comments to make about multi-product firms in this introduction, in the book proper we shall be following the approach in the literature and assuming that each differentiated product is produced by a single firm. This is a strong assumption and it is fortunate that leading theorists in industrial organisation such as Shaked and Sutton have been trying to build good models of multi-product firms.

3 Schmalensee (1982) has shown that being a pioneering brand can also confer a first-mover advantage.

4 See, for example, Helpman (1984) and Helpman and Krugman (1985).

5 Note that, if there were no product differentiation, there could be no product variety. However, differentiation and variety are not the same thing. For example, suppose that there are two products within a group and that the specification of one of them is changed so as to place it further from the other in characteristics space. It would be natural to say that while product differentiation had increased, variety had not.

2 Spatial models of imperfect competition

1 In Chamberlin-type models each brand competes with every other. In a recent paper Perloff and Salop (1985) construct a model in which there is neither a representative consumer nor localised competition. We shall look at this in chapter 7.

2 Transport costs are borne by consumers, each firm quoting a unique mill price. This practice is referred to as 'uniform mill pricing'. There are important issues of price discrimination in spatial markets but these are not our concern here. The interested reader may find a collection of papers surveying the area in the September/December 1982 issue of the *Journal of Industrial Economics*.

184

3 Of course, ensuring the continuity of demand functions is not *sufficient* to guarantee that an equilibrium will exist.

4 Note that if $\alpha = \beta$ (symmetric locations) then (2.4) reduces to the condition that $\alpha = \beta \leqslant (1/4)l$. In other words, the firms must be located outside the quartiles if we are to get a Nash equilibrium in prices.

5 If $\alpha + \beta < l$, we would also get the competitive result if transport costs were zero $(c = 0)$ – see equation (2.10). This is also a case we would want to say involved no product differentiation.

6 Salop also relaxes the assumption of perfectly inelastic demand. He assumes instead that there is an 'outside' good on which consumers spend all their income when the price of the differentiated good exceeds their reservation price. Another example along these lines, but which uses Hotelling's linear market construction, is Friedman's (1983) discussion of the work of Economides.

7 Salant (1986) has shown that in a location model in which firms enter *sequentially* and firms choose quantities rather than prices, the profit functions are quasi-concave and so an equilibrium exists. However, if location and quantity are chosen simultaneously, the profit function is not globally concave and existence remains a problem.

8 An example is Neven's (1985) model which we discuss in the next section. For an alternative early demonstration using the example of two firms located in product quality space see Prescott and Visscher (1977, pp. 386–7). As they mention, the non-existence problem was noted by both Smithies (1941) and Eaton (1976). A further way in which continuity can be restored is to assume that firms are differentiated in the eyes of consumers not just by virtue of different locations but also in terms of their inherent attributes and that consumers are heterogeneous. This means that consumers at the same location will place different valuations on different products (cf. De Palma *et al.*, 1985). Such an assumption can help to eliminate discontinuities in the demand (and profit) functions when the firms' market areas overlap. Finally, Gal-Or (1982) has shown that Hotelling's model may possess a mixed-strategy equilibrium even when a pure strategy equilibrium fails to exist.

9 The same framework can be used to look at the existence of equilibrium in the market for a vertically differentiated good.

10 As elsewhere in this chapter, we are assuming (unless otherwise stated) Nash behaviour. As we shall note below, much of the literature in this area uses alternative solution concepts.

11 See also Prescott and Visscher (1977, pp. 385–8), for another proof of equilibrium in prices and locations in a model with two firms. d'Aspremont *et al.* (1983) generalise their earlier (1979) result by showing that 'under mild assumptions the principle never holds in Hotelling's model if prices adapt themselves in a non-cooperative equilibrium' (p. 20).

12 It implies that marginal utility cost is increasing. For a more extensive discussion of (2.11) see Neven (1985, p. 320).

13 This seems the most appropriate equilibrium concept given the interdepen-

dence of price-location choices. The concept of perfect equilibrium is also discussed and used in chapter 6. See also Neven (1985, pp. 322–3).

14 This point is made by Eaton (1972, p. 269), who attributes it to Lerner and Singer (1937). Eaton and Lipsey (1975) use Hotelling's zero conjectural variation (ZCV) assumption to discuss locational equilibrium for $n > 2$. They find that none exists when $n = 3$ but that it does exist for $n > 3$. Shaked (1982) shows that a Nash locational equilibrium exists for $n = 3$ if firms use mixed strategies.

15 As an alternative to this multi-stage Nash equilibrium concept (and to the multi-stage equilibrium concept to be discussed below) some authors have used a modified ZCV assumption. Novshek (1980) uses a 'no mill-price-undercutting' assumption: 'each firm believes that no other firm will allow itself to be undersold at its own location and that other firms will reduce price if they are undercut at their own locations'. This is used to prove the existence of equilibrium in prices and locations for a circular market. Kohlberg and Novshek (1982) do the same for a bounded linear market in which consumers have linear (rather than Hotelling's perfectly inelastic) demands and where the total market length is 'sufficiently large' relative to the number of firms.

16 In practice, solving for an asymmetric Nash equilibrium in prices is very cumbersome when $n > 2$ and soon becomes unmanageable.

17 They use a model of a one-dimensional market. It has also been used by Lane (1980) for the case of a two-dimensional market to show the existence of a unique equilibrium in product specifications and prices in which firms will charge different prices and produce products with different characteristics. The same concept was also independently used by Hay (1976) in a study of entry deterrence (see chapter 8). Notice too the similarity in terms of sequential entry with the analysis of Salant (1986).

18 The ability to deter entry depends here on the assumption that relocation is prohibitively costly. This will be examined in more detail in chapter 8.

19 The assumptions of this argument can be reversed: firms, rather than consumers, having imperfect information about the spatial distribution of demand. The same conclusions follow. See Graitson (1982) and the references cited therein.

20 See the articles by Capozza and van Order (1978), Eaton (1976), Eaton and Lipsey (1978), Eaton and Wooders (1985), Holahan (1978), Lane (1980), Novshek (1980), Prescott and Visscher (1977) and Salop (1979).

21 We deal with this issue in depth in chapter 8. Much of the literature does not use spatial models. The exceptions are Eaton and Wooders (1985), Novshek (1980) and Shaked and Sutton (1987).

22 References here are the papers by Eaton and Lipsey (1978, 1979), Hay (1976), Lane (1980), Judd (1985) and Schmalensee (1978).

23 In this chapter we outline its features, its comparative statics and its welfare implications. We compare the last of these with those of the 'representative consumer' model in chapter 4. Authors have sought to establish the existence of a deterrence equilibrium by relaxing the assumption of costless relocation in this class of model.

24 As noted in the previous section, one may argue that for any given number of
   firms involved in a two-stage location-price game, symmetric locations are
   optimal Nash locations if, at the last stage, Nash price equilibria are
   anticipated. See also our discussion of Eaton and Lipsey (1978) in chapter 8.

25 All of this implies that consumers are homogeneous inasmuch as they have the
   same valuation of their ideal brand and obtain the same utility from spending
   their (identical) incomes on the outside good.

26 It is of interest to compare this kinked demand curve with that of Sweezy
   (1939). In this case the kink is explained by the existence of the outside good
   even though symmetric 'Nash' conjectures are assumed.

27 As we shall show below, the competitive equilibrium price is equal to
   $[m+(c/n)]$. Thus the price at which the discontinuity in demand occurs is less
   than the constant marginal cost and will therefore never be chosen when there
   are fixed costs around (it may be chosen if marginal costs are decreasing). For
   this reason we have omitted this section of the demand curve in figure 2.13.

28 Totally differentiating (2.29) shows that an increase in m or F will reduce n^k if
   $[cL/2(n^k)^2] < F$. Since $n^m < n^k$ and $[cL/2(n^m)^2] = F$, we can see from (2.26) that
   this condition holds.

29 From (2.29), the effect of an increase in v is exactly the opposite to that of an
   increase in m.

3 Symmetric preferences, the Chamberlinian paradigm

1 Archibald and Rosenbluth (1975) have argued that 'neighbouring effects' are
   likely to be very small if the dimensionality of the characteristics space is large.
   Indeed, with four or more characteristics, a brand may have a large number of
   direct competitors so that the effects of its actions may no longer be localised.

2 See E.H. Chamberlin (1933), *The Theory of Monopolistic Competition*, chapter
   V.

3 The assumption of a fixed and finite size of market underlies both some 'spatial'
   (e.g. Lancaster, 1979, Salop, 1979) and 'symmetric preference' (e.g. Spence,
   1976a,b) models of imperfect competition.

4 It is not always the case that, in the limit, one gets monopolistic rather than
   perfect competition. A point we shall emphasise below is that a major aim in
   the analysis is to explore under what circumstances one or other of these
   limiting equilibria arises.

5 This approach is gradually beginning to be superseded by a properly imperfectly competitive analysis. See, for example, E. Helpman and P. Krugman
   (1985), *Market Structure and Foreign Trade*, Wheatsheaf.

6 A recent paper by Ireland (1985) makes it necessary to comment on and make
   explicit another of the assumptions in our model. We assume that firms are
   risk-neutral. Ireland introduces uncertainty about demand in a Chamberlinian
   model. This has the effect of reducing industry output but its impact on the
   number of firms and hence output per firm is ambiguous. An interesting
   implication of this is that if the welfare loss due to the reduction in industry
   supply because of uncertainty is small then the presence of uncertainty may

actually increase expected net welfare if it results in a more efficient scale of firm because there are fewer firms in equilibrium. This might be expected to occur when products are fairly homogeneous and when there are substantial economies of scale.

7 This follows the treatment in the papers by Spence (1976a), Dixit and Stiglitz (1977) and Koenker and Perry (1981). In Hart (1985a, 1985b), Perloff and Salop (1983) and Sattinger (1984) there is no representative consumer. In Hart, a consumer only likes m ($1 < m < n$) brands, whilst in the latter two papers, each consumer is assumed to like *every* brand.

8 Note too that, in spatial models, the entry of new firms leads to increased congestion in the commodity space and one is likely, in the limit, to get competitive results. This is not the case here. Congestion doesn't increase because the numbers of commodities and characteristics are of the same order of magnitude. (See Dixit and Stiglitz's 'Reply' to Pettengill's 'Comment', *American Economic Review*, 69(5), December 1979, pp. 961–3 and 955–60 respectively).

9 For a discussion of the consequences of using alternative assumptions, see Koenker and Perry (1981) and Yarrow (1985). We shall consider this issue briefly in chapter 4.

10 $\dfrac{\partial q}{\partial p_i} = \dfrac{1}{n^{\sigma/\sigma - 1}}\left[1 + \sum_{i \neq j} \dfrac{dp_j}{dp_i}(p_i/p_j)^\sigma\right].$

11 A free-entry equilibrium is defined by the condition that no existing firm gets negative profits and no potential entrant anticipates earning positive profits were it to enter.

4 Product diversity and product selection: market equilibria and social optima

1 Spence (1976b, p. 408).

2 Recall that net surplus is equal to gross surplus less total costs. Thus net surplus is the sum of consumers' surplus and profits.

3 Here we shall concentrate on the case of substitutes. A discussion of complements can be found in Spence (1976b, section 3). He shows there that in the (Nash) market equilibrium, it is a case of 'too little and too few'.

4 A lucid discussion of these issues can be found in Lancaster (1979, chapter 1). He notes that the conflict between variety and efficiency may lead to an *equity* problem. Think back to the location model and suppose that, on social welfare grounds, it was decided to improve efficiency by reducing variety. Some consumers will lose less than others because brands that disappear may be far from their ideal brand. In the representative consumer case here, everyone loses equally and no equity issue arises.

5 Other early discussions of the issues in this chapter are Kaldor (1935) and Bishop (1967).

6 We are referring here to the large-group equilibrium, Chamberlin's distinctive

contribution. Chamberlin used the standard monopoly and oligopoly models to analyse the small-group case.

7 This is in contrast to what may happen to oligopoly; see Yarrow (1985).
8 Dixit and Stiglitz (1977, p. 304).
9 This case has been examined by Mankiw and Whinston (1986). They also discuss product diversity. Their results for the latter are in line with the results reported in later sections of this chapter.
10 Mankiw and Whinston (1986, p. 49).
11 See, in addition, the interchange between Pettengill (1979) and Dixit and Stiglitz (1979). This did not affect the conclusions that we have discussed above.
12 He also compares the oligopoly solution with the optimum.
13 On this, see Koenker and Perry (1981, pp. 224–6), and Yarrow (1985, pp. 521–3).
14 See Salop (1979, p. 142).
15 Note that the lower an indifference curve, the higher the level of welfare.
16 See, for example, Waterson (1984, p. 9).
17 See also Spence (1976a, p. 409).
18 Spence notes that these examples indicate that 'it is not exactly elasticity that matters, but rather what fraction of net potential surplus for a product is capturable' and that this depends upon 'both the structure of demand and costs'. (Spence 1976a, p. 410).
19 Spence (1976a, p. 410). A similar argument is given by Dixit and Stiglitz (1977, p. 307), where they note that it provides an 'economic reason why the market will lead to a bias against opera relative to football matches and a subsidisation of the former and a tax on the latter, provided the distribution of income is optimum'. A more complete and rigorous analysis of the results of this subsection can be found in Dixit and Stiglitz.

5 Product quality and market structure

1 This assumes that the cost of improving the quality of a good depends on the rate of output. For example, it may be more difficult to maintain quality standards (such as design tolerances) at high output than at low output rates. However, when dealing with vertically differentiated goods, as we do in chapter 7, the focus is on the cost of quality being a fixed cost. This implies $c_{xq}=0$.
2 The gross surplus from a good was defined earlier in equation (5.3).

6 Vertical product differentiation

1 This has been shown for this case by Gabszewicz and Thisse (1986).
2 The lower bound on income has to be strictly positive. This is needed to ensure that there is no consumer who is indifferent between alternative products when they are offered for sale at unit variable cost.
3 A rigorous proof of this is given in Shaked and Sutton (1987). Their Proposition 1 says that in horizontal markets, given some market share $m > 0$,

there exists an economy size (S^*) such that all firms' market shares will be less than m for $S > S^*$ in a price equilibrium in which inside firms earn non-negative profits net of all costs and outside firms find it optimal to stay out. To prove this they first show that an increase in market size involves a reduction in 'distance' between firms. The question of whether or not there is convergence to perfect or monopolistic competition as the size of the economy increases is examined in chapter 7.

4 A complete analysis can be found in Shaked and Sutton (1982b) where the firms' optimal decisions concerning entry, quality choice and price are examined as part of a three-stage game. In this firms decide first on whether to enter, then on the quality of their product and finally on their price. The idea behind this is that these are decisions whose costs are decreasing. While price can be varied at will, modifying a product's specification is a more complex matter and entry requires someone to actually construct a plant.

5 For an analysis that uses a more general utility function see Gabszewicz, Shaked, Sutton and Thisse (1981).

6 A formal proof under the assumptions above of the existence of a Nash equilibrium in prices when n distinct qualities are on offer is given in Shaked and Sutton (1983, pp. 1475–6).

7 In a slightly more general model this would be a more complex expression involving both c_n and c_{n-1}.

8 The choice of quality is considered in section 4.

9 In studying perfect equilibria attention is limited to strategies that do *not* involve threats that the firms have, *ex post*, no incentive to fulfil. A non-technical discussion can be found in Dixit (1982, p. 13) or van Damme (1985).

10 Of course this is equivalent to requiring that no consumer attains a maximum *or* a minimum of utility by choosing q such that $\underline{q} < q < \bar{q}$. When this condition is satisfied all consumers will rank qualities in the same order.

11 See Shaked and Sutton (1983, p. 1481).

12 A similar result has been obtained by Gal-Or (1985) who considered the case of an industry where firms simultaneously choose quality level and *output*. In the Cournot–Nash equilibrium firms choose distinct qualities.

13 See Shaked and Sutton (1982b, p. 30) for a precise statement of how close q_0 and $\bar{q}$ need to be. The closeness of these two goods implies that consumers only spend a small fraction of their incomes on the quality goods.

14 See Baumol, Panzar and Willig (1982).

15 The existing literature on vertical differentiation has not yet been able to provide a way to predict the level of concentration. However it does seem fairly clear that by placing stronger restrictions on $F(q)$ and by specifying particular utility functions one could deduce stronger results as to the level of concentration.

7 Product differentiation and market imperfection: limit theorems

1 Hart (1979, pp. 1–2).

2 Roberts (1980) has also shown that the limit points of monopolistic competi-

tion cannot be restricted to perfectly competitive equilibria, although perfectly competitive equilibria are limit points. Also, Wolinsky (1986) has shown that Hart's conditions can arise when consumers have imperfect information.

3 This restriction is needed in the example but is not needed by the functions in Hart's general proof.

4 For example, see Mas-Colell (1975, p. 263).

5 It is assumed that $nM(n)$ is increasing in n. However, this may not always be the case for $M(n)$ itself.

6 This condition guarantees that the demand curve approaches the price axis fast enough to ensure that in every symmetric equilibrium firms locally perceive a flat dd curve.

7 See also chapter 3, section 3.

8 Recall that F is fixed cost.

9 The distance that minimises the total resource cost of meeting consumers' perfectly inelastic demand.

10 $(L^e/L^*) < 1$ implies *excessive* diversity.

11 This argument is due to Hart. See Hart (1985a, p. 530).

12 The natural question is to ask what it is that places this limit on the brands considered. Wolinsky (1986) shows that this can arise when consumers have imperfect information. His analysis allows for the cost that consumers face in searching out the price and valuation of any brand. He shows that, in the limit, price is bounded away from marginal cost by a magnitude that depends on the cost of information.

13 Notice that we have assumed that the constant equals unity for the sake of simplicity of exposition. This normalisation is not essential.

14 See Hart (1985b, p. 899).

15 The right-hand side is the revenue obtained *if* the share had been ϵ and *if* every buyer had paid Y^+.

16 Shaked and Sutton call these 'fragmented' markets.

8 Product differentiation and the entry process

1 One should be careful here to distinguish between brand proliferation (filling the product space with additional products) and an increase in product differentiation (a reduction in substitutability between existing products). The latter will tend to make entry *easier*. This point has been made by Eaton and Lipsey (1978) and Dixit (1979).

2 For details, see chapter 2, section 2.

3 See chapter 2, footnote 15.

4 See their appendix, p. 468.

5 Recall that g is non-decreasing in d.

6 Neven, Matutes and Corstjens (1988) consider brand proliferation in a Hotelling model. They find that in this model it is always profitable for the incumbent to deter entry by brand proliferation. Moreover they also find that the equilibrium is one in which the brands that are most exposed to entry

competition are strategically used as 'fighting brands'. Their results thus suggest that the Schmalensee analysis is of more general applicability.

7 Implicit in this discussion is the assumption that the colluding group of firms or, a monopolist, have first-mover (asymmetry) advantage. In other words they are first allowed to choose the number of products and set their prices in anticipation of entry. Only then does a potential entrant decide whether or not to enter. We also note in passing that this model may be thought of as providing an explanation for multi-product firms.

8 Remember that R^l is the average profit per brand that will be earned by the multi-product monopolist if there is no relocation after entry and that competition between the entrant and the monopolist is only going to be intense for a small number of the former's brands.

9 As Judd (1985, p. 162) notes, this analysis implies that raising one's exit costs is strategically advantageous since it makes more credible the commitment to stay. He refers to the example where an incumbent firm promises severance pay to employees fired if exit occurred but points out that the actual viability of these strategies is questionable. The reason is that, when another firm enters, it may be in the mutual interest of the incumbent firm and the worker to break the contract and transfer the worker to producing another product.

10 The other assumptions are: a uniform consumer distribution, quadratic transportation costs and finite reservation prices which are the same for all consumers. The latter buy exactly one unit of a brand in equilibrium.

9 The gains from trade under product differentiation

1 See chapter 3, section 2 for a discussion of utility function (9.2). Endowment I rather than w is the notation used in chapter 3.

2 Equation (9.4) is a consequence of the 'large numbers' assumption. As can be seen from (9.3) it is a good approximation when n is very large.

3 See chapter 6, last paragraph of section 2.

4 For good k, $R_k = p_k(y_k - y_{t-1})$ when the income distribution is uniform; these revenue functions are discussed in detail in chapter 6.

5 It can easily be seen that p_2^* is less than the pre-trade equilibrium value of q_2. If before trade q_2 was the low quality good in country k, $k = 1, 2$, its equilibrium price would have been

$$p_2 = \left(\frac{q_2 - q_0}{q_2}\right) a_k > p_2^*,$$

whilst if it was the high quality good in country k (in which case q_1 would also be produced by that country) its equilibrium price would satisfy

$$q_2(y_2 - p_2) = q_1(y_2 - p_1).$$

So, since in this case p_1 will be given by $(q_1 - q_0/q_1)a_k$,

$$p_2 = \left(\frac{q_2 - q_1}{2_2}\right)y_2 + \left(\frac{q_1 - q_0}{2_2}\right)a_k > p_2^*$$

since $y_2 > a_2$.

6 Shaked and Sutton (1982a, p. 5).

7 See Shaked and Sutton (1982a, p. 27, theorem 2).

8 See section 4 on quality competition in chapter 6 for conditions under which R_1 is as indicated in figure 9.2.

9 See Shaked and Sutton (1982a, p. 13); it can be shown, by differentiation, that R_2 has a negative second derivative with respect to q_2 when $V \geqslant b + a/3a$ and that when $V \leqslant b + a/3a$ this second derivative is bounded from above (see Shaked and Sutton (1982a, pp. 37–8)).

Bibliography

Archibald, G.C. and Rosenbluth, G. (1975), 'The New Theory of Consumer Demand and Monopolistic Competition', *Quarterly Journal of Economics*, 80: 569–90.

d'Aspremont, C., Gabszewicz, J.J. and Thisse, J.-F. (1979), 'On Hotelling's "Stability in Competition"', *Econometrica*, 47: 1045–50.

(1983), 'Product Differences and Prices', *Economics Letters*, 11: 19–23.

Auernheimer, L. and Saving, T.R. (1977), 'Market Organization and the Durability of Durable Goods', *Econometrica*, 45: 219–28.

Baumol, W.J., Panzar, J.C. and Willig, R. (1982), *Contestable Markets and the Theory of Industrial Structure*, New York: Harcourt, Brace Jovanovich.

Baumol, W.J. and Willig, R. (1986), 'Contestability: Developments since the Book', *Oxford Economic Papers*, 38: 9–36.

Bishop, R.L. (1967), 'Monopolistic Competition and Welfare Economics', in Kuenne, R. (ed.), *Monopolistic Competition Theory: Studies in Impact*, New York: Wiley and Sons, pp. 251–63.

Bonanno, G. (1987), 'Location Choice, Product Proliferation and Entry Deterrence', *Review of Economic Studies*, 54: 37–46.

Butters, G.R. (1977), 'Equilibrium Distributions of Sales and Advertising Prices', *Review of Economic Studies*, 44: 465–91.

Capozza, D.R. and Van Order, R. (1978), 'A Generalized Model of Spatial Competition', *American Economic Review*, 68: 896–908.

Chamberlin, E.H. (1933), *The Theory of Monopolistic Competition*, Cambridge, Mass.: Harvard University Press.

(1953), 'The Product as an Economic Variable', *Quarterly Journal of Economics*, 67: 1–29.

Dasgupta, P. and Maskin, E. (1986), 'The Existence of Equilibrium in Discontinuous Games, I: Theory and II: Applications', *Review of Economic Studies*, 53: 1–26 and 27–41.

De Palma, A., Ginsburgh, V., Papageorgiou, Y. and Thisse, J.-F. (1985), 'The Principle of Minimum Differentiation Holds Under Sufficient Heterogeneity', *Econometrica*, 53: 767–82.

Dixit, A.K. (1979), 'Quality and Quantity Competition', *Review of Economic Studies*, 44: 587–99.

(1982), 'Recent Developments in Oligopoly Theory', *American Economic Review: Papers and Proceedings*, 72: 12–17.

(1984), 'International Trade Policy for Oligopolistic Industries', *Economic Journal (Supplement)*, 94: 1–16.

Dixit, A.K. and Normann, V. (1980), *Theory of International Trade*, Cambridge University Press.

Dixit, A.K. and Stiglitz, J.E. (1977), 'Monopolistic Competition and Optimum Product Diversity', *American Economic Review*, 67: 297–308.

(1979), 'Monopolistic Competition and Optimum Product Diversity: Reply', *American Economic Review*, 69: 961–3.

Dorfman, R. and Steiner, P.O. (1954), 'Optimal Advertising and Optimal Quality', *American Economic Review*, 44: 816–36.

Drèze, J.H. and Hagen, K.P. (1978), 'Choice of Product Quality: Equilibrium and Efficiency', *Econometrica*, 46: 493–515.

Eaton, B.C. (1972), 'Spatial Competition Revisited', *Canadian Journal of Economics*, 5: 268–78.

(1976), 'Free-Entry in One-Dimensional Models: Pure Profits and Multiple Equilibria', *Journal of Regional Science*, 16: 21–33.

Eaton, B.C. and Lipsey, R.G. (1975), 'The Principle of Minimum Differentiation Reconsidered: Some New Developments in the Theory of Spatial Competition', *Review of Economic Studies*, 42: 27–49.

(1976), 'The Introduction of Space into the Neoclassical Model of Value Theory', in Nobay, A.R. and Artis, M.J. (eds.), *Studies in Modern Economic Analysis*, Oxford: Basil Blackwell.

(1978), 'Freedom of Entry and the Existence of Pure Profit', *Economic Journal*, 88: 455–69.

(1979), 'The Theory of Market Pre-emption: the Persistence of Excess Capacity and Monopoly in Growing Spatial Markets', *Economica*, 46: 149–58.

(1980), 'Exit Barriers are Entry Barriers: The Durability of Capital as a Barrier to Entry', *Bell Journal of Economics*, 11: 721–9.

Eaton, B.C. and Wooders, M.H. (1985), 'Sophisticated Entry in a Model of Spatial Competition', *Rand Journal of Economics*, 16: 282–97.

Friedman, J.W. (1983), *Oligopoly Theory*, Cambridge: Cambridge University Press.

Gabszewicz, J.J. (1985), 'Comment', in Arrow, K.J. and Honkapohja, S. (eds.), *Frontiers of Economics*, Oxford: Basil Blackwell, pp. 150–69.

Gabszewicz, J.J., Shaked, A., Sutton, J. and Thisse, J.-F. (1981a), 'Price Competition Among Differentiated Products: A Detailed Study of a Nash Equilibrium' (I.C.E.R.D. Discussion Paper 81/37, L.S.E.).

(1981b), 'International Trade in Differentiated Products', *International Economic Review*, 22: 527–35.

Gabszewicz, J.J. and Thisse, J.-F. (1979), 'Price Competition, Quality and Income Disparities', *Journal of Economic Theory*, 20: 340–59.

(1980), 'Entry (and Exit) in a Differentiated Industry', *Journal of Economic Theory*, 22: 327–38.

(1986), 'On the Nature of Competition with Differentiated Products', *Economic Journal*, 96: 160–72.

Gal-Or, E. (1982), 'Hotelling's Spatial Competition as a Model of Sales', *Economics Letters*, 9: 1–6.

(1983), 'Quality and Quantity Competition', *Bell Journal of Economics*, 14: 590–600.

(1985), 'Differentiated Industries without Entry Barriers', *Journal of Economic Theory*, 37: 310–39.

Graitson, D. (1982), 'Spatial Competition à la Hotelling: A Selective Survey', *Journal of Industrial Economics*, 31: 13–25.

Grossman, G.M. and Shapiro, C. (1984), 'Informative Advertising with Differentiated Products', *Review of Economic Studies*, 51: 63–81.

Hart, O.D. (1979), 'Monopolistic Competition in a Large Economy with Differentiated Commodities', *Review of Economic Studies*, 46: 1 – 30.

(1985a), 'Monopolistic Competition in the Spirit of Chamberlin: A General Model', *Review of Economic Studies*, 52: 529–46.

(1985b), 'Monopolistic Competition in the Spirit of Chamberlin: Special Results', *Economic Journal*, 95: 889–908.

(1985c), 'Imperfect Competition in General Equilibrium: An Overview of Recent Work', in Arrow, K.J. and Honkapohja, S. (eds.), *Frontiers of Economics*, Oxford: Basil Blackwell, pp. 100–49.

Hay, D.A. (1976), 'Sequential Entry and Entry-Deterring Strategies in Spatial Competition', *Oxford Economic Papers*, 28: 240–57.

Helpman, E. (1981), 'International Trade in the Presence of Product Differentiation, Economies of Scale, and Monopolistic Competition: A Chamberlinian–Hecksher–Ohlin Approach', *Journal of International Economics*, 11: 305–40.

(1984), 'Increasing Returns, Imperfect Markets and Trade Theory', in Jones, R.W. and Kenen, P.W. (eds.), *Handbook of International Economics, Volume 1*, Amsterdam: North-Holland, pp. 326–65.

Helpman, E. and Krugman, P.R. (1985), *Increasing Returns, Imperfect Competition and International Trade*, Brighton: Wheatsheaf Books.

Holahan, W. (1978), 'Spatial Monopolistic Competition versus Spatial Monopoly', *Journal of Economic Theory*, 18: 156–70.

Hotelling, H. (1929), 'Stability in Competition', *Economic Journal*, 39: 41–57.

Ireland, N.J. (1985), 'Product Diversity and Monopolistic Competition under Uncertainty', *Journal of Industrial Economics*, 33: 501–14.

(1987), *Product Differentiation and Non-Price Competition*, Oxford: Basil Blackwell.

Ironmonger, D.S. (1972), *New Commodities and Consumer Behaviour*, Cambridge University Press.

Judd, K.L. (1985), 'Credible Spatial Pre-emption', *Rand Journal of Economics*, 16: 153–66.

Kaldor, N. (1935), 'Market Imperfection and Excess Capacity', *Economica*, 2: 33–50.

Kamien, M.I. and Schwartz, N.L. (1974), 'Product Durability under Monopoly and Competition', *Econometrica*, 42: 289–301.

Kierzkowski, H. (ed.) (1984), *Monopolistic Competition and International Trade*, Oxford University Press.

Kleiman, E. and Ophir, T. (1966), 'The Durability of Durable Goods', *Review of Economic Studies*, 33: 165–78.

Koenker R.W. and Perry, M.K. (1981), 'Product Differentiation, Monopolistic Competition and Public Policy', *Bell Journal of Economics*, 12: 217–31.

Kohlberg, E. and Novshek, W. (1982), 'Equilibrium in a Simple Price-Location Model', *Economics Letters*, 9: 7–15.

Koutsoyiannis, A. (1984), *Non-Price Competition*, London: Macmillan.

Kuenne, R. (ed.) (1967), *Monopolistic Competition Theory: Studies in Impact*, New York: Wiley and Sons.

Lancaster, K.J. (1966), 'A New Approach to Consumer Theory', *Journal of Political Economy*, 74: 132–57.

(1979), *Variety, Equity and Efficiency*, Oxford: Basil Blackwell.

Lane, W.J. (1980), 'Product Differentiation in a Market with Endogenous Sequential Entry', *Bell Journal of Economics*, 11: 237–60.

Leland, H.E. (1977), 'Quality Choice and Competition', *American Economic Review*, 67: 127–35.

Lerner, A.P. and Singer, H.W. (1937), 'Some Notes on Duopoly and Spatial Competition', *Journal of Political Economy*, 45: 145–86.

Levhari, D. and Peles, Y. (1973), 'Market Structure, Quality and Durability', *Bell Journal of Economics*, 4: 235–48.

Levhari, D. and Srinivasan, T.N. (1969), 'Durability of Consumption Goods: Competition versus Monopoly', *American Economic Review*, 59: 102–7.

Mankiw, N.G. and Whinston, M.D. (1986), 'Free Entry and Social Inefficiency', *Rand Journal of Economics*, 17: 48–58.

Mas-Colell, A. (1975), 'A Model of Equilibrium with Differentiated Commodities', *Journal of Mathematical Economics*, 2: 263–96.

Muller, E. and Peles, Y. (1986), 'The Dynamic Adjustment of Optimal Durability' (mimeo, Hebrew University of Jerusalem).

Neven, D. (1985), 'Two-Stage (Perfect) Equilibrium in Hotelling's Model', *Journal of Industrial Economics*, 33: 317–25.

Neven, D. (1987), 'Endogenous Sequential Entry in a Spatial Model', *International Journal of Industrial Organisation*, 5: 419–34.

Neven, D., Matutes, C. and Corstjens, M. (1988), 'Brand Proliferation and Entry Deterrence' (mimeo, INSEAD).

Novshek, W. (1980), 'Equilibrium in Simple Spatial (or Differentiated) Product Models', *Journal of Economic Theory*, 22: 313–26.

Oi, W.Y. (1973), 'The Economics of Product Safety', *Bell Journal of Economics*, 4: 3–28.

Osborne, M.J. and Pitchik, C. (1987), 'Equilibrium in Hotelling's Model of Spatial Competition', *Econometrica*, 55: 911–22.

Parks, R.W. (1974), 'The Demand and Supply of Durability', *American Economic Review*, 64: 37–55.

Perloff, J.M. and Salop, S.C. (1985), 'Equilibrium with Product Differentiation', *Review of Economic Studies*, 52: 107–20.

Pettengill, J.S. (1979), 'Monopolistic Competition and Optimum Product Diversity: Comment', *American Economic Review*, 69: 957–60.

Prescott, E.J. and Visscher, M. (1977), 'Sequential Location among Firms with Foresight', *Bell Journal of Economics*, 8: 378–93.

Roberts, K.W.S. (1980), 'The Limit Points of Monopolistic Competition', *Journal of Economic Theory*, 22: 256–78.

Robinson, J. (1934), 'What is Perfect Competition', *Quarterly Journal of Economics*, 49: 104–20.

Rothschild, M. (1973), 'Models of Market Organization with Imperfect Information: A Survey', *Journal of Political Economy*, 81: 1283–308.

Salant, D.J. (1986), 'Equilibrium in a Spatial Model of Imperfect Competition with Sequential Choice of Locations and Quantities', *Canadian Journal of Economics*, 19: 685–715.

Salop, S.C. (1979), 'Monopolistic Competition with Outside Goods', *Bell Journal of Economics*, 10: 141–56.

Salop, S.C. and Stiglitz, J.E. (1977), 'Bargains and Ripoffs: A Model of Monopolistically Competitive Price Dispersion', *Review of Economic Studies*, 44: 493–510.

Sattinger, M. (1984), 'Value of an Additional Firm in Monopolistic Competition', *Review of Economic Studies*, 51: 321–32.

Schmalensee, R. (1970), 'Regulation and the Durability of Goods', *Bell Journal of Economics*, 1: 54–64.

(1972), *The Economics of Advertising*, Cambridge, Mass.: M.I.T. Press.

(1974), 'Market Structure, Durability, and Maintenance Effort', *Review of Economic Studies*, 41: 277–87.

(1978), 'Entry Deterrence in the RTE Cereal Industry', *Bell Journal of Economics*, 9: 305–27.

(1979), 'Market Structure, Durability, and Quality: A Selective Survey', *Economic Inquiry*, 17: 177–98.

(1982), 'Product Differentiation Advantages of Pioneering Brands', *American Economic Review*, 72: 349–65.

Schwartz, M. (1986), 'The Nature and Scope of Contestability Theory', *Oxford Economic Papers*, 38: 37–57.

Shaked, A. (1982), 'Existence and Computation of Mixed Strategy Equilibrium for 3-Firms Location Problem', *Journal of Industrial Economics*, 31: 93–6.

Shaked, A. and Sutton, J. (1982a), 'Natural Oligopolies and the Gains from Trade' (I.C.E.R.D. Discussion Papers 82/51, L.S.E.).

(1982b), 'Relaxing Price Competition through Product Differentiation', *Review of Economic Studies*, 49: 3–13.

(1983), 'Natural Oligopolies', *Econometrica*, 51: 1469–83.

(1984), 'Natural Oligopolies and International Trade', in Kierzkowski, H. (ed.), *Monopolistic Competition and International Trade*, Oxford University Press, pp. 34–50.

(1987), 'Product Differentiation and Industrial Structure', *Journal of Industrial Economics*, 36: 131–46.

Sieper, E. and Swan, P.L. (1973), 'Monopoly and Competition in the Market for Durable Goods', *Review of Economic Studies*, 40: 333–52.

Smithies, A. (1941), 'Optimum Location in Spatial Competition', *Journal of Political Economy*, 49: 423–39.

Spence, A.M. (1975), 'Monopoly, Quality and Regulation', *Bell Journal of Economics* 6: 417–29.

(1976a), 'Product Differentiation and Welfare', *American Economic Review*, 66: 407–14.

(1976b), 'Product Selection, Fixed Costs, and Monopolistic Competition', *Review of Economic Studies*, 43: 217–35.

(1977), 'Non-Price Competition', *American Economic Review: Papers and Proceedings*, 67: 255–9.

Stahl, K. (1982a), 'Differentiated Products, Consumer Search and Locational Oligopoly', *Journal of Industrial Economics*, 31: 97–114.

(1982b), 'Location and Spatial Pricing Theory with Nonconvex Transportation Cost Schedules', *Bell Journal of Economics*, 13: 575–82.

Stern, N. (1972), 'The Optimal Size of Market Areas', *Journal of Economic Theory*, 4: 152–73.

Su, T.T. (1975), 'Durability of Consumption Goods Reconsidered', *American Economic Review*, 65: 148–57.

Swan, P.L. (1970), 'Durability of Consumer Goods', *American Economic Review*, 60: 884–94.

(1971), 'Durability of Goods and the Regulation of Monopoly', *Bell Journal of Economics*, 2: 347–57.

(1977), 'Product Durability under Monopoly and Competition', *Econometrica*, 45: 229–35.

Sweezy, P.M. (1939), 'Demand Under Conditions of Oligopoly', *Journal of Political Economy*, 47: 568–73.

Van Damme, E. (1985), *New Refinements in the Nash Equilibrium Concept*, Amsterdam: North Holland.

Venables, A.J. (1985), 'International Trade, Trade and Industrial Policy: A Survey' (Discussion Paper No. 74, C.E.P.R.).

Waterson, M. (1984), *Economic Theory of the Industry*, Cambridge University Press.

Weintraub, E.R. (1982), *Mathematics for Economists*, Cambridge University Press.

Wolinsky, A.M. (1983), 'Retail Trade Concentration due to Consumers' Imperfect Information', *Bell Journal of Economics*, 14: 272–82.

Yarrow, G.K. (1985), 'Welfare Losses in Oligopoly and Monopolistic Competition', *Journal of Industrial Economics*, 33: 515–29.

Author index

Subject index